Mr Eternity

The Story of Arthur Stace

By Roy Williams with Elizabeth Meyers

Acorn Press

Published by Acorn Press
An imprint of Bible Society Australia
ACN 148 058 306
GPO Box 9874
Sydney NSW 2001
Australia
www.biblesociety.org.au | www.acornpress.net.au

National Library of Australia Cataloguing-in-Publication entry:

Creator:	Williams, Roy Thomas, 1963– author.
Title:	Mr Eternity: the story of Arthur Stace / by Roy Williams with Elizabeth Meyers.
ISBN:	9780994616654 (paperback) 9780994616661 (ebook)
Subjects:	Stace, Arthur, 1885–1967. Graffiti artists—New South Wales—Sydney—Biography. Evangelists—New South Wales—Sydney—Biography. Eternity.

Other Creators/Contributors: Meyers, Elizabeth, author.

Unless otherwise indicated, Bible quotes are taken from the King James Version of the Bible.

For a detailed list of the sources used for the illustrations in this book, please see page 280.

Editor: Kristin Argall.
Cover design and text layout: Andrew and Jenny Moody.
Printed by Openbook Howden Design & Print.

This book is dedicated by Elizabeth Meyers to her beloved parents,
Rev. Lisle Matthew Thompson and Mrs May Annie Thompson,
who devoted their lives to faithful service of their Saviour and Lord.

I am the vine; you are the branches. If you remain in me and I in you, you will bear much fruit; apart from me you can do nothing.

John 15:5 (NIV)

Contents

Foreword

Mr Eternity looms large in my childhood memories of Burton Street Baptist Tabernacle. Childhood memories can be tricky things, so I checked my recollections with my sister, Judy, who, unlike me, never forgets. We recalled Arthur Stace as a dapper man with hat, tie and jacket; always neatly attired. Sometimes we would note that he was late for church, but he would never just wander in – he would act always like he had been caught up with some serious task. No doubt he was writing the world *Eternity* on some street corner in Sydney. I also recall sitting on his knee knowing, by all the watching eyes, that I was in the lap of a significant person. But to me he was just the dapper Mr Stace. His wife Pearl, always referred to as Mrs Stace, was a very ordered person and although most likeable, as children we certainly watched our ways in her presence.

I now know Arthur Stace to be one of the most interesting and significant figures in Australian Christian life. It's not inappropriate to call him an 'unlikely hero', as he came from a horrid background. The kind of narrative God does great things with. At a time when the church is rediscovering the word 'missional', it could do a lot worse than reflect on Arthur Stace. He is arguably our most creative and artistic missional leader. If I recall correctly, it was artist Martin Sharp who said, at an event, words to the effect that Arthur Stace achieved, in one word, a novel which took Patrick White 100,000 words. He became one of the world's great graffiti artists and one of the few whose work and life lives on. He took the word *Eternity* out of the church and into the streets of Sydney. But more, the word went global as it blazed from the Sydney Harbour Bridge as the pinnacle of our New Year's Eve millennium celebrations, viewed worldwide including in London, New York, Singapore and Hong Kong. The four walls of the church could not contain the message of Arthur Stace. But not only was he missional in an artistic and creative sense, this book clearly shows that he was a respected evangelist who held the attention of crowds in a variety of environments. This book also explodes the myth that Arthur Stace was illiterate, but it does reveal that his copperplate script writing of the word *Eternity* was an inspiration, if not a gift, of God. It was beyond his natural ability.

This is not just a story of God's working in one man's life. (Of course there is his wife, Pearl.) However, the three central characters are Arthur, Baptist evangelist John Ridley and Anglican archdeacon R.B.S. Hammond. Some believe in coincidences, but when you read of the lives of these three men, from different backgrounds and experiences, anyone with a seed of faith will see the extraordinary hand of God. John Ridley was converted at Burton Street Baptist Tabernacle. R.B.S. Hammond delivered the message that led to the transformation of Arthur Stace, who then attended an evangelistic event featuring Ridley at Burton Street. Ridley preached on eternity and cried out 'Eternity – I wish that I could sound, or shout that word to everyone on the streets of Sydney.' That prophetic hope gave birth to Mr Eternity: The 'power' of a sermon.

It's not just a story of people, it's also the story of a church. Burton Street Baptist Tabernacle played a remarkable role in touching people's lives that in turn touched the city and beyond. Fittingly, although the church is no longer there, the building lives on as Eternity Playhouse, courtesy of the Lord Mayor of Sydney, Clover Moore. And it is also a story of how God has interwoven, for his glory, the ministry of denominations, primarily Baptist and Anglican. Some might suggest, 'Lord, do it again!'

This book is a must-read. There is no one who knows the Arthur Stace story better than Elizabeth Meyers. Roy Williams is one of our finest writers. If you have heard of Arthur Stace, this book will sweep away the myths and leave you with the real man. The authors superbly create a narrative that will engage you in a divine drama of how God takes all the cogs and turns them into the finest instrument. It's only on historical reflection, as seen here, that we start to understand the full picture. During the actual time of Arthur Stace we only saw dimly, so it's appropriate that this book is now written. It's a modern miracle story that will inspire and motivate all.

Rev. Dr Ross Clifford AM
Principal, Morling College
President, Asia Pacific Baptist Federation

Introduction: Mr Eternity

That shy mysterious poet Arthur Stace
Whose work was just one single mighty word.
Douglas Stewart

As night fell on 31 December 1999, five million Sydneysiders looked forward to hours of splendid celebration. It was the eve of the twenty-first century; the eve of the third millennium. A feast of live entertainment was planned, much of it on Sydney's majestic, incomparable harbour.

An estimated one million people clustered on the foreshores, residents and tourists alike.[1] Others took to the water in boats of all kinds. There had not been a scene like this since the Bicentennial festivities of Australia Day 1988. Countless lights sparkled and shone, in many colours of the rainbow; the water rippled; stars of the Australian music industry performed at harbourside venues. The highlight was a performance in the Opera House forecourt of Icehouse's classic song 'Great Southern Land.' It was reworked and expanded for the occasion by its composer, Iva Davies, as part of a colossal 25-minute work, 'Ghost of Time.' The musicians took their final bows a few minutes before midnight.

By now, literally billions of people were watching on television, their attention fixed on Australia's premier city. The first of January 2000 would arrive in Sydney before dawning in any other comparable city on Earth.

At ten seconds to midnight the countdown began. Then, as the new millennium arrived, there came a massive fireworks display – perhaps the most spectacular ever seen in Australia – that lasted 24 minutes. The focal points were Sydney's two matchless icons of engineering: the Harbour Bridge and the Opera House. At the end, a fiery cascade erupted downwards from the Bridge's deck. The bells of a dozen churches pealed loudly.

And then, as the smoke cleared, it came into view – emblazoned in gold letters just below the apex of the Bridge's towering arch. The first written word of the third millennium, in distinctive copperplate script:

Eternity

The crowds cheered with gusto. This was a word deeply and affectionately associated with the history of Sydney – and with one man in particular. He was not the first person to write 'eternity' around the streets of Sydney,[2] but he was certainly the most prolific. He did it using chalk or crayon every day for almost 35 years, perhaps half a million times in all.

His name was Arthur Malcolm Stace. He had died 32 years before, but was far from forgotten.

§

May Thompson, 84 years old on New Year's Eve 1999, watched the television broadcast from the comfort of her bed. She was a frail, silver-haired old lady now, a widow of more than three decades, living alone in a small house in the lower Blue Mountains of New South Wales.

May had known Arthur Stace intimately in life. For fourteen years, from 1951 to 1964, her late husband, Lisle M. Thompson, had been Stace's beloved pastor at the Burton Street Baptist Tabernacle in the Sydney suburb of Darlinghurst. It was the Rev. Thompson, in June 1956, who persuaded Arthur to 'go public.' But for Thompson, it is possible, even likely, that Arthur Stace's identity would never have been known.

The sight of *Eternity* on the Harbour Bridge had moved May Thompson to tears and rekindled myriad memories, sweet and sad and everything in between. As soon as the television broadcast concluded, she reached for the phone by her bed and called her oldest daughter Elizabeth Meyers. Elizabeth, too, had known Arthur Stace well. She had met him at the age of nine, as an impressionable girl, and was a young married woman when he died. Now 58, happily married to her husband Lionel and with two grown-up daughters of her own, Elizabeth was extremely close to her aged mother. She recalls part of their conversation that night.

'Arthur would have felt very humbled by that,' May said, the catch in her voice betraying a certain melancholy. But she also felt enormous satisfaction, and something of a sense of closure. 'Elizabeth, I believe Arthur's story could be written now.'

For many years May had hoped, and intended, to write the story herself. She had gathered a large amount of information, but time and circumstances had defeated her. The millennium celebrations had renewed her determination to see it done.

§

It had not come as a surprise – to May or the people of Sydney – when *Eternity* lit up the Harbour Bridge that memorable night. A fortnight or so earlier, workmen had begun erecting the metal frames holding the letters to the eastern side of the Bridge. After a few days, it was clear where things were leading. Stories began appearing in the media in anticipation.[3]

May Thompson was interviewed by the *Sydney Morning Herald*'s Malcolm Knox for an article that appeared on 29 December. It included a thumbnail sketch of Arthur Stace's life that was accurate as far as it went. Crucially, Knox emphasised *the* key point about Stace – he was an evangelical Protestant Christian for whom *Eternity* was a one-word sermon (based on Isaiah 57:15). He would have approved heartily of May Thompson's remarks to Knox:

> The millennium has many people thinking about time, but Eternity only lies in the hands of the Lord. I wonder what the average person thinks of Arthur's 'Eternity'? I think of accountability to the Almighty. It's useful to get people thinking about how they will spend Eternity.[4]

(The designer of the Bridge, J.J.C. Bradfield, would have adored it all, by the way. Apart from being an inveterate publicity hound, Bradfield had a mischievous sense of humour and was a serious practising Anglican. He once described the Bridge as 'a fane of beauty expressive of the divinity and spirit of God, of the "I AM" who spoke to Moses from the burning bush.'[5])

By 30 December, the full word *Eternity* was visible on the Bridge. Another distinguished Australian journalist, David Marr, wrote a reflective front-page story for the *Herald*. It appeared on New Year's Eve under the headline 'From here to Eternity', but dealt far more ambivalently than Knox's had done with the Christian implications of Arthur Stace's message.

Earlier that year, Marr had published a book, *The High Price of Heaven*,[6] lambasting what he saw as the excessively 'wowserish' fixations of the Australian churches down the years. 'One thing about tonight is clear,' he asserted in the *Herald* on 31 December, 'there's no sense that the fireworks will mark a great Christian anniversary.'[7] It was true, as Marr proceeded to explain, that our calendar years are numbered from the year of Christ's birth. But, as Marr also noted, those responsible for creating the dating system in the fifth and seventh centuries AD[8] got their calculations slightly wrong. Jesus of Nazareth was born in or about 5 BC.

Marr's tone reflected the cynical attitude toward Christianity of a large proportion of the Australian population, especially those in the 'better educated' classes. That trend has intensified since 2000.

The artistic director of the millennium celebrations was Ignatius Jones, formerly the lead singer of Australian shock-rock band Jimmy and the Boys, and by 1999 one of the world's most innovative and sought-after event organisers. It was Jones' inspired idea to use *Eternity* on the Bridge, and, at the time, he explained his reasons:

> It's incredibly Sydney. It symbolised for me the madness, mystery and magic of the city. On the one hand there's the meaning of the word in its temporal sense and on this night of fellowship and good cheer it shouldn't just be about one night. The word says that this celebration should be eternal in human life.
>
> But it also says a lot about Sydney that Arthur Stace, who grew up in a brothel, came back from war shell-shocked and became an habitual criminal and alcoholic, should be able to reinvent himself and try to bring joy and meaning into people's lives. This is a quintessentially Sydney message and one we want to spread.[9]

Jones made no mention of religion, but his sentiments were capable of appealing to believers and unbelievers alike.

And that is how *Eternity* was received on 1 January 2000. In the days that followed, there was scarcely a word of protest and plenty of delighted praise.[10] Expatriate author Peter Carey, watching from New York, had felt 'insanely proud and happy at this secret message from my home.'[11] A fortnight later, a local Sydney personality, Leo Schofield, wrote with approval in his *Sunday Telegraph* column that 'no-one will quickly forget ... the impression it made on all Sydneysiders.'[12]

That impression remains firm to this day. During the summer of 2016–17, the word '*Empathy*' began to appear in chalk on the streets of Sydney in Arthur's familiar style. A group known as Empathy Nation was responsible, its vision 'to see empathy become a part of everyday life – in our families, workplaces and politics.'[13]

§

There are several reasons why a biography of Arthur Stace is timely. The fact that 2017 marks the fiftieth anniversary of his death – and the two-hundredth anniversary of the founding of Bible Society Australia – is largely coincidental.

No biography of Stace has been written before. There have been numerous short sketches, usually derivative of others and often marred by factual errors. A good many misconceptions have developed about Arthur Stace and it is time they were dispelled. The true facts are engrossing enough; there is no need for embellishment.

To take a fairly trivial example, Stace did not 'grow up in a brothel', as Ignatius Jones suggested back in 2000. It is a fact, however, that as a young man Stace worked in and for a brothel. As we shall see in Chapter 4, this establishment was in Surry Hills and was owned and operated by his older sister Minnie.

Similarly, in January 2000 the *Sunday Telegraph* announced the 'discovery' of Stace's grave in Botany cemetery. 'The location was revealed only when a reader contacted ... Leo Schofield last week,' a journalist reported.[14] In truth, the gravesite was never 'lost.' Those who knew and loved Arthur always remembered where his mortal remains had been buried. Indeed, May Thompson had been present at the burial service in October 1969 – she gave the eulogy – and later paid for the handsome headstone that is still maintained there.

If these errors were minor, others have been more serious. An enduring myth about Stace is that he was illiterate; that his ability to write the word *Eternity* was some kind of supernatural gift. A resourceful writer-historian, Pauline Conolly, tried to scotch this notion in 2009;[15] but still it persists. Again, as we shall see, the truth is more nuanced – yet none the less fascinating for that.

Most importantly, Arthur Stace was not a 'weirdo.' Several modern-day commentators have felt free to label him as mentally ill – 'almost certainly schizophrenic', offered one in 2006[16] – but this was just not so. He was unusual, certainly, but the same could be said of every prodigious achiever in human history. The Rev. Bernard G. Judd, a friend of Arthur's for some 30 years, came closest to the mark during an on-camera interview in 1994: 'He was a thorough-going, reasonable, rational Christian ... He was indomitable. He was not a fanatic, he was not obsessed. He had a purpose, and nothing could stop him.'[17]

Judd objected to Arthur being 'lumped in' with run-of-the-mill attention-seekers – the narcissists and the kooks. Sydney has certainly had its share of those.

Another way of putting it is this: Arthur Stace was an ordinary man who did one extraordinary thing. But, on top of that, he lived through extraordinary times.

Like, say, A.B. (Bert) Facey, author of that artlessly gripping memoir *A Fortunate Life*, Stace was a living embodiment of an Australia that no longer exists. Both were quintessential working-class[18] battlers. Both had limited schooling and endured unhappy, disrupted childhoods. Their lives were shaped by the economic depression of the 1890s,

Federation, the rise of the Australian Labor Party, World War I, the 'roaring' twenties, the temperance movement, the Great Depression. True, Facey lived a sober, law-abiding life from cradle to grave while Stace was a reformed alcoholic and petty criminal. But their key character traits were the same: modesty, frugality, decency, a certain laconic style.

Both Facey and Stace experienced wholly unexpected fame late in their lives, and had something like sainthood conferred upon them in death.

The great difference between them concerned religion. Facey lost any faith he once had on the hills of Gallipoli: he was an atheist ever after.[19] Stace, who served on the Western Front as a stretcher-bearer, converted in August 1930 to evangelical Christianity. From that moment, his faith was the moving force behind everything he did. It is important to remember that the *Eternity* mission was but one aspect – if by far the most famous – of his 'life in Christ.' In the words of John Starr, long-time secretary of the Burton Street Baptist Tabernacle and a close friend of Arthur in later life, 'his gratitude for salvation and his zest for service had only one focus, to please God alone. He was truly humble.'[20]

This book aims to tell Stace's story in full – its sad and disgraceful aspects as well as the quirky and admirable. Many episodes have never been recounted previously. May Thompson spent her last three decades safeguarding and expanding the documentary record of Stace's life. When she died in 2002, she passed the torch to her daughter Elizabeth, who has continued the process with remarkable doggedness and skill. Between them, mother and daughter also kept track of every appropriation of the *Eternity* story since Stace's death, whether religious, cultural or commercial. I will detail these in the last two chapters.

Finally, I intend *Mr Eternity* as a tribute to three great Australian Christians – men of the church who ministered to Arthur Stace and turned his life on its head. Their names were R.B.S. Hammond (1870–1946), John Gotch Ridley (1896–1976) and Lisle M. Thompson (1910–64). Hammond was of the Church of England; Ridley and Thompson were Baptists. Following his conversion in August 1930, Stace worshipped for about nine years at Hammond's St Barnabas' church on Broadway; after that, for the best part of three decades, his spiritual home was the Burton Street Baptist Tabernacle in Darlinghurst.

In the course of telling this story, two distinctive strains of Christianity will emerge. Both have been of crucial importance in our history. Sometimes they are seen as contradictory; in fact they are, or should be, complementary.

One strain might be termed 'charitable' or 'practical' Christianity, with its emphasis on the doing of good to others in this earthly world. In short: the Golden Rule. The other strain is 'personal' or 'salvation-based' Christianity. Here the emphasis is on the fate, in the afterlife, of the individual's immortal soul.

The focus of Arthur Stace's *Eternity* crusade was individual salvation. It was the same with his open-air street missioning and other forms of evangelism. But as I hope also to show, he did not neglect other, more worldly causes. Far from it. He was a loving son and brother, a devoted husband, and a loyal friend. He performed countless acts of private charity. He understood to the depth of his being that faith without deeds is dead. He never tired of telling people that it was a kindly minister's offer of 'a cuppa tea and a rock cake' that brought him to faith in the first place.

Roy Williams
October 2017

1. Born unto trouble

The childhood shows the man
As morning shows the day.
John Milton, 'Paradise Regained'

By the normal rules of the world, Arthur Malcolm Stace was doomed from the start to a life of sorrow. His early childhood was one of deprivation and depravity.

Born on 9 February 1885 in a dingy terrace house in the working-class Sydney suburb of Redfern[1] – one of a string of rented properties that his embattled parents called home – Arthur knew little but suffering. During the previous six years, each move his family made had been a step *down* the socio-economic ladder. And there would be more tribulations to come.

Outwardly at least, Arthur's father cut a fine figure. William Wood Stace, 29 years old when Arthur came into the world, was an Englishman of good breeding. Well-educated and pleasantly spoken – and tall, dark, and handsome to boot[2] – he may have struck casual observers as a decent, productive citizen. But the truth was otherwise. William's basic problem was that he was unskilled – he possessed neither professional qualifications nor the practical know-how of an artisan.[3] It seems that he was unable or unwilling to live by his wits, or to toil away full-time as a manual labourer.[4]

In short, he could never earn a sufficient income. He was a well-meaning wastrel. And he lived in an era when the social safety net was thin. Ultimately he took solace in the bottle.

Arthur's mother, Laura Lewis, was a very different person. Four years younger than William, she was a native-born Australian of convict/farming stock, raised in the Windsor district of New South Wales some 40 miles (70 kilometres) to Sydney's west. She had little schooling and few social graces. Apart from a determined temperament, her best asset was her physical beauty. As a very young woman Laura had been a winsome sight: petite and fair, with attractive blue eyes. In a different life she might have aged gracefully and blossomed into a caring, competent wife and mother.

In nineteenth-century Australia, most women lost their looks much more quickly than they do today. Harsh sunlight, multiple childbirths, backbreaking domestic chores, poor food and medicine – all took their toll. But Laura Lewis must have aged more rapidly than most.

Arthur was her sixth child. As a teenager in Windsor, before she met William Wood Stace, Laura had already given birth to two babies (in both cases the father is unknown). One had died within days, but Clara, almost nine when Arthur was born, had become part of the Stace family. Baby Arthur's other siblings – like him, the progeny of William and Laura – were Minnie (almost five when Arthur was born), William John (three) and Samuel (17 months).

Arthur's arrival was a turning point of sorts. Virtually since their first meeting back in 1879, William and Laura had 'lived in sin' – they had cohabited while remaining unmarried. In 1885, for reasons that can only be guessed at (a desire for 'respectability'?), they decided to tie the knot. The wedding took place on 13 October that year at Christ Church St Laurence[5] in George Street, a mile or so from the CBD in what is now Railway Square. This venerable sandstone church remains a Sydney institution, distinctive for its Anglo-Catholic tradition. (Well over a century later, it would also be the venue for a notable chapter in the *Eternity* story.)

In terms of religious observance, William and Laura's marriage ceremony seems to have been a one-off. Although they identified as 'Church of England' in official documents, Christian worship was hardly a feature of the Stace family's life.

1.1. Inner-Sydney slum, late nineteenth century, of the sort in which Arthur Stace grew up as a small boy from 1885 to 1892.

Arthur's infancy was, of course, highly formative – yet he would not have retained any long-term memory of the relevant events. It seems clear that Laura received little or no support from her people, the Lewis family in Windsor; we know that William moved his family about with unfortunate frequency. Within months of Arthur's birth they had left the house at 16 Morehead Street, Redfern, to live at Bradley's Rocks, off Sussex Street in the city. Over the next few years they occupied premises in Petersham (Constitution Road), Newtown (Angel Street) and Alexandria (Kings Clear Road).[6] These, like Redfern, were tough, mainly working-class areas, all within a few miles of each other. The housing, or far too much of it, was cramped and unsanitary. The more affluent middle classes had been escaping this part of Sydney since the 1850s.

Taken on the whole, inner Sydney by the 1880s was a less than edifying place. The harbour's natural grandeur was despoiled by outflows of raw sewage. There was as yet no functional city railway. Noisy steam trams and horses cluttered the streets, which had never been properly laid out: they were alternately dusty or muddy, depending on the weather. Murky gas lighting was still the norm at night. Crime rates were high. Worst of all, the gulf between rich and poor was unconscionable. In his classic account of the period, *Wild Men of Sydney*, Cyril Pearl wrote of 'an uncouth sprawling seaport of 288,000 people and 3,167 pubs. There was a Hogarthian flavour about its brutality, its boozing, its corruption; the gallows and the triangles cast long shadows.'[7]

During the first half of 1888 – the centenary year of colonisation of New South Wales – the Stace family may have enjoyed a brief period of optimism. In April Laura gave birth to another child, a girl named Ellen.[8] In May they were joined in Sydney by William's older brother, Malcolm Vincent Stace, whose wife was also named Ellen. It seems at least possible that the new baby was named after her aunt. Certainly, Arthur Malcolm Stace must have taken his middle name from his paternal uncle.

Malcolm Stace was a surgeon, an Englishman of some eminence, who had come to Sydney to set up in private practice. He and Ellen (who were childless) moved into a house in Regent Street, Newtown, the suburb in which his younger brother's family was then living.[9] This, surely, was no coincidence. Presumably Malcolm's familiar presence was reassuring for William; apart from fraternal companionship, William may also have harboured hope of financial assistance. At any rate, Malcolm must have brought with him cheering news from the home country – in particular, greetings from their widowed mother Jane Stace and their married younger sister, Georgina Eustace. Georgina's husband was also a surgeon, and by this time the couple had three little daughters (Georgina, Dorothea and Katherine) – posh first cousins for the Stace children. Perhaps presents and photographs were passed around.

If there was a short idyll, it did not last long. In quick time the Stace family fell apart.

On 26 March 1889, baby Ellen died at the age of just eleven months.[10] The cause of death was infantile diarrhoea and 'debility': her little body, quite probably undernourished, could not cope with the infection that had set in. No doctor had attended her for nine days.[11] Arthur was then four years old, and Ellen's sudden, ghastly death may well have been his first clear long-term memory.

On 8 October of that year, Arthur's half-sister Clara was arrested. The police charged her with 'habitually wandering around the district of Redfern in no ostensible lawful occupation.'[12] She was 13 years old, so this may have been code for prostitution. At any rate, she was clearly a vagrant and truant.*

The police had probably encountered Clara before and were certainly unimpressed on this occasion: the word 'bad' was written next to her name in the register. The Redfern Police Court ordered that she be sent forthwith to the Industrial School for Girls at Parramatta,[13] a state-controlled reformatory home set up in April 1887 for delinquent or neglected children. Clara fell into both categories. It was a grim place, run along authoritarian lines and thoroughly uncongenial for inmates in every way.[14] Riots were frequent and notorious: a serious one took place in the year after Clara arrived.[15]

If Clara's parents put up a fight before their child was sent to Parramatta, there is no record of it. Arthur, now four and a half, must by then have been old enough to take in the abrupt departure of his oldest sister.

---

* She ought to have been attending the so-called Ragged School in Waterloo, a charitable institution set up in 1886 by Protestant clergy and laymen to educate impoverished children resident in the area.

Things went from bad to worse in 1890. Yet another baby was born – a girl, Dora (known as 'Dolly'). Perhaps Laura could still summon up some fond maternal feelings, but more likely she and her struggling husband sighed at the thought of another mouth to feed. Any faith that William had been placing in his older brother was extinguished in 1890, when Uncle Malcolm and Aunt Ellen departed for England, never to return.[16] It appears that Dr Malcolm Stace had not much enjoyed his sojourn in the colonies. There is no surviving evidence of any medical practice that he may have carried on, but there is a police record of the theft of his hunting watch. An expensive silver 'Lecomte' Geneva model was reported stolen in late 1888, but never recovered.[17]

By October 1890 the Stace family had moved into yet another rented house. This one – at 42 Fountain Street, Alexandria[18] – was no more salubrious than the others. It may have been even worse. Certainly, it would be the last place in which the family lived together.

They survived there for two years, during the onset of a severe economic depression across the Australian colonies. Banks failed and unemployment soared. In the words of Manning Clark, it was a 'time of tumult' which 'cast a dark shadow aslant the Australian dream ... the cities of Australia were being likened unto the cities of dreadful night.'[19] If William Wood Stace had not been able to find regular gainful employment during the (relatively) prosperous 1880s, his situation in the early 1890s would have seemed next to hopeless.

At one stage in 1892 he was trying his luck as a 'picture canvasser',[20] but this cannot have raised more than a pittance. In or about the same year William had resorted to applying for 'outdoor relief' from the Benevolent Society of New South Wales.[21] This took the form of weekly handouts of food (flour, milk, sugar, tea, bread), and, in accordance with the prevailing standards of Victorian charity, there was a rigorous system of interview and inspection. The aim was to ensure that only the poorest families received help, and then only in times of extreme hardship – 'merely to prevent people starving.' A culture of 'dependency' among the idle underclass was to be discouraged at all costs.[22]

As an adult, Arthur Stace's entrenched memories of boyhood were centred upon these two wretched years at 42 Fountain Street. As best things can be reconstructed, it was a nightmare world of hunger and want, cruelty and neglect. For by this time – and probably for some years beforehand – both his parents were incurable alcoholics. It was as a small boy of six or seven that Arthur tasted his first strong drink, from the dregs of his father's glass.

1.2. William Wood Stace, Arthur's father, yells drunkenly at his wife Laura while the Stace children cower under the house.
DAVID LEVER, *SANCTUARY*, OIL ON BOARD, 2000/01.

William and Laura screamed abuse at each other habitually. William had a violent streak when in his cups. As a defence mechanism, the children often took shelter under the house, sleeping beneath hessian sacks – even in winter. This was preferable to witnessing their parents' wars at close quarters.[23]

All his life Arthur Stace suffered chronic respiratory problems. He never grew taller than five feet three inches (160 cm) and never weighed more than ten stone (63 kg) – often considerably less. He was a frail wisp of a man. And the root causes are self-evident. Such little spare money as the Stace family possessed was squandered on grog. When the children complained of lack of food (the Benevolent Society's handouts only went a little way), they were ordered to go out and find it for themselves. And they did! Led by the resourceful tomboy Minnie (by then 11 or 12, and in Clara's absence at Parramatta Industrial School the oldest of the siblings), they scavenged in garbage bins. They stole milk from doorsteps and verandas, bread and cakes from bakers' carts, and lollies from shop counters.[24]

1.3. Arthur Stace, aged 6 or 7, steals bread from a neighbour's doorstep in the company of his older sister Minnie.

DAVID LEVER, *DAILY BREAD*, OIL ON BOARD, 2000/01.

Indeed, they stole anything they thought they might be able to sell. On 7 August 1890, oldest brother William Stace, aged 10, was charged at Redfern Police Court with the theft of a quantity of fencing.[25]

It is hard not to feel sorry for Laura, despite her evident failure as a mother. Her life in these years can only have been a misery.

In December 1891 she was the victim of an assault by one Mary O'Donnell – the circumstances of the incident are not known, but they were serious enough to come to the attention of the authorities.[26] A month later, on 27 January 1892, Laura's mother Margaret Lewis died of a stroke.[27] Though she and Laura were probably estranged, this can only have been a source of more sadness. And later in 1892 – early in October – came the cruellest cut of all. William Wood Stace, 37, a wreck of a man at the end of his tether, abandoned his wife and children.

Laura waited a fortnight or so before reporting her husband's desertion to the Redfern police. In those days it was a criminal offence for a male breadwinner to abscond. Stace's whereabouts were unknown. Promptly, a warrant was issued for his arrest.[28]

It may have been the very same afternoon that Laura returned to Alexandria from reporting William's desertion – or possibly or few days later – that the final blow fell. On 28 October 1892, the landlord at 42 Fountain Street served her with a notice of eviction. This ruthless man did it himself, in the company of two police officers. The rent was unpaid and Laura had no way of paying it, so under the harsh legal system of that era, she and her five children were literally turned out on the street. *There and then.* A kindly neighbour took them in overnight.[29] For Arthur Stace, aged seven, these events must have been horrifying.

Next morning, Laura bit the bullet. Any vestige of pride gone, she hustled her brood along to the Sydney Benevolent Asylum in George Street (close to present-day Broadway). But this time it was not for temporary outdoor relief. Laura could cope no longer: she had decided to give her children up to foster care.

§

How had it come to this?

So far, we have been witness to the immediate causes of Laura and William's downfall. In order to understand their tragedy fully, and the whole incredible story of their son Arthur Malcolm Stace, it is necessary to go back much further in time. The sharp reader may be wondering why William Wood Stace ended up such a failure when his older brother and younger sister stayed affluent members of the English upper middle class. Why did Laura's family in Windsor never step in to help?

The answers – at least some of them – are to be found in previous generations. Arthur Stace always spoke sparingly of his parents' backgrounds – and seems to have been largely silent as to his grandparents'. Most of the details that follow were unknown during Arthur's lifetime, certainly to the general public, but also to many of the people who were closest to him. It is probable that Arthur himself was unaware of certain facts. We do not know how much he was told as a child – or how much he remembered of what he had been told.

2. The sins of the fathers

The past is a foreign country; they do things differently there.
L.P. Hartley, *The Go-Between*

William Wood Stace, Arthur's reprobate father, had once had glowing prospects. And much had been expected of him.

His father was Walter Samuel Stace (1824–69), a colonel in Queen Victoria's Royal Engineers.[1] Military service was a tradition in the Stace family. In June 1815 Walter's grandfather, William Stace (1755–1839), served as Chief Commissary of the Royal Artillery during the Battle of Waterloo, the iconic encounter that decided the Napoleonic Wars in Britain's favour.[2] For his contribution to that victory, William was appointed a Companion of the Order of the Bath (CB);[3] later, from 1823, he served as Storekeeper of the Royal Arsenal at Woolwich.[4] It seems certain that William Wood Stace was named after this distinguished ancestor.

William's mother, Jane Matilda Stace (née Pasley), came from an even more eminent family. Her father, Sir Thomas Sabine Pasley KCB (1804–84), was a senior officer in the Royal Navy who served across the globe in various capacities and ultimately achieved the rank of full admiral. He was also a member of the British aristocracy – the 2nd Baronet Pasley of the county of Craig in Dumfries, no less.[5]

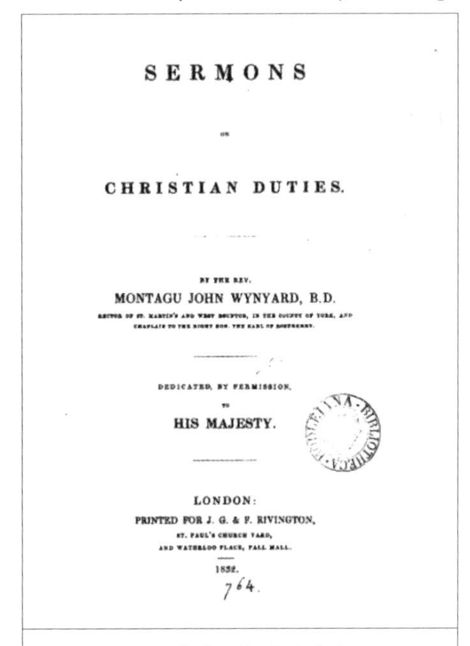

SERMONS

ON

CHRISTIAN DUTIES.

BY THE REV.

MONTAGU JOHN WYNYARD, B.D.

DEDICATED, BY PERMISSION,

TO

HIS MAJESTY.

LONDON:

PRINTED FOR J. G. & F. RIVINGTON,

ST. PAUL'S CHURCH YARD,

AND WATERLOO PLACE, PALL MALL.

1832.

764.

2.1. Title page of a book of Christian sermons by the Rev. Montagu John Wynyard B.D. (1781–1857), Arthur's great-great grandfather. Rev. Wynyard presided at the marriage of Arthur's paternal grandparents, Walter Stace and Jane Pasley, in 1851.

The marriage of Walter Stace and Jane Pasley, on 16 June 1851, was a major social event. It took place at the parish church of St John Pater, in Pembrokeshire, south-west Wales.[6] In the 1840s Pembroke Dock had become an important military town, the site of a naval dockyard and fortified barracks. The fathers of both bride and groom were distinguished senior officers, and the presiding prelate, the Rev. Montagu John Wynyard (the bride's grandfather) was a chaplain to Queen Victoria herself.[7]

So William Wood Stace was of fine pedigree. And when he entered the world, on 17 May 1855, it was in a notably exotic location – the island of Mauritius in the Indian Ocean, about 700 miles (1130 kilometres) east of Madagascar.

Mauritius had been in British hands since 1810: it was a spoil of the Napoleonic Wars and an important strategic possession in the Southern Hemisphere. During 1851, at its capital, Port Louis, the Royal Engineers completed the construction of an imposing 16-gun

2.2. Government House (top) and naval citadel (bottom, atop hill in background) at Port Louis, Mauritius, birthplace in 1855 of William Wood Stace, Arthur's father. Captain Walter Stace, Arthur's grandfather, commanded the citadel in the mid-1850s.

citadel. Three years later, in 1854, Walter was promoted to the rank of captain and dispatched from England to take command of it. Given that the Crimean War was raging back on the Continent,[8] this was a plum post in a non-combat role. Walter was accompanied by his wife Jane and their infant son Malcolm. Baby William's arrival the following year made them a family of four.

Their stay on Mauritius was short. Within a few years, Captain Walter Stace was stationed in an even more colourful place: the remote South Atlantic island of St Helena, where Napoleon Bonaparte himself spent his final years in exile. There, in September 1858, Jane gave birth to their third child and only daughter, Georgina.[9]

It had been a peripatetic existence. But by 1861 the family was back in England at a prestigious London address – 2 Belitha Villas, in Islington. They were living with Walter's sister Ann and her husband, the Rev. William Vincent.[10] Here, again, we can detect a hint of serious Christianity in the *Eternity* backstory. William Vincent occupied the pulpit at Islington's Holy Trinity Church, in Cloudesley Square. This was – and is – an imposing greystone edifice with tall spires and beautiful stained-glass windows. It seems almost certain that William Wood Stace attended services there as a boy. His brother, Malcolm, had taken his middle name, Vincent, from their clerical uncle.

2.3. 2 Belitha Villas, Islington, London, childhood home in the 1860s of Arthur's father, William Wood Stace. William's uncle, the Rev. William Vincent, occupied the pulpit at nearby Holy Trinity Church in Cloudsley Square.

Later in the 1860s the Staces left London and struck out on their own again. Walter, promoted to lieutenant-colonel in 1867,[11] took up a post in or near the Somerset town of Bath. This was another highly congenial spot. (Bath had been the home of Jane Austen, and, in his retirement, of the first governor of New South Wales, Arthur Phillip.) The Staces resided in Sion Hill Place, a row of nine four-storey Georgian terraces designed by the noted architect John Pinch the Elder.[12]

Further details are scant, but it cannot be doubted that William Wood Stace enjoyed a privileged boyhood. Both the London and Bath houses were spacious and handsome, and almost certainly staffed by domestic servants. William, like his older brother Malcolm, must have received a decent private education.

What went wrong for William? The turning point, perhaps, was the sudden death of his father in September 1869. Colonel Walter Stace was just 45 when he died, having recently retired on full pay.[13]

2.4. Sion Hall Place, Bath, later childhood home of William Wood Stace. After his father Walter's death in 1869, William continued to live there with his widowed mother and two siblings until joining the 5th Royal Lancashire Regiment in 1874. Three years later he resigned his commission and ventured to Australia.

He left his wife and family only reasonably well-off – his estate was valued at less than £450.[14] Probably with the help of Pasley relations, Jane was able to remain at 4 Sion Hill Place for a few years. But her position had become precarious. Older son Malcolm evidently knuckled down, soon afterwards commencing medical studies. Daughter Georgina was just eleven.

Of the three siblings, William seems to have been affected the most. He was a vulnerable and impressionable teenager when his father died and evidently had a restless temperament.

By late 1874, still only 19, he had left home and enlisted in the 5th Royal Lancashire Regiment in Burnley (hundreds of miles to Bath's north).[15] This move was consistent with family tradition, on both the Stace and Pasley sides, and William soon attained the rank of sub lieutenant. But his military career was brief. On 20 March 1877, he resigned his commission.[16]

His reasons for doing so can only be guessed at. Perhaps he simply did not fancy the military life; perhaps he was rebelling against the burden of family expectations. One suggestive fact stands out. Under the terms of his late father's estate, he was entitled – probably once he attained the age of 21 – to an annual allowance of £50. This was not a princely sum even then (the equivalent of about $7,000 in today's money), but it was enough to spoil him. Perhaps imagining that he might make his fortune in the southern colonies – or perhaps just looking for fun and adventure – he decided to travel to Victoria. In retrospect, it was a feckless, reckless thing to do.

On 22 October 1877, he departed Portsmouth as a cabin passenger on the SS *City of Santiago*. It was an uneventful voyage in pleasant company. Just under two months later, on 19 December 1877, the vessel arrived in Melbourne where William disembarked.[17]

It is likely that William spent at least part of 1878 in Melbourne, then the biggest and most prosperous city in Australia. But his activities can only be a matter for speculation. By mid-1878 he was in Sydney: he was a passenger on a ship, the SS *City of Brisbane*, which embarked from Circular Quay on 12 July on a journey north to Queensland.[18] But his stay there must have been short. Later in 1878 he was back in Sydney, living in rental accommodation in Rushcutters Bay Road, Woollahra,[19] a mile or so east of the CBD.

During this period, William missed some big family events back in England.

The first, in September 1878, was the marriage of his sister Georgina. The groom, Edward Eustace, was a surgeon major in the Royal Army Medical Corps, and, at 37, almost twice his bride's age. Georgina, 19, now had her future secured. Soon she would become a mother and set off with Edward to a posting overseas, in Gwalior, India. It appears that her widowed mother, Jane Stace, travelled to India with her. In the back of both their minds was some comforting knowledge: Edward's older brother was the owner of the Newstown estate in County Carlow, Ireland, and thus a man of means.[20]

The prospects of Malcolm Stace, William's older brother, also appeared bright. In February 1879, at age 25, he passed his final medical exams and was admitted to the Royal College of Physicians of Edinburgh.[21] The following year, 1880, he married an eligible young lady named Ellen Cleve at St George's, Hanover Square – a church in London's Mayfair district, built in the reign of Queen Anne and renowned for its 'high society' weddings. Around the same time – perhaps seeking to emulate his new brother-in-law, Edward Eustace – Malcolm began a period of service in the military as a surgeon in Her Majesty's Fleet.[22] (As it happened, his naval career was brief: he retired 'unfit' within a few years[23] and entered private practice – hence his sojourn in Sydney in the late 1880s. But that is beside the point. Malcolm by 1879 was *respectable*.)

Was William Wood Stace, languishing in Australia, already thought of as the family's 'black sheep'? Perhaps not yet. But he was shortly to make the most fateful decision of his life.

§

The exact date and circumstances of their meeting are lost to history. But sometime in the first half of 1879, probably in April or May, in or near Rushcutters Bay in Sydney, William Wood Stace encountered Laura Lewis.

Mutual sexual attraction was almost certainly immediate. As we saw in Chapter 1, both William and Laura were good looking. And Laura, 19, had every incentive to seduce him, or at least to succumb easily to whatever advances he may have made. She was alone in Sydney with a three-year-old daughter to care for – the girl Clara, her illegitimate offspring from an encounter in Windsor. How Laura could have hoped to survive in rough-and-tumble Sydney is anyone's guess: most likely she did not know herself. William Stace, with his handsome bearing and appearance of affluence, must have looked a wonderful catch.

At any rate, by June 1879 Laura was pregnant with his child. And William, to his great credit, stood by her. Later he would sink to the sorriest of depths, moral as well as material, but that one honourable choice cannot be taken away from him. The *Eternity* story pivots upon it.

William and Laura decided to make a life together, moving to the semi-rural suburb of Ryde. The rents would have been cheaper there than in Rushcutters Bay and the surroundings more pleasant. Their baby, a girl, was born in a house on Twin Road on 3 March 1880.[24] They named her Minnie.

It is hard to escape the conclusion that William Wood Stace was a kind-hearted man. Until Laura fell pregnant, he was an unattached Englishman in his mid-twenties, of fine breeding and with everything to live for. He must have been extremely tempted to send Laura packing. At any time he might have returned to England alone. But he did not. Why? Innate decency and the pangs of conscience surely came into it, but another factor was the sheer horror of Laura's life story to that point. Only a pitiless monster could have failed to be moved.

For Laura had fled Windsor in extraordinary circumstances. She was the third of ten children in a dysfunctional family. Her father, John Lewis, a farmer, was a vicious brute prone to drunkenness and violence. Her long-suffering mother, Margaret Lewis (née Mehan), may have cracked under the strain. On 29 August 1876, at the family home in Richmond, 42-year-old Margaret fed her granddaughter Clara – then a three-month-old baby – a deadly poison. Clara suffered severe external and internal injuries, but survived.

The Windsor police charged Margaret with attempted murder. On 15 September 1876 she was admitted to Windsor Gaol, but was released on bail pending her committal hearing ten days later.[25] The account of that hearing, published in the *Sydney Morning Herald*, boggles the mind:

> Laura Lewis, daughter of defendant, and mother of the child, was a single woman; on the 29th of August last, [Laura] left her child in bed at her mother's house, in Richmond; the child had a bad cold but was otherwise in good health; after placing the child in bed, [Laura] went to Mr Eather's next door, and was absent about ten minutes; whilst at Eather's her sister Rebecca called her, and she went to her, at her mother's, and saw her mother with the child in her arms; the child's mouth seemed all scalded, and it was shivering with cold; [Laura] asked her mother what she had been giving to the child, and she said, 'A drink of tea;' [Laura] said to her, 'You gave the child scalding tea;' she dressed the child and gave it a dose of castor oil, and afterwards, at her mother's request, went for Dr McPhee.[26]

Medical investigations had later revealed that the liquid Clara ingested was not hot tea but carbolic acid. There was a jar of it in the house, prescribed a few months earlier by a local doctor for application to an abscess.[27]

What really happened? Possibly, in a moment of delusion, Margaret had imagined that the child was better off dead. Yet she denied intent to kill. On balance, it was likely a genuine accident in a chaotic household. Although Margaret was committed to stand trial,[28] it seems clear that, subsequently, the charge was dropped.[29] Margaret resumed her life in Richmond.

Yet she may have been safer in gaol. A few years later she was brutally beaten by her husband, sustaining multiple broken bones. At Windsor court on 18 February 1880, John Lewis was convicted of inflicting grievous bodily harm on his wife and sentenced to six years' hard labour 'on the roads'.[30]

These two fine citizens would be Arthur Stace's maternal grandparents.

§

It is no wonder, then, that Laura Lewis had set out from Richmond on her own. Her family had failed her utterly, and William Wood Stace soon became her world. But William just could not cope.

Their experiment of living in Ryde ended quickly. Within months of Minnie's birth in March 1880, they were back in the harsh surrounds of inner Sydney, most likely because the area offered better employment prospects for William. For a few years they occupied a small rented terrace at 24 Walker Street, Redfern: it was there that Arthur's older brothers were born, in 1881 and 1883 respectively.[31] The first son, William John, was named after his father. The second son's name, Samuel Seaward Stace, had a nautical flavour – and a nice alliterative sound.

It is clear even from such slender details that William Wood Stace was a man of some wit and sensibility. And that, at least when sober, he retained a measure of dignity.

It was the scourge of alcohol that ruined him, though it is unclear when his drinking began. For anyone with a weakness for the bottle, Sydney in the 1880s was a bad place to be. In the words of Nathaniel (Nat) Gould, a talented English journalist and novelist who ventured to New South Wales at that time and became turf editor of the *Referee*:

> An enormous amount of liquor, good, bad, and indifferent, is consumed in Sydney. The bad quality of much of the liquor sold has a good deal to do with the drunkenness seen there. Drink is expensive, and runs away with a vast amount of money. In most cases a drink costs double, sometimes treble, the amount it does in England. A man must earn very good wages to indulge at all freely in drinking. In summer the heat makes working men thirsty, but they seem to forget that the more they drink the more they require.[32]

Gould also observed, in words that might have been written about William Wood Stace: 'It is not the native-born Australian who is the heavy drinker, although he can take his share; it is the man who comes out to make a living there. It is the principal reason why he fails to make that living.'[33]

William's drinking may well have been habitual by the time Arthur was born in 1885. Already, by then, his responsibilities were heavy. But Malcolm's departure from Sydney, sometime in 1890, was perhaps the final straw. His older brother was returning, not merely home, to dear and familiar England, but to the sort of life that the Stace brothers had been groomed for. Their widowed mother was not wealthy enough in her own right to bail out William and his antipodean family, even if she had felt so inclined. The ghost of 'what might have been' surely haunted William to the grave. *Why oh why had he ever resigned his army commission?*

As for Laura, the curse of alcohol addiction already ran in her family. As we have seen, her father John Lewis was a violent drunkard. (So was her great-grandfather, an ex-convict named Isaac Cornwall: on New Year's Day 1817, he had been shot dead in a drunken fracas while wielding an axe.[34])

So alcoholism was in Laura's genes. But for her there was an additional factor: the steady loss of faith. It must have been soul destroying. On top of the grind of daily life, she mourned the death of baby Ellen in March 1889 and confronted the dawning realisation that William would not be her saviour. Her parents, too, cannot have been of much, if any, help. We do not know how Laura's relationship with her mother was impacted by the poisoning episode of 1876, but such hard evidence as there is suggests they remained estranged. Margaret died of a stroke in January 1892, aged 55. For years afterwards several of Laura's siblings published fond 'in memoriam' notices on the anniversary of their mother's death.[35] Laura never did.

And so we return to where we left Laura at the end of Chapter 1 – with her decision in October 1892 to give up her children to foster care.

3. The road to perdition

All of us who are worth anything, spend our manhood in unlearning the follies, or expiating the mistakes of our youth.
Percy Bysshe Shelley

The Benevolent Society of New South Wales was a vital institution in nineteenth-century Sydney. Established in 1818 by Edward Smith Hall,[1] a great Christian philanthropist who had been close to Governor Lachlan Macquarie,[2] its principal aims were 'to relieve the poor, the distressed, the aged, the infirm,' and to 'encourage industrious habits.'

One of its main centres of operation was the Sydney Benevolent Asylum, a large, sprawling building which backed onto the old Sydney burial ground in Devonshire Street.

By the 1860s, the chief purpose of the Asylum was assisting pregnant women, both married and single, during their confinement.[3] But from 1881 it served an additional purpose, following enactment in that year by the New South Wales parliament of the State Children's Relief Act. This legislation established a system of 'Boarding Out' – the placement of orphans and other unwanted children in foster care, along lines previously implemented with success in Victoria and South Australia.[4] The system was administered by a government agency, the State Children's Relief Board, under the presidency of another prominent nineteenth-century Christian in Sydney, Arthur Renwick. Carers were paid an allowance by the state: the going rate around this time was £2.5s per quarter.[5] For the foster-child, where they ended up was a matter of luck (or providence).

Strictly, the Benevolent Society was a separate, private body. But it worked closely with the Board because the Asylum was frequently the first port of call for desperate people in Sydney.[6]

Deserting Wives and Families, Service, &c.

Sydney.—A warrant has been issued by the Central Police Bench for the arrest of Matthew Clarke, charged with disobeying a Magisterial order for the support of his wife. Offender is 60 years of age, 5 feet 8 inches high, gray hair and heavy gray moustache, stout build, three or four blue spots on back of each hand; a labourer; an Irishman.

Redfern.—A warrant has been issued by the Redfern Bench for the arrest of William Wood Stace, charged with deserting his wife, Laura Stace, of 42, Fountain-street, Alexandria. Offender is an Englishman, 44 years of age, 5 feet 10 or 11 inches high, thin build, dark-brown hair, fair complexion, moustache and small side levers; dressed in dark-gray sac coat, blue serge trousers, and blue tie; a picture canvasser.

Redfern.—A warrant has been issued by the Redfern Bench

3.1. Notice in the *New South Wales Police Gazette* of the desertion of William Wood Stace in early October 1892.

On Saturday 29 October 1892, Laura Stace was such a person. She arrived at the Asylum in the morning with five children in tow – Minnie (12), William (11), Samuel (9), Arthur (7) and Dora (2). Then she told her story, which was recorded by a clerk in immaculate handwriting:

> Husband William Wood Stace, labourer, deserted three weeks ago, and a warrant has been issued for his arrest. The family were

turned out of their home by the landlord last night for the non-payment of rent. They were sheltered by neighbours till today.[7]

3.2. The Sydney Benevolent Asylum, to which a desperate Laura Stace took her five children on 27 October 1892. The family had been evicted from their home in Alexandria the previous day for non-payment of rent.

Laura's scattered state of mind is perhaps best evidenced by one tiny but telling detail: she misstated Arthur's age. Her youngest son was seven (indeed almost eight) years old – not six, as she told the clerk.

Stace Laura (née Lowis) 38 yrs C E Natives. Husband, William Wood Stace,
Minnie 17 yrs labourer, deserted three weeks ago, and
William John 11 yrs a warrant has been issued for his
Samuel Steward 9 yrs arrest. The family were turned out of
Arthur 6 yrs their home by the landlord, last night for
Lord 2½ yrs the non payment of rent. They were sheltered
by neighbours till today. (Last address: 33
Fountain Street, Alexandria)
Mrs Stace was in receipt of out door relief.

3.3. Register of the Sydney Benevolent Asylum, 27 October 1892. Arthur's age is incorrectly recorded as 6.

The family was admitted to the Asylum as a case of 'emergency.'

The Stace children, if they had remained in the dark until then, must have learned their fate over the weekend. For their mother stayed only two nights. On Monday 31 October 1892 Laura left the Asylum, accompanied only by Dora. The clerk made this ominous notation: 'Mrs Stace will endeavour to gain a livelihood with her infant.'[8]

That left Minnie and the three boys. The Asylum would then have notified the State Children's Relief Board and awaited further instructions. In the meantime, the Stace boys at least had the benefit of regular meals, clean clothes and a bed to sleep in. They also had their older sister's company, but not for long. A month later, on 26 November 1892, Minnie was released – or released herself – from the Asylum's care.

The Boarding Out scheme was confined to children *under* the age of twelve when first admitted,[9] making Minnie ineligible. Although the written record is silent, it may be surmised that Minnie feared meeting the same fate as Clara: an indefinite stay at the dreaded Industrial School for Girls at Parramatta. Minnie, it appears, preferred to take her chances on the streets. If nothing else, she possessed spunk and resource. (And according to her own lights, she succeeded. As we shall see, by the turn of the century she would be running a busy brothel in Surry Hills.)

The three Stace brothers spent Christmas 1892 together in the Asylum. But just a few days afterwards, on 29 December, Arthur was wrenched from William and Samuel's company. A foster carer had been found for him under the Boarding Out scheme, a middle-aged widow named Catherine Campbell who lived in the inland town of Goulburn, some 120 miles (190 km) to Sydney's south-west.[10] Arthur was discharged to the temporary supervision of a Boarding Out officer, whose task was to deliver him safely to Mrs Campbell in Goulburn. Almost certainly they travelled there by train.

3.4. Goulburn Railway Station, late nineteenth century, at which a seven-year-old Arthur arrived in late December 1892. He lived in foster care in Goulburn with Mrs Catherine Campbell until late 1899.

For seven-year-old Arthur, it must have been a lonely, nervous journey. Probably he envied his two older brothers, for whom foster care places had not yet been found: in the meantime, they got to stay together at the Asylum. As it happened, William and Samuel would wait several years before being 'boarded out', and eventually both were assigned to homes on the south coast of New South Wales not far from each other.[11] In January 1896, twelve-year-old Samuel was sent to Jamberoo and the care of a married couple, Henry and Dora Noble.[12] William waited until June 1897, when he was 15, before being assigned to a single man named George Swan in the nearby town of Berry.[13]

§

Arthur Stace spent seven years in Goulburn under Mrs Campbell's care. Unfortunately, even with the benefit of hindsight, little can be stated with complete assurance about this period of his life. In the

1950s, when Arthur publicly revealed certain details of his boyhood, he said nothing about his time in Goulburn.[14]

Nevertheless, a few pieces can be fitted together. We know that when Arthur arrived at her home, Mrs Campbell was 57 years old and had one late-teenage daughter, Lillian, still living with her. Her other ten children were grown up and had moved away. It seems likely that Mrs Campbell had a strong maternal instinct.

Two other inferences may safely be drawn: that Arthur attended primary school in Goulburn, with reasonable frequency,[15] while also performing many chores for Mrs Campbell. At least in theory, attendance at school was compulsory under the Boarding Out scheme; but the opportunity of obtaining free labour was a strong motive for prospective foster carers.[16] As Arthur Renwick explained:

> It is always impressed upon the guardians that the object of the system is not to 'coddle' the children ... they must also be qualified as far as they may be in their youth to go out into the world and fight the battle of life with credit to themselves and advantage to the commonwealth.[17]

Some guardians had mercenary motives and overworked their charges. But to be fair to Mrs Campbell and Lillian, there is no evidence of mistreatment of Arthur. His silence about them in later life is explicable on a number of innocent grounds, foremost among them the probability that his enforced move to Goulburn was a source of deep-seated and long-lasting grief. However dysfunctional the Stace family was, it must still have been a dreadful shock for a boy of seven to be wrenched from his home, and especially from the company of his siblings. In Mrs Campbell's household he was the only child. We will return to this issue in Chapters 14 and 15.

Nevertheless, it remains arguable that Arthur was better off in foster care in a country town than he would have been back in inner

Sydney with his parents. The same applies to William and Samuel. It is true that – to put it mildly – the boys did not go on to make the most of their chances. But they all grew up in a relatively healthy physical environment. And whereas at least two of the Stace sisters (Clara and Minnie) were illiterate, certainly as teenagers and probably also as adults,[18] the two younger boys (Samuel and Arthur) went to school and learned to read and write.[19] How often (if at all) they received letters from their parents, or from each other, is unknown.

Back in Sydney, neither William nor Laura Stace picked up their act. They did resume living together: by 1898, probably earlier, they shared an address at 5 Moore's Lane in Balmain.[20] But their married life was no happier, even in the absence of their children. The drinking and violence continued. In late March 1897, William was convicted of assault for the 'knocking down' of Laura – a sordid, ignominious incident that was reported in the Sydney press.[21]

It cannot have helped that William suffered a series of bereavements. In March 1893 his younger sister Georgina died in England,[22] followed two years later, in September 1895, by his mother Jane.[23] (They were the aunt and grandmother that Arthur Stace never knew.) And in October 1900, William lost the final link with his past. His older brother Malcolm – the surgeon, he of the stolen 'Lecomte' hunting watch – died in Portsea, Hampshire, aged just 47.[24] Throughout this time, William was spiralling into the abyss. The death of his mother brought with it no compensating inheritance.

Laura's life was similarly bleak. In November 1894, at Central Police Court, she was convicted of drunk and disorderly conduct and sentenced to a short term of imprisonment in Darlinghurst Gaol.[25] This was embarrassing enough, but four years later she was involved in a much more squalid criminal episode.

It appears that, by this time, Laura was plying her trade as a prostitute in Sydney's Haymarket district. On 1 December 1898 she lured a male customer to Balmain, where the two of them consumed 'sundry glasses of ale.' Later, at her house in Moore's Lane, Laura robbed the man of a watch and chain, and some cash, before striking him with an axe! The police were summoned. A week later, at Balmain Police Court, Laura was convicted of robbery and assault and sentenced to three months' imprisonment.[26] She served her time at Biloela Gaol on Cockatoo Island[27] – an infamous hellhole.

ASSAULT AND ROBBERY AT BALMAIN.

At the Balmain Police Court to-day, before Mr. M'Farlane, a woman named Laura Stace, residing at 5 Moore's-lane, Balmain, was charged with stealing from the person of John Bain the sum of 13s 6d, and a watch and chain, valued at £4 3s 6d, on the 1st instant. From the evidence given it appears that the complainant met the accused in George-street, near the Haymaket, and accompanied her to her home in Balmain. On reaching that suburb they had sundry glasses of ale. When they arrived at accused's place he was relieved of the cash, and afterwards, when she tried to eject him, the watch and chain disappeared, but were subsequently found by the police secreted in the back yard. Accused was sentenced to two months' imprisonment in Biloela Gaol. The same accused also pleaded guilty to assaulting the prosecutor, John Bain, by opening his forehead with the blade of an axe, and was ordered to be sent on to Biloela for another term of a month.

3.5. Newspaper report of an assault and robbery committed by Arthur's mother, Laura Stace, at Balmain in 1898. Arthur was still in foster care in Goulburn.

In the middle of all this, Laura had lost custody of Dora. Perhaps it was that humiliation which finally drove Laura into prostitution. In August 1896 the little six-year-old girl had been admitted to Sydney Hospital with a 'spinal injury.' Although the record does not reveal how or by whom the injuries were inflicted – or how serious they were – the authorities acted quickly. Soon afterwards, Dora was placed into foster care with a Mrs Brown, of Marsden Street, Parramatta.[28]

Meanwhile, Clara's progress had been wayward. From the Parramatta Industrial School, in May 1893, she was apprenticed as a domestic help to a married couple named Channier, in Marshall Street, Marrickville.[29] Evidently the post was not to Clara's liking: she absconded on 14 November 1894 and a notice was issued a week later in the *New South Wales Police Gazette* giving her physical description ('medium height, good-looking, fair hair and complexion').[30] It seems she was apprehended, or that she returned to the Industrial School at Parramatta of her own accord. Either way, she stuck it out there for almost another year, before the authorities determined she had turned 18 (in fact, she was already 19). On 21 October 1895 she was discharged from the School and placed in service with a Mrs McDonnell in the town of Young.[31]

But that didn't last long. By August 1897, aged 21, Clara was back in inner Sydney and in the advanced stages of pregnancy. The father was a 32-year-old Cantonese man named John Go-Hing, a produce merchant. It is to be remembered that the Chinese were a despised race in late nineteenth-century Australia. The small, tight-knit Chinese community in Sydney dated back to the days of the gold rushes, but the White Australia Policy was just around the corner. The fact that Clara and Go-Hing were not married was an added complication. In many eyes, Clara's pregnancy would have seemed the ultimate disgrace.

Even so, Clara kept the baby – a boy. On 5 October 1897 he was delivered safely at the Sydney Benevolent Asylum and named Henry.[32] John Go-Hing stuck by Clara and subsequently his extended family rallied around her in a way that her own parents had never done. She was welcomed into their homes and treated with dignity. Two years later, in 1899, she and John Go-Hing had a second child, a daughter (Ethel Edith).[33]

As we shall see, from a most unlikely beginning – not least her narrow escape from poisoning as a baby, at the hands of her grandmother – Clara's story would have a happy ending. Of all the Stace children, only Arthur went on to lead a more fulfilling life.

§

Let us now focus our attention back on Arthur. By December 1899 he was almost 15 years old. His school days – such as they had been – were over. So was his time in Goulburn in the care of Mrs Campbell.

Under the Boarding Out scheme, boys of Arthur's age and background were expected to obtain gainful employment.

We know that Arthur took up his first job in late October 1900 at a coal mine on the south coast.[34] But where did he spend the interim ten months? The records of the Benevolent Society are silent, but it is possible that he returned to Sydney and sought out his parents. In later life he would speak of being a 'Balmain boy', and in 1900 William and Laura Stace were still living in Balmain, in Moore's Lane.[35] They were living alone – Clara had been taken in by the Go-Hing family, Minnie was at large, William was now a free man, and Samuel and Dora were still in foster care – so there would have been room for Arthur.

If he was in Balmain during those ten months, what he got up to is anyone's guess. Most probably he frittered his time away, demoralised by the frequently drunken behaviour of his broken parents.

3.6. Mt Kembla coal mine, at which a teenage Arthur worked from October 1900 to May 1902. On 31 July 1902 an explosion at this mine killed 96 men and boys.

In October 1900 he began another chapter of his life. He was assigned by the State Children's Relief Board to the care of new foster parents – a married couple named Thomas and Maria Smith.[36] They lived on the western outskirts of Wollongong at Kembla Heights and had four daughters, Maria's by her first marriage to a man named Craddock.[37] The Mt Kembla mine was within walking distance of the Smiths' home: almost certainly that is where Arthur worked.

For Arthur, this must have been a time of rapid readjustment – and, most likely, profound anxiety. Apart from the obvious reason (the disconcerting effect of any major change), there were two extra factors at play.

First, the Smith family was not a happy one. In late November 1900, just a month after Arthur's arrival, Maria Smith confronted her husband of four years with the charge that he had 'taken liberties' with Maud, his oldest stepdaughter. Thomas Smith denied it, but he left the family home immediately and never returned. In June 1901 Maria filed for divorce on the grounds of adultery, alleging 'improper conduct' on Smith's part with Maud at 'the Cordo' (the nearby Cordeaux river).[38] Maud gave evidence against Smith and the divorce was granted three months later. Arthur had gone from one dysfunctional family to another.

The second factor contributing to his unease was, surely, the nature of his work. Coal mines in early twentieth-century Australia were extremely dangerous and unwholesome. The shifts were long, the conditions gruelling, and accidents frequent. Back in March 1887 at the nearby Bulli mine, a huge gas explosion had killed some 81 men and boys.

Arthur, of course, started at the bottom, and it must have been a tough initiation. According to one authoritative account,

> from the first day a boy went into the pit there was a pecking order through which he progressed to the coalface. On his first day at

> work a young boy might be lucky to get a job as a token boy on the surface. Every miner had his own identifying number stamped on the leather token and the token boy would take these from skips and hang them on allocated hooks for reuse. The next step was being sent underground and given a job as a trapper, opening and closing ventilation doors for the wheelers and horses.[39]

We do not know whether Arthur began as a token boy or a trapper. But we do know what he did after receiving his first week's wages. He went along with his workmates to a local pub – most likely the Mount Kembla Hotel, established in 1898 – and shouted them a mug of beer.[40] On the same occasion he downed his first 'man's drink.'

It was the beginning of a catastrophic addiction. As Arthur recalled decades later, drinking 'became [his] regular habit, and as early as 15 years of age he was carted off to jail drunk ... Pleadings and threats by the police were of no avail.'[41] So, by early 1901 – just after Australia had become a federated nation – Arthur Stace was on the road to perdition.

In his sober periods, he continued to work by day at the Mt Kembla mine. After his stint as a token boy or trapper he would have progressed to the next stages:

> From there [a boy] would become a clipper, clipping on full and empty skips. After some experience he would be taught spragging, jamming the wheels on the skips. This could be a very dangerous job and many boys and men lost their fingers doing it ... Most boys spent their first years as token boys, trappers, greasing the dummy dodds that controlled the hurling rope, clipping, spragging skips and then, when their turn came, they became wheelers.[42]

A wheeler's job – performed with the help and company of a pit-pony – was to transport the empty skips to the miners at the coalface, and to bring the full skips back to the surface.[43]

It is unlikely that Arthur had progressed to the stage of wheeling by the time he left the Mt Kembla mine's employ. This was in early May 1902, after only 18 months, when he was removed from the household of Maria Smith/Craddock by the State Children's Relief Board.[44] Conceivably Maria had complained about Arthur returning to her home drunk. She had four daughters to consider, after all, and may have been gun-shy after her experience with Thomas Smith.

Arthur was still only 17 and was assigned to new foster carers, Alex and Janet Dalgleish.[45] Aged in their late 50s when Arthur came to live with them, with no children of their own,[46] they resided in the small township of Balgownie, some ten miles to Wollongong's north, near the Mt Pleasant coal mine. In more ways than one, this was a providential move for Arthur. Unlike Thomas and Maria Smith, the Dalgleishes were a stable married couple. They had emigrated from Dunfermline in Scotland in 1886 and become productive, respected citizens.[47] Probably (for Dunfermline was a mining town) Alex Dalgleish had worked at the nearby Mt Pleasant mine after his arrival in New South Wales; later, in about 1900, he and Janet opened a general store at Balgownie. It appears the store failed, for Alex was declared bankrupt in the first half of 1902;[48] this may well have been a factor in him and Janet taking in a foster child. Be that as it may, it is likely that they made their best efforts to provide a steadying influence for Arthur. And it seems probable (though the Benevolent Society's records are silent) that Arthur began work at the Mt Pleasant mine.

Just under three months later, on 31 July 1902, a calamity befell the Illawarra mining community. A devastating underground explosion at the Mt Kembla mine – where Arthur had been working earlier in the year – killed 96 men and boys and injured dozens more. To this day it remains, in terms of loss of life, the worst industrial accident in Australian history. Subsequent enquiries blamed negligent management practices.[49]

Arthur may have felt the shockwaves of the blast while working at nearby Mt Pleasant. It is probable that he knew some of the victims. Certainly, along with the whole Illawarra community, he must have grieved their collective loss. Surely the thought also passed through his mind: 'It could have been me.' In his later Christian life, one imagines that Arthur should have responded with special understanding to Luke 13:4. (Jesus posed a rhetorical question about a disaster of his day: 'Or those eighteen, upon whom the tower in Siloam fell, and slew them, think ye that they were sinners above all men that dwelt in Jerusalem?')

In July 1902, however, the combination of existential shock and melancholy cannot have helped Arthur's worsening drinking problem. Nor would contact with his older brothers. William and Samuel Stace were still living in the Wollongong area after their own earlier discharges from foster care; no doubt the three brothers met from time to time. But they were not good influences on each other. All of them had developed serious drinking problems and Sam had strayed into a life of petty crime. In July 1904, in Kiama Police Court, he was tried and convicted of theft – he had pilfered tools from his employer of 13 months, a carpenter from Jamberoo.[50]

According to the official records, Arthur was released from the care of Mr and Mrs Dalgleish on 24 January 1904,[51] but it is possible he left the Wollongong area sooner. As an old man, he recalled 'humping his bluey at 18 between Newcastle and Tamworth', and seeking work as a railway ganger.[52] He had turned 18 on 9 February 1903.

At any rate, by this time, he was a lost soul. By his own admission, 'no employer would keep him, so he moved from job to job, from town to town – always finding a new job – a new hotel – a new policeman – and a new jail!'[53]

Sometime in 1905 he had had enough. He decided to return to Sydney and try his luck there.

4. And lead us not into temptation

Nearly everyone in the world has appetites and impulses, trigger emotions, islands of selfishness, lusts just beneath the surface.
John Steinbeck, *East of Eden*

When Arthur came back to Sydney in 1905[1] he faced two immediate tasks: finding a job and finding somewhere to live. It is likely that he found a home first. In 1905, his beleaguered parents were living at 192 Riley Street, Surry Hills, and his sister Minnie was at 39 Brisbane Street in the same suburb.[2] Arthur must have moved into one house or the other.[3] Possibly he switched between both.

Surry Hills was then among the most crowded and unsavoury places in Sydney. More than 30,000 people lived and worked in the district – a tangle of commercial, industrial and residential development. Pubs and brothels abounded, as did organised crime. Riley Street itself, home to William and Laura Stace, was 'notorious as Sydney's worst thoroughfare and Underworld battleground.'[4]

According to historian Christopher Keating, 'properties in Surry Hills exhibited all the old defects characteristic of inner-city rental housing.'[5] Nearly half the buildings had broken drains and sewer connections; few had indoor toilets, functioning windows or adequate ventilation; almost none were properly proofed against rising damp. Typically, a five-room house in Surry Hills had just one tap – in the backyard by the toilet. There was no garden, gas or electricity. Food was cooked on wood- or coal-fueled stoves.[6] During 1900, in the wake of an outbreak of bubonic plague, moves had begun in progressive quarters to 'clean up' inner-city Sydney suburbs such as Surry Hills. But the process took decades.

4.1. Riley Street, Surry Hills, early twentieth century, in which Arthur's parents lived in 1905 when 20-year-old Arthur returned to Sydney. Riley Street was notorious as Sydney's worst thoroughfare and underworld battleground.

Minnie by this time was married. In November 1903, aged 23, she had wed a man two years her senior, John Joseph Harmon.[7] This was *not* a 'marriage up': Harmon was a labourer, and he and Minnie had been living together before their wedding, in Surry Hills. That may be one reason why the ceremony took place at the Unitarian Church in Pitt Street[8] rather than within the Church of England.[9] Another possible reason is that Minnie was by then running a brothel.[10]

We know from Arthur's admissions later in life that he worked in and for Minnie's brothel when he lived in Surry Hills. But this may not have started immediately. In 1905, economic conditions were good. It was an opportune time in which to seek honest work – even for an unskilled man of 20 like Arthur. The Depression of the 1890s was by then a memory: the national unemployment rate was low and falling. Arthur was engaged by the City Council, most probably as a day labourer, and worked intermittently for three years.[11]

But his problems with alcohol continued, and he began not only to drink in pubs, but to work for them. In Lisle Thompson's words, he

> became a tout for a local pub [in Surry Hills], carrying drink from the pub to houses of ill-fame located in this area. [He] carried drink to the various two-up schools, one of which was run in an upstairs room of his sister's house of ill-fame. Arthur was employed as a scout to warn the two-up school of any approach by the police – one night he was severely reprimanded and let go.[12]

It seems probable, too, that Arthur was having frequent sex with prostitutes – Minnie's girls or girls in other brothels, or both.

Any hope of positive parental influence was long gone. William Wood Stace was now a grey-haired ruin of 51, in the final stages of his life. Three of his stated occupations around this time were in bizarre contrast: 'chainman' (a kind of glorified surveyor), 'tea agent' and 'sculptor'.[13] None can have been profitable. In October 1906 he deserted Laura again, and a warrant was issued for his arrest.[14]

The year 1908 was a very bad one for the Stace family – a turn for the even worse.

Dora turned 18 and was released from foster care. Within a few years she would be back living in inner Sydney with an illegitimate child (Eileen) to look after.[15] At some stage, like Minnie before her, she resorted to prostitution. She 'ran [a] house of ill-fame for many years'.[16]

William Wood Stace did not survive the year. On 23 June 1908 he was admitted to the care of the government-run Liverpool Asylum for the Infirm and Destitute. After a stay of 17 days he absconded, only to be readmitted five days later, on 15 July. Thereafter he remained in the Asylum for six weeks, until he was transferred[17] to the Parramatta Hospital for the Insane. He died there on 25 November 1908. The cause of death was 'general paralysis of the insane.'[18]

Deserting Wives and Families, Service, &c.

Newtown.—A warrant has been issued by the Newtown Bench for the arrest of Harold Coutie, charged with being a neglected child. He is about 10 years of age, reddish hair; dressed in dark knicker clothes and tweed cap; barefooted. Complainant, Inspector J. W. Chalmers, State Children's Relief Department.

Darlinghurst.—A warrant has been issued by the Water Police Bench for the arrest of William Wood Stace, charged with wife desertion. He is 58 years of age, 5 feet 10 inches high, slight build, gray hair and moustache; usually dressed in a light-tweed coat and vest, dark trousers and black hard hat. Complainant, Laura Stace, 192, Riley-street.

4.2. Notice in the *New South Wales Police Gazette* of the desertion of William Wood Stace in early October 1906. His age is stated incorrectly as 58. He was only 51.

It appears that throughout this period, none of William's family knew where he was. When he entered the Asylum in June, he could still name his children but he could not remember – or did not know – Laura's address. In the Asylum's records, there appears the horribly sad notation: 'Wife Unknown.'[19] Later in the year he lapsed into insensibility. The clerk at Parramatta Hospital who acted as the informant for his death certificate had very few details to supply. While in the hospital, William had been unable to name his parents, wife or children. All he could recall was that he had 'five children living.'[20] (This suggests that he did not count Clara as his.) He was buried in an unmarked grave in the Church of England section of Rookwood cemetery.

No notices were published in Sydney newspapers announcing his death or details of his funeral. It is probable that none of the Staces knew of his fate until at least six months later. On 25 May 1909, a city solicitor, the executor of William's will, published a notice in the *Evening Star* asking for any of William's relatives to contact him.[21]

Apart from his father's death, 1908 was also an especially bad year for Arthur. Indeed, it was a watershed. He was dismissed by the City Council – and understandably so. During his three years' employment, he had 'lost half of this time off work through the effects of alcohol.'[22]

4.3. Arthur works as a cockatoo (look-out) for a brothel in Surry Hills, c. 1910.
DAVID LEVER, *COCKATOO*, OIL ON BOARD, 2000/01.

The next eight years were the vilest of Arthur Stace's life. He was now a mean drunkard without any lawful means of supporting himself. Consequently, he 'abandoned himself to the underworld ... where he was known to and knew the criminal population of Sydney.'[23] He was used by gangs of thieves and robbers to act as a look-out – his tiny frame made him lithe and unobtrusive. Many years later he would make a chilling confession. During this period of his life he developed a 'vicious spirit': if ever he had a bad turn done to him, he would pay a standover man to give the offender a brutal beating. 'I would watch and it didn't affect me,' he admitted.[24]

It appears that Arthur still maintained contact with at least two of his siblings at this time – brother Samuel and sister Minnie. But neither was a positive influence.

Sam was still living on the south coast. On Australia Day 1909 he married a local woman, Edith Geary, and settled with her in the northern Wollongong suburb of Woonona.[25] But Sam had acquired an addiction to alcohol that would ultimately become even worse than Arthur's. It may have been on a visit to see Sam, in June 1909, that Arthur went on a drunken binge which landed him in the Wollongong Court on a charge of riotous behaviour.[26] The incident occurred at nearby Balgownie, where Arthur had lived with the Dalgleishes as a teenager – he had probably looked up some old drinking mates.

Minnie had separated from John Harmon[27] and was still running a brothel. In mid-1910 she was convicted of 'vagrancy'[28] – a euphemism for prostitution – and served a short period in gaol. Many years later, Arthur could still recall the grisly aftermath of his sister's stint inside.

Apparently, Minnie had been dobbed in to the police by one of her girls. According to Arthur, she exacted revenge on the informer: 'She did a stretch and when she came out she took her to Centennial Park and got her drunk and then cut her throat with the wine bottle ... that is the answer to that old crime.'[29]

Yet there was always a loyal, loving side to Minnie. On 25 November 1909, the first anniversary of her father's death, she arranged publication of an 'in memoriam' notice in the *Sydney Morning Herald*:

> In sad and loving memory of my dear father William Wood Stace,
> who departed this life November 25, 1908.
> Inserted by his loving daughter, Minnie Harmon.[30]

Laura published a similar notice.[31] She, even more so than Minnie, had found it within her heart to forgive.

Laura's own sad life was now petering to an end. In June 1910, her brute of a father, John Lewis, died of 'senile degeneration [and] heart failure.'[32] He was 79. It seems unlikely that Laura shed any tears for him, but the occasion may still have evoked feelings of loss and regret. Better news for Laura came the following year. From the distribution of William's estate in England, she received £50 (evidently the last annual allowance to which William had been entitled in his lifetime)[33] – enough to keep her going for a little while longer.

Laura knew she was dying. She was suffering malignant cancer and 'cachexia' – weakness and wasting of the body due to severe chronic illness. In February 1912 she made a will, meagre though her estate was. Perhaps she wished to convey a message of some sort: her no-good sons received nothing. Two-thirds of her estate went to Minnie and one-third to Clara. Dora also missed out.

In mid-April 1912 – around the time the *Titanic* sank – Laura admitted herself to Sydney Hospital in Macquarie Street. Her final weeks must have been agonizing: she died on 13 May 1912.[34] Curiously – can it be that the events were related? – Clara married her de facto husband John Go-Hing on the very same day, 13 May 1912.[35]

Arthur was aware of his mother's passing. We do not know if he visited her in hospital, but almost certainly he was kept 'in the loop', probably by Minnie. On 15 May he joined with his oldest brother, William, in publishing a funeral notice in the *Sydney Morning Herald*. Their friends were 'respectfully invited' to attend their mother's funeral that afternoon at Rookwood cemetery.[36]

And a year later, on the anniversary of Laura's death, Arthur published an 'in memoriam' notice of his own:

> In loving memory of my dear mother, Laura Stace,
> who departed this life May 13, 1912.
> Far and oft my thoughts do wander
> To a grave not far away,

Where they laid my darling mother
Just one year ago today.
Inserted by her loving son, Arthur Malcolm Stace.[37]

STACE.—In memory of my dear mother, Laura Stace, who departed this life May 13, 1912.
I did not know what pain she bore,
I did not see her die;
I only know she passed away,
And never said "Good-bye."
Inserted by her daughter, Dora Stace.

STACE.—In loving memory of my dear mother, Laura Stace, who departed this life May 13, 1912.
Far and oft my thoughts do wander
To a grave not far away,
Where they laid my darling mother
Just one year ago to-day.
Inserted by her loving son, Arthur Malcolm Stace.

STACE.—In loving memory of my dear mother, Laura Stace, who departed this life May 13, 1912. Inserted by her loving daughter, Minnie.

STACE.—In loving memory of our dear mother, Laura Stace, who departed this life May 13, 1912. Inserted by her loving daughter, Clara Gohing, and grandchildren, Harry and Ethel Gohing. Rest in peace.

STACE.—In loving memory of our dear mother, Laura Stace, who departed this life May 13, 1912.
You will roam, and times will fly,
Every leaf shall fade and die,
Every rising sun shall set,
But you, mother, we never shall forget.
Inserted by her loving son and daughter-in-law, Sam and Edie Stace.

4.4. 'In memoriam' notices published in the *Sydney Morning Herald* on 13 May 1913, the first anniversary of Laura Stace's death. Arthur paid for a poem 'in loving memory of my dear mother.'

But these were the briefest grace notes in Arthur's otherwise dismal life. Both his parents were dead, prematurely so. Clara excepted, his siblings were mired in various forms of degradation. Arthur was to spend three more years in Sydney's underworld (perhaps working occasionally as a labourer[38]) before journeying even further into hell, on the battlefields of France.

Where would he find salvation?

5. He that doeth

Not every one that saith unto me, Lord, Lord, shall enter into the kingdom of heaven; but he that doeth the will of my Father which is in heaven.
Matthew 7:21

What hope was there for people like Arthur Stace?

On one fashionable view, such people were victims of their genes and their environment. Across the Western world, in the years leading up to World War I, so-called 'social Darwinism' was a gathering force. Its ethos was ruthless. The riff-raff of human society must be allowed to die out ('survival of the fittest'). And, ideally, the process should be hurried along by such means as birth control, sterilisation and euthanasia.[1]

But not everyone felt that way. There were at least two forces in Edwardian Australia dedicated to improving the lot of the downtrodden. The first was in the arena of secular politics. The Political Labour Leagues (the forerunners of the ALP) had been active in all the colonies since the early 1890s as the electoral arm of the trade union movement. They enjoyed rapid success at the polls, and they were soon – albeit, at first, from opposition – exerting substantial influence on the ruling parties of wealth and privilege. Their swelling numbers in the lower houses of all Australian parliaments could not be ignored. Slum areas of the kind that Arthur Stace had grown up in – inner-Sydney suburbs like Redfern, Newtown, Alexandria, Balmain and Surry Hills – were among the first to elect Labor members.

Eventually these representatives of the working class began to form governments. The first was in Queensland in 1899, though that administration lasted only a week. But the trend was inexorable. Not long after Federation, the ALP held office nationally (in 1904, 1908–09 and 1910–13). It also won power at state elections in South Australia (in 1908), New South Wales (in 1910) and Western Australia (in 1911).

The period 1891–1914 saw the emergence of some fine national and state leaders in Australia, on both sides of politics. In New South Wales, important and long-overdue social reforms were achieved by the likes of George Reid[2] and J.S.T. (Jim) McGowen.[3] Federally, two prime ministers stood out: Alfred Deakin (Protectionist/Commonwealth Liberal) and Andrew Fisher (Labor). The best governments, whatever their political stripe, were dedicated to the amelioration of poverty and injustice. Among the most important reforms to be implemented were industrial and minimum wage laws; factories and shops legislation, leading to improvement of the worst of working conditions for the lowly paid; tariff protection for vulnerable Australian industries; the introduction of old-age pensions; town-planning initiatives; increased public works spending; and – a big one – the enfranchisement of women.

Deakin, Fisher and McGowen – and several other significant leaders besides – had something else in common. They were deeply religious men, devoted *in their inner being* to service of their fellow citizens.[4]

This brings us to the second force working for the welfare and betterment of people like Arthur Stace: the Christian churches. Let it never be forgotten that the churches had been active in these fields since 1788. Throughout most of the nineteenth century – before any government-funded social safety net existed in Australia – it was the churches, and religiously motivated individuals, who provided charity to the afflicted. We have already seen the crucial role played in Arthur's life by bodies such as the Benevolent Society of New South Wales.

But Christian charity only ever went so far. The churches and associated institutions competed for scarce private funds. As historian Stephen Barton has explained, 'the proportion of wealthy citizens [in Sydney] was small, and many of those who made substantial fortunes were self-made men more inclined to safeguard their fortune than distribute some of it to the less well off'.[5] There were lots of urgent and worthy causes but not enough philanthropists. In the 1860s, the secretary of the Benevolent Society lamented that 'so few people are subscribers and the same people subscribe to them all.'

Funding issues aside, there was also a flaw in the churches' approach to dispensing charity – especially on the Protestant side. It lay in their attitude to the 'vices of the poor.' Desperate men and women, even children, tended to be judged as 'deserving' or otherwise. Too much Christian charity was cold and sanctimonious, or tied conditionally to the (outward) moral behaviour of prospective recipients. Often this lessened its effectiveness.

With these thoughts in mind, it is time to introduce a new character in the *Eternity* story.

§

Robert Brodribb Stewart Hammond (1870–1946) was the first of three indomitable Christian men who, collectively, made the legend of Arthur Stace. Indeed, Hammond was one of the greatest Australian Christians of the first half of the twentieth century – perhaps *the* greatest.

By 1910, during Arthur's descent into the Sydney underworld, Hammond was honing the personal skills, and forging the network, that twenty years later would rescue Arthur from perdition.

Hammond was born in Brighton, Victoria, on 12 June 1870, the third son of prosperous parents. He attended Melbourne Grammar School and shone as a sportsman (especially in Australian Rules football) before moving on to university.[6] The turning point of his life came in 1890–91, when he was converted to serious Christianity by the influence of two visiting British evangelists, both giants of their day. A Scot, Henry Drummond (in 1890[7]), and an Irishman, George C. Grubb (in 1891[8]), electrified young colonial audiences with their passionate, progressive messages.

Of the two, Grubb was the more vital in Hammond's formation. Grubb's mission 'emphasised the attainment of a higher life of holiness, and transformed evangelicalism from a low church account of past events to focus upon the revitalising power of the Holy Spirit. These were Hammond's spiritual roots.'[9] He took to heart an insufficiently emphasised warning of Jesus, the one quoted at the outset of this chapter:

> Not every one that saith unto me, Lord, Lord, shall enter into the kingdom of heaven; but he that doeth the will of my Father which is in heaven (Matthew 7:21).

'He that doeth' became Hammond's creed.[10]

What did this entail? In Hammond's mind, it was the idea that there is much more to real faith than self-satisfied 'belief'. Faith without deeds is dead (James 2:20). Christianity must be lived out constantly in conduct of the sort that Jesus exhibited on Earth – conduct that he expects his followers to try to emulate, however imperfectly (John 8:29–31, 15:10, 14). Like most Christians, Hammond believed that Jesus will judge each of us by the way we treat others, and pre-eminently by our treatment of 'the least of these' (Matthew 25:45).

Let it be emphasised that Hammond was thoroughly orthodox in most aspects of Protestant theology. But he did much more than talk about it. In the words of his principal biographer, Bernard G. Judd, he was a man of 'disturbing drive.'[11] He trained for the ministry in the Church of England and was ordained in 1894. After service at various small parishes in Victoria, he moved to Sydney in 1899 to take up a three-year post at St Mary's, Balmain, as curate to the Rev. (later Canon) Mervyn Archdall.

5.1. Rev. R.B.S. Hammond in or about 1899, the year he came to Sydney.

(Here we encounter one of several coincidences in the *Eternity* story. As we saw in Chapter 3, Arthur Stace may have been living in Balmain, with his parents, from late 1899 to October 1900. Thirty years before their most vital meeting, it is quite possible that he and Hammond passed each other in the streets of Balmain.)

Hammond's first mentor in Sydney was not the Rev. Mervyn Archdall, who was a hidebound, sectarian old stick,[12] but the incumbent at nearby St Paul's, Redfern. The Rev. (later Archdeacon) Francis Bertie Boyce (1844–1931) was a charismatic figure of considerable fame and influence. Included among his parishioners was none other than 'Honest' Jim McGowen, ex-boilermaker, leader of the NSW Labor Party, future premier of the state, and, at St Paul's, the long-time Sunday school superintendent.[13]

Boyce had a strong interest in social justice. He was a vociferous advocate of 'slum clearance' – that is, improved housing conditions for the working classes and progressive town planning.[14] But his pet issue – not, in his eyes, unrelated to social justice – was temperance. He saw all around him the devastating effects of alcoholism on working-class people, and he was determined to do something about it by legislative means.

The Women's Christian Temperance Union was another powerful body. It attracted strong support, from all strata of society, because women and children were frequently the chief victims of drunken violence and neglect. (The Stace family was a case in point.) Many of the pious women who established the Temperance Union were also the pioneers of female suffrage in Australia. The two causes went hand in hand.[15]

In due course, Hammond also became a champion of temperance. But first he had to establish himself in Sydney as a respected and effective minister of the church. In April 1902, aged 31, he began a three-year post as curate of St Philip's, Church Hill. This was one of the city's foundation churches, located near the Rocks district not far from Circular Quay and Darling Harbour. Hammond soon found himself preaching in the open air to some tough, worldly customers.

'He did it,' wrote Bernard Judd, 'with a combination of downright, positive dogmatism seasoned with a dash of infectious humour.'[16] Consider this example:

> The place was at the foot of Margaret Street at the waterfront alongside the Union Company's wharf. A telegraph boy stood looking curiously at the speaker whilst a luggage porter paused in his trunk-shoving to listen. A lorry driver, with a great load of wool towering above, halted his horses whilst four gentlemen playing 'Crown and Anchor' left off robbing one another to catch what was said. The speaker was speaking of 'A Way of Life', and speaking

> in a way that was arresting, persuasive and forceful. For he was attacking 'booze' in its stronghold ... 'Who's this cove?' inquired a gentleman who sat on the kerb. 'He's the new Curate up at St Philip's,' replied the telegraph boy.[17]

Another of Hammond's admirers recalled:

> On this occasion in the park opposite St Philip's he saw a crowd of wharf labourers who were on strike. They were being addressed by one speaker after another and [Hammond] asked if he might be allowed to say something. They demanded to know what was the subject of his talk and his reply was: 'About a man who went on strike because his wages were too high!' They were both amazed and interested and gave him permission. And so, standing on an upturned packing-case, he delivered one of his characteristic talks on 'The wages of sin is death, but the gift of God is Eternal Life'.[18]

In Bernard Judd's view, Hammond's 'unique life-long ministry to men really commenced with his curacy at St Philip's.'[19]

By mid-1904, Hammond was ready for bigger challenges. Early in June he married Jean Marion Anderson, a union that would last for almost 40 years. Sadly, however, it began in traumatic circumstances. He and Jean lost their only child (a son, Bert) within 12 months. The boy was born in late June 1905 but died four weeks later. Jean was inconsolable and remained a recluse for the rest of her life.[20]

It has been suggested that Hammond's intense devotion to evangelism, charity and social justice constituted, at least in part, a sublimation of his feelings of helplessness and grief.[21] However that may be, he threw his energies into his new role within the church. For seven years, from August 1904, he was the organising missioner for its Mission Zone Fund, which operated within the congested inner-city areas of Waterloo, Woolloomooloo, Surry Hills, Redfern and Darlington.

This was Stace family territory. From 1905, when Arthur returned to Sydney following his days as a coalminer, he lived much of the time in Surry Hills where Minnie ran her brothel.

Neither Arthur nor Minnie would have realised it at the time – or, most likely, been thankful if they had. But during the decades that followed, Hammond, and others of like mind, were working tirelessly to address the spiritual and material problems that had destroyed their parents and which now beset them. Chief among these problems was the scourge of alcohol.

Under the leadership of Boyce and Hammond, and equivalent figures in other Protestant churches,[22] temperance became a major political issue in New South Wales. On 9 December 1905, the Liquor Act (NSW) came into force. This ground-breaking legislation provided for a radical form of 'local option', the right of citizens within each state electorate to decide by referendum whether liquor licences in their electorate should be continued, reduced in number or extinguished entirely.[23]

In the lead-up to the September 1907 state election, at which the first such referendums were held, Hammond founded a weekly newspaper called *Grit*. It was an effective organ of the temperance cause and gained wide circulation.

The results of the 1907 poll were gratifying. Across New South Wales, 179,000 votes were cast for extinguishment of all liquor licences (i.e. prohibition) and another 75,000 for reduction – a total of 254,000 votes in favour of change of some kind. Some 209,000 votes were cast for continuation of the status quo. True, no single electorate cast the requisite 60 per cent majority for prohibition. But in only 25 of the state's 90 electorates did a majority vote for continuation. In the remaining 65 electorates, a majority voted for either prohibition or reduction – which amounted, in effect, to a vote for the milder alternative, reduction. As a result, some 286 hotels were closed across

GRIT.

A PAPER FOR THE PEOPLE.

Registered at the General Post Office for transmission by Post as a Newspaper.

Vol. 1.—No. 1. SYDNEY, THURSDAY, MARCH 28, 1907. Price One Penny

Stay on Top—Pull them Up

EVERY year since the beginning of human life on this planet the spirit of charity has grown.

Every year and every century have seen more and more men and women anxious to help others.

To-day, with all the greed for money, all the foolish pursuit of wealth unneeded, we see a steadily increasing army of human beings anxious to work and live for others, IF THEY ONLY KNEW HOW.

This is an encouraging world. It is a bad place for pessimists. It is a world getting better constantly.

Poverty is diminishing. DRUNKENNESS IS DIMINISHING RAPIDLY. Crime grows less and less.

AND HUMAN AMBITION BECOMES CONSTANTLY NOBLER, which is the most hopeful sign of all!

The man of great wealth in times past thought only of spending his money in self indulgence. He wanted armies of servants, of slaves. He craved the flattery and submission of the ignorant.

Now the man who has made the [illegible] hundreds of millions actually apologises for his wealth. He tries to make other men his equals in ability, instead of trying to pull them down. He encourages science, endows universities, he fights with his money, consciously or unconsciously, against the very conditions THAT MADE HIM POSSIBLE, BY MAKING POSSIBLE HIS EXPLOITATION OF THE MANY FOR THE BENEFIT OF HIMSELF.

There is an army of earnest men and women in this world anxious TO LEAD GOOD, UNSELFISH LIVES.

They want to DO something rather than TO BE SOMETHING.

Of such men and women many have written:

"I feel that I have no right to be comfortable and happy, to enjoy life, while I know that so many are in want. I am ashamed of myself and of all other prosperous people when I see how the poor suffer in spite of their willingness to work, and especially when I see the children that have no chance."

How many have asked themselves whether they ought not at least to try to live up to the Golden Rule, get rid of their wealth and share their lot with the poor?

WHAT IS THE DUTY OF A MAN OR A WOMAN IN THIS WORLD?

What is the best thing that an earnest human being can do?

It is better to be Strong Yourself, and PULL UP THE WEAK, than to Go Down to the Pit and be Weak with Them

5.2 The first issue of *Grit*, Hammond's weekly newspaper, published on 28 March 1907.

New South Wales and 46 wine licenses withdrawn.[24]

Of course, this was only scratching the surface of a deep-seated problem. The vote for change tended to be lowest in electorates – such as Arthur's – that needed change the most. And, as it happened, the 'local option' vote in 1907 proved to be the high-water mark. For temperance campaigners, the results of the 'local option' polls of 1910 and 1913 were discouraging.[25]

Another priority would emerge: shortening the opening hours of hotels and bottle shops across the whole state. In due course, Hammond threw himself into that cause as well. But he did not confine his efforts to the political arena. He also got down and dirty.

On 10 January 1913, after four years of pleading with the authorities to grant him permission, he began a practice that continued for decades – talking to prisoners in the so-called 'drunks' yard' of the Central Police Court in Liverpool Street while they waited to make their appearance before the magistrate.[26] He did this, sometimes, as many as four mornings a week.[27] In this way, Hammond was brought directly into contact with some of the lowest of Sydney's low, including inebriates like Arthur Stace. He ministered to them, and, whenever possible, offered practical help. He also urged them to sign a pledge to give up alcoholic drink for good. Hammond was proud to wear the label of 'wowser'.[28] But he was not a wowser in the pejorative sense of that term. He was motivated by compassion and a desire to lift people up.

Nor was he a one-issue obsessive. He was well aware that alcohol addiction was only one of many problems besetting Sydney's inner-city poor. Others were unemployment, low wages, homelessness, cold, hunger, sickness and bereavement. 'What these hard up men need more than anything else,' he often said, 'is hope. If you can infuse hope into a man who feels like giving up, you have gone a long way to introducing him to the Saviour.'[29]

Throughout its 36-year history, the pages of *Grit* were not devoted to the temperance question alone. The first issue, published on 28 March 1907, outlined Hammond's overarching worldview: 'It is better to be Strong Yourself, and PULL UP THE WEAK, than to Go Down to the Pit and be Weak with Them.'[30]

Consistently with this ethos, Hammond practised friendly evangelism and set up hard-headed programs. He conducted open-air meetings and visited people in their homes. In 1908, in Newtown, he opened the first of his 'Hammond Hotels' – or 'Pilgrim's Houses' as he first called them. They were places where desperate men could get clean clothes, something to eat and drink, and emergency accommodation, as well as instruction in the gospel. Hammond's reasoning was as follows:

> I was deeply impressed by the fact that Zaccheus was a wonderful man ... It then dawned on me that his conversion was not due to a sermon, but a kindly invitation to a meal.* Men who were 'down

---

* Cf. Luke 19:1–10.

> and out' are more susceptible to hospitality than to sermons, and the one can provide as good an opening to help a man's soul as the other.[31]

(As we shall see in Chapter 9, on 6 August 1930 these words would apply *exactly* to the pitiful circumstances of Arthur Stace.)

Hammond's seven-year stint as Mission Zone Fund organiser ended in late 1910. But he continued the same sort of work in another guise, as rector of two churches in Surry Hills: St Simon's and St Jude's (from 1909) and St David's (from 1913).[32] These had been regarded as near-hopeless congregations, but Hammond revitalised them. He gathered a large and devoted following within Surry Hills and adjoining suburbs. Numbers at services increased tenfold.[33]

5.3. St David's Anglican Church, Surry Hills, at which Hammond served as rector from 1913 to 1918. It is now a community hall.

§

Arthur Stace was not among the souls saved by the Rev. R.B.S. Hammond in this period. Arthur was mired in booze, petty crime and other degradations. But his life – along with the lives of most other Australians – was about to take a different turn. We come now to the seminal event of modern history and its relevance to the *Eternity* story.

6. The lot is cast into the lap

Perhaps the greatest tragedy of [World War I] was not the deaths of those who had everything to live for but the lives of those for whom a single chance to do something different was worth dying for.
Richard White, 'Motives for Joining Up'[1]

Britain declared war on Germany on 4 August 1914. The news reached Sydney around lunchtime the next day, but already, for all practical purposes, Australia was also at war.

A federal election campaign was on foot, and, as ever, it was fiercely contested. A few days earlier, the Liberal prime minister, Joseph Cook, had declared on the hustings:

> Whatever happens, Australia is part of the Empire right to the full ... I want to make it quite clear that all our resources in Australia are in the Empire and for the Empire and for the preservation and security of the Empire.[2]

Cook got no argument from the opposition leader, Labor's Andrew Fisher.[3] There were few votes to be lost by appeals to jingoism and none to be won by caution or reserve. Or so the politicians reasoned.

They were probably right. For most citizens, Australia's participation was a given – even cause for outright celebration. Some worried that the war might be over before Australian soldiers could be trained and sent to the front.[4] Jingoism sprang from innocence and complacency as well as genuine loyalty to the mother country.

Within the mainstream Christian churches, there was almost no dissent from prevailing community 'wisdom'. In fact, some clergymen welcomed war as an opportunity for national spiritual renewal.[5] In Sydney, Protestant leaders arranged united services of intercession at which the empire's cause was lauded and all eligible men urged to do their duty.

On Sunday 9 August, Archbishop Wright declaimed at St Andrew's Cathedral:

> We have a spirit of confidence when we look at the reason why this Empire is at war ... We stand for our plighted word, and our word has ever been our bond. This has been the strength of our race. May it ever be for the generations to come.[6]

The next day, recruiting offices opened in Sydney and 2000 men enlisted. Within weeks the number had risen to 10,000.[7]

It must be doubtful whether Arthur Stace shared much, if any, of this early enthusiasm. In 1914 he was back living in Surry Hills, at 237 Commonwealth Street, possibly with his youngest sister Dora.[8] He was frequently drunk and still mired in a life of sin.

In any case, he could not have enlisted even if he had wanted to. At the beginning of the war, the recruitment standards for the Australian Imperial Force (AIF) were strict: only men with excellent physique were wanted. Apart from anything else, at 5 foot 3 inches tall, Arthur was way too short.[9]

§

Just a few miles from Surry Hills, in the rich harbourside suburb of Darling Point, there lived a jaunty 17-year-old boy named John Gotch Ridley. Known to his family and friends as 'Jack', he adored all things martial and was eager to enlist as soon as he could. The official minimum age in August 1914 was 19, but this would not have stopped him. Many under-aged youths joined up. But, frustratingly for Jack, his parents were reluctant. Though staunch admirers of the British Empire, they adopted a wait-and-see approach with their precious son.[10]

Jack Ridley would see action in due course. A lot of it. He would also grow up to become a distinguished Baptist minister, and, after R.B.S. Hammond, the next most important person in Arthur Stace's Christian life. Some would insist that he was *more* important, given his pivotal if unknowing role in inspiring Arthur's *Eternity* mission.

A little background is in order. Ridley was born on 8 September 1896, when Arthur (then 11) was in foster care in Goulburn. His parents, Thomas (Tom) and Ellen Ridley, were an upper-middle-class couple of impeccable reputation and considerable wealth. Tom was an executive at the publishing and magazine distribution company Gordon & Gotch,* and eventually became chairman of its New South Wales board. He was also a keen amateur cricketer and actively involved in the affairs of St Mark's, Darling Point, then (and now) one of Sydney's most salubrious Church of England congregations. Tom's wife Ellen was a homemaker, 'a gracious lady of the old school.' They had four children, of whom Jack was the youngest.[11]

The Ridley family lived at 'Walmer', a lovely house at 50 Mona Road (almost opposite St Mark's) with sweeping views of the harbour. Theirs was a 'peaceful and happy, though strictly disciplined' home[12] – the antithesis of Arthur's in almost every way.

---

* Hence Jack's middle name, Gotch.

When war broke out Jack Ridley was working for Gordon & Gotch, learning the ropes as a bookseller. Prevented from enlisting in the AIF straight away, he rose to the rank of lieutenant in the so-called Militia,[13] the pre-existing civilian forces which had been formed throughout Australia after Federation. Then two huge events intervened.

The first was the Gallipoli campaign, beginning on 25 April 1915. When news of the exploits and the plight of the Anzacs reached Sydney, Ridley, like many other idealistic young men of his mindset and social station, became still more determined to do his bit for King and Empire.

The second event – completely life-changing for Ridley – was his conversion to evangelical Christianity.

This happened in August 1915 at the Baptist Tabernacle in Burton Street, Darlinghurst, a mile or so from the Ridley home in Darling Point and the epicentre of the *Eternity* story. Opened in April 1887,[14] and later expanded, the Tabernacle building was designed to be spacious and functional rather than grandiose. An eminent architect and foundation member of the congregation, J.J. Stone, had provided his services for free; the costs of land and construction were met by donations from other members, including a prominent draper, William Buckingham. By 1915 the congregation was thriving.[15]

What was Jack Ridley doing there at all? To that point, his faith had been formal only. As a boy, he had received solid biblical teaching at a Presbyterian Sunday school, but overall had found the experience there 'solemn' and 'tiresome'.[16] During his teenage years, he was far more interested in sport, the Boy Scouts, and, above all else, matters military.

In that dark winter of 1915, Jack was drawn to the Tabernacle at the urging of his grandmother. She had been 'rocked' by a sermon about the war delivered by the Tabernacle's resident pastor, the Rev. William Lamb (1868–1944).[17] A New Zealander, then in his mid-

40s, Lamb had arrived at Burton Street in September 1911 at the height of his fame and powers. He was renowned for a musical and fluent preaching style, as well as a pre-millennialist interpretation of Scripture[18] – the idea that the return of Christ will be preceded by certain dramatic, unusual events (wars, famines, earthquakes, etc.) followed by a 1000-year period when Christ will reign on Earth in peace and righteousness.[19]

Premillennialism is a minority Christian position even among evangelicals, but it has enjoyed bursts of popularity down the centuries. For much of the twentieth century, Burton Street was renowned for hosting regular 'Second Advent' conventions devoted to this subject.

Jack Ridley knew nothing about the Baptist church, let alone premillennialism, when he went along to the Tabernacle in August 1915. He was drawn by the prospect of an interesting sermon about the war. 'I would go anywhere for information about this tremendous world conflict,' he later admitted.[20]

He got far more than he bargained for. In Ridley's words, many years later:

> That night I listened spellbound to a minister of God with a message from God delivered with the power of God. For the first time I realised that real religion necessitated a definite acceptance of Jesus Christ as one's personal Saviour; and meanwhile every moment of delay in making that decision increased the danger of being left behind at the sudden Second Coming of the Lord.[21]

Within a fortnight, Ridley had 'come forward' at Burton Street and made an open confession of Christ.[22]

His new religious fervour was matched by a heightened desire to serve in the AIF. Finally – the key breakthrough – his mother relented.[23] Jack was permitted to enlist and was accepted as a private into the 1st Battalion, 11th Reinforcements. After a short period of training at Liverpool – an eye-opener in more ways than one for an earnest, sheltered young toff from Darling Point[24] – he set sail from Sydney on Tuesday, 5 October 1915 aboard the T.S.S. *Themistocles*. His family was there to wave him off, along with sundry aunts, uncles, cousins and friends.[25]

Jack Ridley was one of those recruits who left home to fight despite having everything to live for.

6.1. John Gotch Ridley in AIF uniform, World War I.

The voyage to Egypt took four weeks. Ridley kept a diary; almost a century later, it was published in book form as *Born to be a Soldier* and makes compelling reading. Frequently he expressed surprise and disgust at the amount of gambling, swearing, smoking and drinking among his fellow recruits. He yearned to excel. He attended Christian services, and at one of them addressed his first ever meeting – a nervous seven-minute stutter.[26] When his ship reached the Red Sea he was full of wonder – 'I can hardly realise ... [this is] where Christ parted the waters to allow the Chosen People to pass through'[27] (cf. Exodus 14:21).

After disembarkation at Suez there followed another

period of training. This one was intense – it lasted for several months and coincided with the Anzacs' evacuation from the Dardanelles in December 1915. Henceforth it was common knowledge that the AIF's focus would switch to France and the Western Front, long since locked in a fearful, bloody stalemate. On 14 February 1916, Jack was 'taken on strength' into the newly formed 53rd Battalion. Roughly half its members were new recruits from Sydney such as him; the rest were surviving veterans from the 1st Battalion who had fought at Gallipoli.[28] It was an honour for Jack to be made a sergeant with responsibility for a squad of men.[29]

A week later, on 21 February 1916, the Germans launched a massive attack at Verdun.

§

Back in Australia, divisions in society were beginning to open up. The failed campaign at Gallipoli had cost almost 8000 Australian lives. Even Sydney's ever-bombastic *Daily Telegraph* admitted that the retreat was 'a dramatically disappointing anti-climax.'[30] With many more reinforcements now needed on the Western Front, recruiting standards were relaxed. Eligible men who had not already 'answered the call' were subjected to strong moral pressure to do so. Those who refused, even hesitated, were labelled 'shirkers' or worse. The prospect of conscription loomed.

For Arthur Stace, volunteering for service in the AIF seems to have been a last throw of the dice. He was one of those 'for whom a single chance to do something different was worth dying for.'[31] The minimum height had been lowered to five feet two inches, so he was no longer automatically ineligible.[32] He had little to lose and much to gain: self-respect. And at six shillings a day, the AIF pay was good.[33]

On Thursday 16 March 1916, Arthur presented himself for enlistment at the Royal Agricultural Society's grounds in Prince Alfred

Park. His 'attesting officer' that day – the man who took down his details and assessed his application – was Major David A. Storey, who had been educated at the elite Sydney Grammar School and wounded at Gallipoli.[34] Storey was a hero now, and evidently a man of some breeding: perhaps he took pity on the shabby little fellow before him who tipped the scales at a mere 9 stone 5 pounds (60kg). We know that Arthur understated his age by five years (he was 31, not 26) and fibbed about his place of birth (Redfern, not Kogarah). He gave his occupation as 'labourer' (though he had scarcely worked an honest day since 1908) and his address as 'C/- Haymarket Post Office.' He also claimed to have served for five months in a volunteer rifle unit, which seems unlikely.

Presumably he was gilding the lily in hope of maximising his chances of being accepted. If so, the tactics succeeded. Arthur passed muster and joined the 19th Infantry Battalion, 16th Reinforcements, as a private.[35] The next day, his name appeared in print in Sydney's *Evening Star* newspaper – he was listed as one who had 'answered the call.'[36] Surely he felt a little pride.

§

Let us take stock of the situation of each of our three main characters – Arthur, Jack Ridley, and R.B.S. Hammond – as the first half of 1916 unfolded.

Hammond, at 46, was too old to fight and in any case exempt as a minister of religion. On top of his missioning duties in Surry Hills, he was engaged in a different kind of struggle, at least tangentially related to the war effort: further reform of New South Wales liquor laws.

On 14 February 1916, some 5000 AIF soldiers in camp at Liverpool and Casula had initiated a sort of drunken mutiny. It became a three-day riot and pub crawl involving hijacked trains, destruction of

A ... RALIAN MILITARY FORCES

AUSTRALIAN IMPERIAL FORCE.

Attestation Paper of Persons Enlisted for Service Abroad.

No. ~~1220~~ 5934 Name STACE. A.M.
Unit
Joined on 16-3-16

Questions to be put to the Person Enlisting before Attestation.

1. What is your Name? ... 1. Arthur Malcolm Stace

2. In or near what Parish or Town were you born? 2. In the Parish of ~~Cogra~~ Kogarah
near the Town of Sydney
in the County of Cumberland

3. Are you a natural born British Subject or a Naturalized British Subject? (N.B.—If the latter, papers to be shown.) ... 3. Yes

4. What is your age? ... 4. 21 years.

5. What is your trade or calling? ... 5. Labourer

6. Are you, or have you been, an apprentice? If so, where, to whom, and for what period? ... 6. No

7. Are you married? ... 7. No

8. Who is your next of kin? (Address to be stated) 8. Mrs. Minnie Hamilton (Sister) ~~24 Jones St Pyrmont~~ 166 Bourke St Pyrmont NSW

9. Have you ever been convicted by the Civil Power? 9. No.

10. Have you ever been discharged from any part of His Majesty's Forces, with Ignominy, or as Incorrigible and Worthless, or on account of Conviction of Felony, or of a Sentence of Penal Servitude, or have you been dismissed with Disgrace from the Navy? ... 10. No

11. Do you now belong to, or have you ever served in, His Majesty's Army, the Marines, the Militia, the Militia Reserve, the Territorial Force, Royal Navy, or Colonial Forces? If so, state which, and if not now serving, state cause of discharge 11. 5 months St Georges Rifles Resigned

12. Have you stated the whole, if any, of your previous service? ... 12. Yes

13. Have you ever been rejected as unfit for His Majesty's Service? If so, on what grounds? ... 13. No

14. Do you understand that no Separation Allowance will be issued in respect of your service beyond an amount which, together with Pay, would reach eight shillings per day? ... 14. Yes

15. Are you prepared to undergo inoculation against small-pox and enteric fever? ... 15. Yes

I, Arthur Maurice Stace ... do solemnly declare that the above answers made by me to the above questions are true, and I am willing and hereby voluntarily agree to serve in the Military Forces of the Commonwealth of Australia within or beyond the limits of the Commonwealth.

*And I further agree to allot not less than two-fifths three-fifths of the pay payable to me from time to time during my service for the support of my wife wife and children

Date 16/3/16 Arthur Malcolm Stace
Signature of person enlisted.

6.2. Arthur's application to join the AIF, 16 March 1916. Many of the details he supplied were incorrect.

2

CERTIFICATE OF ATTESTING OFFICER.

The foregoing questions were read to the person enlisted in my presence.

I have taken care that he understands each question, and that his answer to each question has been duly entered as replied to by him.

~~I have examined his naturalization papers, and am of opinion that they are correct.~~

(This to be struck out except in the case of persons who are naturalized British Subjects).

Date 18/3/16.

David A Storey Maj
Signature of Attesting Officer.

OATH TO BE TAKEN BY PERSON BEING ENLISTED.*

I, Arthur Malcolm Stace swear that I will well and truly serve our Sovereign Lord the King in the Australian Imperial Force from 18/3/16 until the end of the War, and a further period of four months thereafter unless sooner lawfully discharged, dismissed, or removed therefrom; and that I will resist His Majesty's enemies and cause His Majesty's peace to be kept and maintained; and that I will in all matters appertaining to my service, faithfully discharge my duty according to law.

SO HELP ME, GOD.

Arthur Malcolm Stace
Signature of Person Enlisted.

Taken and subscribed at R A S Grounds in the State of N S Wales this 18th day March of 1916, before me—

David A. Storey Maj
Signature of Attesting Officer.

*A person enlisting who objects to take an oath may make an affirmation in accordance with the Third Schedule of the Act, and the above form must be amended accordingly. All amendments must be initialled by the Attesting Officer.

6.3. Official certification of Arthur's application by his attesting officer, Major David A. Storey, a Gallipoli veteran.

property and skirmishes with police, ending with gunfire in the streets of inner Sydney[37] (coincidentally, Arthur's home patch*). The incident, dubbed 'Black Monday', evoked widespread shame. There were renewed calls by temperance campaigners for prohibition, at least for the duration of the war. In the end, the Labor Government of W.A. Holman agreed to hold a referendum on the closing time of pubs and bottle shops throughout the state.[38] The date of the poll was 10 June 1916. Voters were presented with two main choices: 6pm (the temperance campaigners' preference) or 9pm (the 'compromise' position of the liquor industry). The status quo was 11pm.

6.4. Street in Surry Hills, c. May 1916, in the lead-up to the New South Wales referendum on the closing time of hotels. An advertisement by the liquor interests for 9 o'clock closing appears in the background. On 10 June 1916 the citizens of New South Wales voted for 6 o'clock closing, an endorsement of the campaign led by R.B.S. Hammond.

The temperance campaign was led by Hammond and the result was a personal triumph. The citizens of New South Wales approved 6 o'clock

* Arthur could not have participated in the riot as a trainee soldier because it happened a month before he enlisted. It is possible that he witnessed its closing stages as a civilian, once it reached the pubs and streets of inner Sydney.

closing by a wide margin.[39] Soon afterwards the law was amended accordingly, and it would remain unchanged until 1955. The votes of women, and churchgoing Protestant men, had been decisive.

Arthur Stace was still in Sydney – in the AIF camp at Liverpool, in fact – when the referendum was held. In retrospect, if Arthur bothered to vote at all, it seems probable that he voted for 9pm closing (or even 11pm). This despite the fact that alcohol had done him so much harm already.

We may be sure that if Sgt J.G. Ridley could have cast a vote in the referendum (he was too young), it would have been for 6 o'clock closing. During all his time in training, first at Liverpool and later aboard ship and in Egypt, he had been repulsed by the drunkenness and debauchery of so many comrades. His diary makes that clear. But by June 1916 his thoughts were elsewhere. The 53rd Battalion arrived in France towards the end of the month, and by 10 July it had reached the front.[40]

7. The furnace of affliction

I am right in the thick of it now, banging and booming all around, with shells flying overhead. Yes, I know now what the 'Horrors of War' are, and I know also what the 'comfort of Christ' is, and the great nearness of His presence in this awful inferno.
J.G. Ridley, letter to his mother from the trenches, 18 July 1916[1]

John Ridley wrote those words on the eve of the Battle of Fromelles, the AIF's legendary introduction to trench warfare on the Western Front. The context is important.

In response to the German assault on Verdun in February 1916, the Allies decided to launch a huge counter-assault of their own – in the region of the River Somme in Picardy, in northern France. The Battle of the Somme began on 1 July 1916, the bloodiest day of the war. Around 20,000 British soldiers were killed and another 40,000 wounded.[2] The Germans suffered about 6,000 casualties. It was inconceivable slaughter. And it would continue for months.

The AIF was pitched into this maelstrom at Fromelles (or Fleurbaix), a flat marshy area to the north of the Somme. The planning was 'rushed and confusing.'[3] Sgt Ridley and his comrades were not in good hands, and, as Jack's letter to his mother makes clear, they knew that their lives hung by a thread. Ridley later recalled: 'Eternity seemed to hover above [me] and about [me] in World War I, and the one great necessity to this newly converted soul was preparation for his meeting with God.'[4]

Ridley was unusual in that he worried, not only about the fate of his own soul, but that of others. 'War is an awful thing,' he wrote in his diary, 'but what is more awful is that so many who are here facing death, care not for the One who can save them.' He took comfort in prayer and from contemplation of the daily Bible verses set out in the tract he carried with him everywhere, *A Threefold Chord*.[5]

One of the verses that strengthened him most was 2 Samuel 22:4: 'I will call on the Lord, who is worthy to be praised; so shall I be saved from mine enemies.'[6]

7.1. AIF troops from John Ridley's 53rd battalion in the trenches at the Battle of Fromelles, 19 July 1916. Ridley was shot that day through the jaw, tongue and throat, but survived. 2,000 of his comrades were killed.

The appointed day for the AIF attack at Fromelles was Wednesday 19 July 1916. Ridley's 53rd Battalion was up early, and British shells began raining down on the German line at 9am. But the men had to wait in the trenches for another nine agonising hours, until 6pm, before receiving their orders to charge.

Ridley's written account of the next few minutes is stunning, and worth reading in full. Somehow he dodged and scrambled a few hundred yards, muddy ear-shattering carnage around him. With a few mates, he fell into a water-logged ditch and took cover. Then this:

> I can't explain properly how it all happened. We were forcing our way down the stream when I must have raised my head slightly, when crash! Bang! It was a terrible smack, it makes me shiver when I think of it ... It stunned me with the force of it and for a moment I hardly knew I had been hit. Then the blood rushed out of my mouth and down my face in torrents. I dropped back into the ditch and managed to make a noise to Elliott who turned and saw me. He seemed staggered for a moment, but I was in agony, nearly choking ... Elliott got the bandage round my head but the blood was coming so fast he exclaimed to MacDonald, 'It's no good, Mac, it's useless.'[7]

In fact, the wound was not fatal. Ridley had been shot through the jaw, tongue and throat, and he thought he was dying ('I wondered what my first view of Heaven would be like'). But comrades got him to safety, and his injuries, though severe, were treated at a dressing station, later at a field ambulance, and later still at a French hospital. Within a few days he had been transported back to England, where he spent several months recuperating at Edmonton Military Hospital in North Middlesex.[8] He was helped along by many letters from family and friends back home, including the Rev. William Lamb of the Burton Street Baptist Tabernacle. He also received devoted personal care from two colleagues of his father's at the London office of Gordon & Gotch.[9]

It should be noted that the AIF attack at Fromelles was, in a military sense, a 'disastrous failure.'[10] On that fateful night there were some 5,500 Australian casualties, including almost 2,000 dead. According to one authoritative source, 'this is believed to be the greatest loss by a single division in 24 hours during the entire First World War. Some consider Fromelles the most tragic event in Australia's history.'[11] A trifle unnecessarily, an English doctor remarked to Ridley: 'Do you know you have had a very close shave, lad?'[12]

Ridley himself drew profound lessons. 'My life [was] saved,' he wrote in hospital, 'by the Grace of God to do Him service in the years which are to come.' He added, with an eye towards *Eternity*:

> General Sherman of the Union Army in the [American] Civil War said 'War is Hell', but I think that war is but a minor vision of that place of Eternal Judgment, and what saddens me is that so many who live through the inferno of horror do not stop to thank their Great Deliverer.[13]

By late 1916 he had recovered sufficiently to rejoin the 53rd Battalion in France.[14] Probably he could have come home. But according to his disappointed yet immensely proud father, 'his conscience told him to go back and finish his work for King, Empire and God.'[15]

§

By this time – late 1916 – Arthur Stace was also in uniform. He had embarked from Sydney on 7 October on HMAT *Ceramic* and reached Plymouth on 21 November. Once in England, there was little time for further training: the 16th Reinforcement of the 19th Battalion was needed on the Western Front. Arthur boarded the SS *Princess Clementine* on 23 December, and within a week was on the march in France. On 5 February 1917 he was 'taken on strength' into the 19th Battalion for service in the field.[16]

With his slight physique and mediocre health, it is hard to imagine that Arthur could ever have been an effective combat soldier. Clearly his superiors recognised this, and at an early stage he was marked out for duty as a side drummer in the 19th Battalion's band.[17] In practice, many bandsmen became stretcher-bearers:

> The answer to why [bandsmen were stretcher-bearers] is not simple and for every theory there is a contradictory example. In general terms the band provided an organisation that was well-suited to performing the medical (stretcher-bearer) role. It had the necessary numbers and rank structure to allow personnel to be distributed among the companies of an infantry battalion. The band was able to train in their medical role while the rest of the unit trained in their infantry role. In action, the band was not required to perform so the band could be employed in other tasks. Stretcher-bearing certainly didn't offer a safe option. In fact a number of unit commanders withdrew their bandsmen from stretcher-bearing duties because of the number of casualties and used them in roles such as mortar sections in order to keep a band.[18]

Arthur's war records establish that he was in the field with the 19th Battalion in northern France from early February to late April 1917. During this period, according to the Australian War Memorial, 'the 19th was involved in the follow-up of German forces after their retreat to the Hindenburg Line, and was one of four battalions to defeat a counter-stroke by a German force, almost five times as strong, at Lagnicourt.'[19]

The official records do not specify that Arthur acted as a stretcher-bearer. But that is what he later said, *after* he had become a reformed man,[20] and such service would have been consistent with regular practice in the AIF. There is no good reason to doubt his account.

7.2. Arthur Stace served as a stretcher-bearer on the Western Front from early February to late April 1917, before contracting pleurisy.

DAVID LEVER, *STRETCHER-BEARER*, OIL ON BOARD, 2000/01.

The role played by stretcher-bearers was of incalculable importance. In 1918, the AIF magazine published this anonymous tribute by an Australian soldier:

> Stretcher-Bearers! Stretcher-Bearers!
> Seeking in the rain
> Out among the flying death
> For those who lie in pain,
> Bringing in the wounded men –
> Then out to seek again.
>
> Out amongst the tangled wire
> (Where they thickest fell)
> Snatching back the threads of life
> From out the jaws of Hell;
> Out amongst machine-gun sweep
> And blasts of shatt'ring shell.

For you no mad, exciting charge,
No swift, exultant fight,
But just an endless plodding on
Through the shuddering night;
Making ('neath a star-shell's gleam)
Where ere a face shines white.

Stretcher-Bearers! Stretcher-Bearers!
To you all praise be due,
Who ne'er shirked the issue yet
When there was work to do;
We who've seen and know your worth
All touch our hats to you.[21]

John Ridley had special reason to admire the role played by stretcher-bearers in World War I. Arthur was not a Christian when he served in 1917. Yet many years later, shortly after Arthur's death, Ridley still wondered whether 'stretcher-bearing did not, at odd times, bring before his mind the transient nature of this life and the trenchant mystery of the life to come.'[22]

It would be surprising if such thoughts did not pass through Arthur's mind. One day, feeling very ill, he was making his way to a doctor's tent when a German shell exploded near him. He was hurled yards into the air, his eyes and lungs seared by the exploding gas.[23] By 19 April he had been admitted to a field hospital (56th C.C. Stn) suffering bronchitis. Two days later he was transferred to a general hospital in Rouen, and there, another week later, diagnosed with pleurisy. Soon afterwards he embarked for England on HMS *St George*. On 1 May 1917 he was admitted as an 'invalid' to the 1st War Hospital in Birmingham.[24]

The AIF's custom was to notify an ailing soldier's next-of-kin. When Arthur enlisted in Sydney, he had given his sister Minnie's name and address. On 17 May 1917, the AIF's standard form letter was sent to her in Pyrmont. She was illiterate, but presumably had someone read it out: if so, she learned that Arthur had been admitted to hospital in England 'suffering pleurisy' and that 'in the absence of further reports it is to be assumed that satisfactory progress is being maintained.'[25]

Possibly Minnie passed this news on to the other Stace siblings. But it seems unlikely that she did much else. Being illiterate, she could not write to Arthur and there is no evidence that Arthur wrote any letters to her, or to anyone, during his overseas service.[26] Nor is it likely that he received any letters – unless the odd one from his brothers. The contrast with John Ridley is stark. He wrote prolifically to loved ones back home and enjoyed a steady stream of correspondence in return. Arthur was alone.

§

The rest of John Ridley's war was traumatic – but highly distinguished and critical to the *Eternity* story. After rejoining the 53rd Battalion, he saw active service through 1917 and 1918, including at Polygon Wood and Messines. His finest hours as a soldier came near the end of the war, from August 1918, during the Allies' crucial last push against the German line under the command of John Monash.

The 53rd Battalion was involved in the vital campaigns at Péronne (1–3 September) and Bellicourt (20 September–2 October). By this time Ridley had been promoted to the rank of lieutenant, and at Bellicourt he performed acts of conspicuous bravery that earned him the Military Cross:

> On many different occasions he organised parties for the carrying forward of ammunition and rations to the Line, although this necessitated crossing ground heavily swept by artillery and machine gun fire. His action in leading forward several parties with ammunition and bombs undoubtedly saved the situation forward as the supply there had been entirely exhausted. He also collected

> a party of volunteers and searched the whole of the ground covered by the attacking troops and brought in wounded thereby saving several lives. Throughout the operation his energy, cheerfulness and gallantry set the finest possible example to all his men.[27]

(Three of the wounded that Ridley saved were Germans who had been left behind in a captured trench.[28])

Ridley may have been a bit of a prig when the war began, but by its end he was greatly and deservedly respected. One comrade paid him this tribute:

> [His] influence for good was immense ... I say of him most sincerely that he is one of the most perfect Christians I have ever met. A mere boy in years ... he remained as pure and unsullied as when a schoolboy, inspired by patriotic enthusiasm and confidence in God ... Brave as the bravest, cool and manly in action, Jack Ridley was beloved by officers and men.[29]

Ridley, then, was a hero. He had fame and status. During the voyage back to Australia in April–May 1919 on the SS *Kildonan Castle*, he rubbed shoulders with A.B. 'Banjo' Paterson and enjoyed a long one-on-one chat in the dining saloon with C.E.W. Bean, Australia's celebrated war correspondent.[30] Shortly afterwards he received a personal letter of congratulations from General (later Field Marshal) W.R. Birdwood, one of the most senior officers in the British high command.[31]

But it was not only on the battlefield that Ridley had excelled. He had also come into his own as an evangelist and pastor. Inspired by two New Testament texts – Matthew 18:20 and Romans 8: 35, 37[32] – he led a prayer and Bible study group within the 53rd Battalion. It started in July 1917 with just a handful of men but grew steadily, at various times attracting as many as 40 or 50 members. The group became extremely tight-knit, but there was intermittent grief: at Péronne alone, more than half their number were killed or wounded.[33]

As far as the *Eternity* story is concerned, perhaps the most crucial outcome of the war was Ridley's decision to dedicate his life to the Baptist church. It was a devoted fellow Christian in his prayer group who first planted the suggestion, in the late summer of 1917. Ridley hesitated at first because he had always imagined a career in the military. But after much soul-searching, he yielded to his conscience a few days later. He told his friend: 'if the Lord spares me through this war, I promise I shall give myself to Him for full-time service.'[34]

When he arrived home in Sydney on Friday 9 May 1919 – to an ecstatic welcome from family and friends – he had already made up his mind to study for the ministry.

§

For Arthur Stace, the rest of the war was an anticlimax.

On 18 May 1917, still recovering from pleurisy but out of immediate danger, he was transferred from the 1st War Hospital in Birmingham to the 3rd Auxiliary Hospital in Dartford, Kent. This was a pleasant place, set in tranquil country surroundings. According to one contemporary account, 'the huts were rather nicely fitted out, being heated with steam and having baths and lavatories with hot and cold water laid on. A fine recreation room was provided for reading and writing.'[35]

For Arthur, it was probably the most comfortable place he had ever lived in. He recuperated there for two months before being discharged on furlough.

The spectre still loomed of a return to the Western Front. On 1 August 1917, he reported for duty at No. 2 Command Depot in Weymouth, on England's south coast. A week later he was on the march – a 51-mile trek north-west from Weymouth to No. 3 Command Depot at Hurdcott on the Salisbury Plain. One wonders how his scarred lungs handled that. At Hurdcott he continued his convalescence, but did so in the knowledge that if and when the powers-that-be so decreed, he could be pitched back into full-scale preparation for a return to the trenches. The command depots (other than the one at Weymouth) were for soldiers released from hospital who were expected to be fit enough to return to active service in due course.[36]

7.3. HMAT *Takada*, the hospital troop ship that transported Pte Arthur Stace back from World War I in early 1919.

7.4. SS *Kildonan Castle*, the vessel on which Lt J.G. Ridley M.C. returned from World War I, two months after Arthur. Ridley's fellow passengers included C.E.W. Bean and Banjo Paterson.

For whatever reason – probably continued ill-health – Arthur never got that call. If he had, he would first have been sent to the Overseas Training Brigade at Perham Down (later Longbridge Deverill).[37] That never happened. But nor was he permitted to return home. Instead, on 1 June 1918, he was 'taken on strength' into the AIF's HQ Depot in London. There, for the rest of the war, he performed menial administrative duties. It was only after the Armistice that he rejoined the 19th Battalion for repatriation to Australia, departing England on Christmas Day 1918 on HMAT *Takada*.

The *Takada* reached Sydney on Sunday 16 February 1919 and passed quarantine.[38] The next day there was a lengthy report in the

Sydney Morning Herald, but needless to say, no mention of Pte Arthur Stace.[39]

The contrast with the triumphant return of Lt J.G. Ridley M.C. could scarcely have been starker. Arthur's record was perfectly honourable, but, by the standards of the day, nothing out of the box. It is most unlikely that anyone was there to meet him. The AIF had sent a letter to Minnie notifying her of the date of her brother's expected arrival – but by then she was living in Broken Hill. The letter never reached her.[40]

A few months later, on 2 May 1919, Arthur was officially discharged from the AIF. He was medically unfit and entitled to a small pension.[41] In addition to 'pleurisy', his file had been marked 'DAH' – disordered action of the heart. In those days, this was a euphemism for shellshock. Today the condition is known as PTSD – post-traumatic stress disorder.

8. Lost in the wilderness

The 1920s was Australia's 'mean decade' ... an uncertain, cautious and shabby era ... War had shattered the possibly naïve, but nonetheless constructive, idealist national mood of the previous decades without substituting anything very positive in its place.
Russel Ward, *Australia Since the Coming of Man*[1]

If the 1920s was Australia's 'mean decade', it was, for Arthur Stace, the lost decade. Very little is known of his day-to-day activities throughout these years. What can be reconstructed is sad – pitiful, in fact.

He did manage to survive the outbreak of Spanish influenza that struck down Sydney in the first half of 1919 and killed some 6,000 people. On 3 February 1919, just a fortnight before Arthur arrived back from the war, premier W.A. Holman had issued an official warning: 'A danger greater than war faces the State of New South Wales and threatens the lives of all.' For some months, citizens were required to wear a face mask when outside their homes. Bans were placed on public meetings, including church services. Some schools and hotels were closed.[2] Given Arthur's weak chest and the fact that young and middle-aged men were disproportionately affected, it must be accounted lucky – or miraculous? – that he lived through it.

Arthur's plight in the 1920s was a common one for returned soldiers. Many from the middle classes prospered, and wage-earners and their dependents were reasonably protected by trade unions. But lots of others fell through the cracks. The lingering psychological effects of war were poorly understood. Most vulnerable were those from the working class who came back maimed or sick, or stayed unemployed. Along with many single women, and the non-white, they constituted society's underclass.[3]

Arthur did not resume his pre-war life in Sydney's criminal underworld.[4] It appears that he did almost nothing at all, except mooch about and drink.

8.1. Darlinghurst Gaol as it stands today. During the 1920s, Arthur Stace spent many nights in the cells there after being arrested for drunkenness.

At first he hung around with some of his old companions in Sydney's wharf areas, mingling with the returned soldiers ('we waited until the next shipload ... came in and lived on them until they were broke').[5] Later he lived in Surry Hills.[6] His drinking became increasingly heavy: there were times he was so drunk he could not walk or stand up.[7] Sometimes he slept on benches in the Domain, wrapped in newspapers.[8] Periodically arrested for drunkenness, he became a regular 'overnighter' in police cells.[9] Darlinghurst – home by the 1920s to the infamous 'razor gangs' of madams Tilly Devine and Kate Leigh – was one of his favourite haunts.

There is one surviving letter from this period, written by Arthur to the AIF on 15 August 1927. For its bleak pathos, and incidental proof of Arthur's standard of literacy, it bears quoting in full:

> Dear Sir,
>
> Would you kindly forward on a Duplicate discharge for Arthur Malcolm Stace as I have lost mine through no fault of my own it has been lost three weeks to day. I am a pensioner & cannot put in for the German Verge fund* without it so will be pleased if you will forward on as soon as possible thanking you for same.[10]

What of Arthur's brothers and sisters? Minnie was still living in Broken Hill in the first half of 1919, so Arthur could not have moved in again with her, at least not immediately. Minnie did come back to Sydney later in 1919, in October, to attend the funeral of John Harmon (the husband from whom she had separated some years earlier).[11] But after that her whereabouts, and the extent of her contact with Arthur, are uncertain. In May 1925 she married[12] a timber worker named Alexander Campbell and moved with him to Cordeaux Dam in the Nepean area.[13]

As for the others, Clara was travelling in China with her husband and daughter until June 1920,[14] and thereafter stayed close to the Go-Hing family. William and Dora's activities are unknown. Sam, still living in the Wollongong region, pops up occasionally in the historical record – but always for bad reasons.[15]

---

* The private benefactor of this fund was a man named German Verge (1838–1920), a wealthy recluse from the Macleay River district. He bequeathed the bulk of his estate (some £125,000) to trustees for the benefit of returned soldiers in NSW.

379 Riley St
Surry Hills NSW
15/8/27

Dear Sir.

Would you kindly forward on a Dupicate discharge for Arthur Malcolm Stace as I have lost mine through no fault of my own it has been lost three weeks to day. I am a pensioner & cannot put in for the German Verge fund without it so will be pleased if you will forward on as soon as possible thanking you for same

I.A.M.

5943 A. M. Stace
19th Batt. 5th Brigade
Sydney.

8.2. Letter from Arthur Stace to the AIF in August 1927. Clearly, he was not illiterate.

Like Arthur, Sam had enlisted in the AIF during the war[16] but returned to bad habits in peacetime. He was a throwback to his father, William Wood Stace, a family man consumed by addiction to alcohol. Many times during the 1920s, Sam's long-suffering wife Edith applied for and obtained 'prohibition' orders against him under the Liquor Act, at least once with Sam's consent. Theoretically, these orders prevented him from setting foot on licensed premises – but invariably he flouted them. He was a slave to grog. At last he snapped to a judge: 'I'll get it and drink it until I die.' He did.[17]

Arthur's salvation was never going to come from his family. Nor (though his war pension kept him alive) from governments. And certainly not from his few 'mates', a motley assortment of drinking buddies. As the 1920s wore on, Arthur's stocks got lower and lower. By his own admission, 'beer drinking became wine drinking, wine drinking became whisky drinking, whisky led to gin and rum and rum finally to methylated spirits.'[18] He said in later life that he often spent more time lying in the gutter than out of it.[19]

§

The two men who would change Arthur's life forever – R.B.S. Hammond and John Gotch Ridley – faced challenges of their own in the 1920s. Let us begin with Ridley, who, like Arthur, spent much of the decade suffering from the insidious effects of war. They had that much in common.

As we saw in Chapter 7, Ridley returned to Sydney a feted hero. Gladly he spent a few weeks back at his beloved 'Walmer', the family home in Darling Point. But before long he was restless. His father urged him to recuperate at leisure for a period of at least twelve months, but Ridley refused. According to his biographer, Harold E. Evans, 'the zealous young warrior said, "No, father. I have been called to the ministry and must go ahead at once" ... [He] sprang into study and service with all the ardour and energy of [his] war-weakened body.'[20]

A key figure in his early labours was the Rev. William Lamb of Burton Street Baptist Tabernacle in Darlinghurst. Ridley had soaked up Lamb's pre-millennialist message. The point is critical to the *Eternity* story, for, as Ridley later wrote in his laudatory biography of Lamb, 'One feels that the very word "ETERNITY" might well be chosen as the watchword of his ministry.' Ridley recalled:

> How frequently in Tabernacle times he selected hymns like: 'Eternity is drawing nigh'; 'O, the clanging bells of time'; 'Where will you spend Eternity?'; 'I sat alone with life's memories'; 'Jerusalem, the Golden'; 'A few more years shall roll'; and 'The sands of time are sinking.' Like George Whitefield, he had Eternity stamped upon his eyeballs.[21]

During his lifetime, Lamb defended his heavy emphasis on questions of eternity and Christ's second coming. 'Not any other phase of the Divine message,' he once insisted, 'has yielded such satisfactory results in soul-winning as this has done in my whole ministry.'[22] In January 1920 he launched a weekly newsletter, *The Advent Herald*, devoted to these themes. It would continue to be published until Lamb's death in 1944.

Another important influence on Ridley in the 1920s was the Rev. John Complin, the minister at Sydney's Central Baptist Church in Bathurst Street from 1918–29 and a former member of the Salvation Army. A passionate, ultra-patriotic evangelical, Complin had served as a young man under General William Booth himself. Ridley was introduced to him by a mutual friend in the spring of 1919 and soon afterwards joined the Bathurst Street congregation.[23]

While Ridley studied for the ministry, he began to serve with the NSW Baptist Home Mission Department at the Maroubra Baptist

Church, in Storey Street.[24] He preached the Sunday service there on several occasions in 1920–21 and was soon popular with the growing congregation.[25] But in mid-1921, at the age of 26, his world collapsed. In the language of the day he suffered a complete nervous breakdown. Any concentration was agony; even prayer and reading became difficult. His head ached, he could not sleep properly, and often he felt exhausted – unaccountably so. He was 'low as hell.'[26] Without doubt, he endured severe bouts of clinical depression and PTSD.

What brought it on? The sudden death of his father on 10 March 1921[27] must have been a shock. A nasty dental operation was also a catalyst. But there can be no question as to the root cause: his war service had caught up with him. Not just the head wound inflicted at Fromelles, but the whole awful experience. In his own words:

> The War had presented an heroic side to balance its horrors; now, in this breakdown, there seemed to be nothing heroic, nothing to balance, nothing to compensate, nothing but helplessness and, for a time, hopelessness.[28]

John Ridley, in his own way, had fallen as low as Arthur Stace. His mother rallied to his side, but many 'friends' and acquaintances questioned his manhood. Doctors recommended rest and relaxation for an indefinite period – a total change of scene.[29]

Early in the summer of 1921–22, accompanied initially by his mother, Ridley travelled to Condobolin, a small township on the Lachlan River in the central west of New South Wales. At a large property in the vicinity he began a stint as a jackeroo and station hand. It was sweltering work, but the horseriding, solitude and wide open spaces gradually soothed his mind and body. After a time, he was able to read his Bible: he found special comfort in John's Gospel and the Psalms.[30] But it was far from a total cure, and when he returned to Sydney he was still in a weakened state.

By May 1924 he had recovered sufficiently to dabble again in evangelism. He made his way to the Blue Mountains – the town of Blackheath – and enjoyed a brief period of ministry in the local Baptist church.[31] A New Testament verse caught his eye and got him thinking: 'But watch thou in all things, endure afflictions, *do the work of an evangelist*, make full proof of thy ministry' (2 Timothy 4:5).[32]

Disobeying medical advice, he decided to become an itinerant evangelist – a 'bush missioner'.[33] After buying a horse ('Gypsy') and a second-hand wagon, he left Blackheath in the company of a man named Kearney and spent three months touring towns, hamlets and homesteads in the outback of the state. Everywhere they went, Ridley preached the gospel to whoever would listen. In all, he and Kearney covered 1,000 miles and distributed 20,000 tracts. It was a tough slog, but John Ridley had found his calling.[34]

In Blackheath he also found a wife – a wonderful one.

Dorothy Chapman was 19 years old when she met Ridley. He had stabled his horse at her home, 'Hiawatha', a charming property not far from Blackheath Railway Station. Dorothy's father, Professor H.G. Chapman, was a prominent man – head of cancer research at Sydney University – and he and his wife had raised a smart, outgoing, attractive daughter. But Dorothy 'knew nothing of the Lord',[35] and at first she and Ridley were drawn to each other by a shared passion for the outdoors. On their rides and walks together, he witnessed to her earnestly: soon she had fallen in love with both him and Christ.[36]

Perhaps Dorothy yearned for wholesomeness and stability, for her parents' marriage was a sham. In 1916 Chapman had taken a lover – a typist/secretary at the Royal Society of New South Wales – and separated from his wife. He lived at the University Club in Castlereagh Street while maintaining flats in the city and at Bondi; the family homes were at The Spit and Blackheath.[37] Apart from maintaining a double life, Chapman lived prodigally and was a public advocate of the consumption of alcohol.[38] One wonders if he baulked at the prospect of a fervent, squeaky-clean Baptist as a son-in-law. Despite his privileged upbringing, Ridley had little money of his own and no obvious occupation: he was not even an ordained minister of a church, and his ongoing health problems continued to prevent him from studying.

But love conquers all. On 18 August 1926 Dorothy Chapman married John Ridley at the Baptist Church in Blackheath.[39]

8.3. John and Dorothy Ridley, late 1920s/early 1930s, standing next to the gospel van in which they regularly toured New South Wales as Baptist missioners during the first nine years of their marriage.

Intermittently over the next nine years, husband and wife travelled together around New South Wales in a four-cylinder Ford caravan-type vehicle – a 'Gospel waggon.' They visited people in their homes, distributed tracts, held open-air meetings, and, when invited, conducted indoor services. It was not always plain sailing, but Ridley could take a joke. One year in Cootamundra, in early November, he offered a man a tract. 'Will this tell us who'll win the Cup?' was the instant reply. Ridley enjoyed repeating the story.[40]

Eventually the Ridleys became part of network known as the 'Australian Bush Crusade' and John's reputation grew as a speaker/evangelist.[41] By 1929, at their home base in Sydney, he had become an elder at the Central Baptist Church in Bathurst Street. Both he and Dorothy were 'great favourites [there] with the pastor and the people.'[42]

The stage was set for Ridley to play his part in the *Eternity* story.

§

For the Rev. R.B.S. Hammond, the 1920s were also critical formative years. As we saw in Chapter 6, he did not serve in World War I but continued his missionary and social justice work in the inner suburbs of Sydney, based in Surry Hills. Then, during the year the war ended, 1918, he moved to a new parish – St Barnabas', Broadway, even closer to the CBD. His first day there was Sunday 1 July 1918.[43]

Hammond was now 48 years old and at the peak of his powers. He needed to be, for St Barnabas' was a dwindling congregation. Founded in 1856 by a former drunkard-turned-evangelist named Thomas Smith, it had enjoyed rapid growth in the latter nineteenth century before going backwards just as quickly around the time of Federation.[44] Yet before long, using the skills he had honed over the previous 20 years, Hammond completely reinvigorated the place. By decade's end it had become a major centre of charity and evangelism in Sydney, and Hammond had entrenched his reputation as a 'Mender of Broken Men'.[45]

Three aspects of Hammond's ministry in this period bear special mention because of their direct future relevance to the *Eternity* story. The first was his decision – made at the very outset – to hold a Men's Meeting at St Barnabas' every Wednesday night without fail. A general invitation was issued to all and sundry to hear the gospel, share a bite to eat, and if so inclined, join 'the Brotherhood.'[46] The Brotherhood's card of membership set out three non-negotiable conditions:

1. PERSONAL: Having decided to accept Jesus Christ as a Personal Saviour, I will begin the day with prayer, and daily read a portion of the Holy Scriptures, and abstain from all intoxicating liquors.

2. IN RELATION TO THE CHURCH: I will, whenever possible, attend the Men's Meeting at St Barnabas', and also some place of public worship on Sunday – St Barnabas' for preference.
3. FOR OTHERS: I will try to influence at least one man each week to attend the meeting. I will donate weekly to the funds of the Brotherhood, as much as my means will allow, for the financing of the various objects of the Brotherhood.[47]

By 4 July 1923, the fifth anniversary of the first Wednesday night meeting at St Barnabas', some 431 men had signed this card. By the end of the decade, the number was over 1,000 – and climbing.[48] It is to be stressed that the men concerned came from all walks of life. They ranged from eminent city professionals to 'wasters' and 'loafers', and everything in between. Hammond did not play favourites. Nor did he extend fellowship only to the 'worthy'. He tried to live by the injunction of Jesus in Luke 6:35: 'for He is kind unto the unthankful and to the evil.'[49]

The second matter worthy of note is Hammond's continued commitment through the 1920s to the cause of temperance. In 1919, and again in 1922–23, he visited North America to attend conferences on alcoholism and make a study of prohibition. Shortly after his return from the latter trip, he received a long personal letter from the great William Jennings Bryan (1860–1925), three-time Democratic candidate for president of the United States and one of the most influential left-wing* Christian populists of all time. Addressing his note to 'my dear Hammond,' Bryan praised his Australian friend's deep knowledge of the subject, engaging style of presentation and 'unselfish devotion to the welfare of your people.'[50]

* That is to say, 'left-wing' on issues of war and peace and economic justice – radically so. But Bryan, like Hammond, was a staunch social conservative. He drew his electoral support from the Bible belt.

The praise was merited. Back home, Hammond continued his dogged, selfless work in the drunks' yard at Central Police Court in Liverpool Street. On 9 January 1928, the fifteenth anniversary of these activities, he was congratulated by the acting chamber magistrate, a Mr Goldie. By then Hammond had persuaded some 26,194 men to sign his 'total abstinence' pledge.[51] Of course, some reoffended – including Arthur Stace. But a good many did not. And the very existence of the tough cases convinced Hammond to try even harder.

In the lead-up to the New South Wales prohibition referendum on 1 September 1928, he played a leading role in prosecuting the 'Yes' case. The proposal was defeated easily[52] – and, with the benefit of hindsight, this was perhaps the right decision. If the American experience was any guide, prohibition would not have eradicated the vile scourge of alcoholism. Black letter law can only go so far. But the campaign in New South Wales served a good purpose in further educating the population as to the evils of excessive drink. Likewise in other Australian states.

For his part, Hammond remained convinced that 'temperance does not mean moderate indulgence in all things – evil as well as good. It means a moderate and disciplined use of good things and a complete avoidance of what is hurtful and harmful.'[53] At an individual level, for people like Arthur Stace, he was right.

Finally, the third aspect of Hammond's tireless work in the 1920s: practical charity for Sydney's underclass through the provision of meals, clothes, accommodation, job-placement services and such wise. From his base at St Barnabas', Hammond built up a formidable system. Among other things, he persuaded some of his wealthy middle-class parishioners 'not to be selfish or self-satisfied but deeply and habitually generous to the needy.'[54] He also befriended sympathetic governors and politicians, conservatives with a conscience. These men helped to publicise and fund his causes.

According to Stephen Judd:

> In all, Broadway spent £1000 each year in the 1920s in the relief of poverty, far more than any other Sydney Anglican parish or diocesan agency. It was the acknowledged leader in social services, and the conduit through which much Anglican and inter-denominational poverty relief was channeled in Sydney. It was also a success which would put Hammond's social services, as they became known, at the forefront of relief through the troubled 1930s.[55]

Which brings us to another epochal event – the Wall Street stock market crash of October 1929, which brought on the Great Depression.

9. From darkness to light

Verily, verily, I say unto thee, Except a man be born again, he cannot see the kingdom of God.
John 3:3

The Great Depression produced human misery in Australia on a scale not seen before or since. It was considerably more severe than the Depression of the early 1890s – the one that had crushed William Wood Stace's spirit and broken up his family – and affected many more people. The Australian population had doubled since 1890, from 3.2 million to 6.5 million in 1930. And the rate of unemployment – which reached a staggering 30 per cent at its peak in 1932 – was unprecedented.

Governments both state and federal were soon floundering. The Scullin[1] Labor administration in Canberra had been elected in October 1929 on a reformist platform, but much of that was ditched as the economic crisis deepened. In New South Wales, Labor premier J.D. (Jack) Lang was undeterred: he continued to propose socialist measures and was stymied at every turn. Both Lang and Scullin faced implacable opposition from both within and without their own caucuses (and from each other). The forces of capital and privilege – banks, business, landlords, the upper houses of parliament, most of the mainstream press – were unanimous in urging strict 'austerity'. The hopes of millions for a kinder, more equitable society were soon in ruins.[2]

As 1930 opened, R.B.S. Hammond was stepping up his charitable efforts and John Ridley his fiery, whole-hearted evangelism. (The two men actually appeared together on 22 January, at Sydney Town Hall, as consecutive speakers at a United Intercessory Service[3] – this may well have been the day they met for the first time.) Meanwhile, Arthur Stace was living at yet another temporary address, 1 Mort Street in Surry Hills.[4] His fortunes had reached rock-bottom. Three incidents from this time remained seared in his memory in later life – it is not clear exactly when they occurred, or in what order, but it seems certain they all shortly preceded his conversion experience.[5]

Once he checked himself into a voluntary psychiatric clinic, Broughton Hall at Rozelle.[6] Established in 1921 by a far-sighted physician, Dr Sydney Evan Jones, Broughton Hall specialised in the treatment of World War I veterans of modest means who were suffering from mental illness of some sort, but not certifiably insane. 'The grounds and gardens were part of the therapy to divert patients from neuroses to normality.'[7] In Arthur's case, the treatment was to no avail. Not even the frightening prospect of committal to the asylum next door, Callan Park, cured him of his destructive ways. But at least he escaped the fate of his father, who had died in a mental asylum.[8]

The second incident was an appearance at Central Police Court on yet another charge of drunk and disorderly conduct. Arthur had spent the night before in a holding cell, and, in light of his dire record, the magistrate tried a threat: 'Don't you know I have the power to put you in Long Bay Jail or the power to set you free?' Arthur replied meekly: 'Yes, sir.'[9] He was let off lightly that time and released back into the community, possibly because he had signed the Rev. Hammond's 'total abstinence' pledge that day[10] or because his voluntary admission to Broughton Hall, though unsuccessful, demonstrated a serious effort to reform.

Despite his lenient treatment from the magistrate, Arthur felt no joy or relief. 'He knew he needed something which the magistrate didn't have the power to give – power to stop drinking, power to overcome a vile heredity, power to throw off the effects of a slum environment'.[11] In despair, possibly straight after leaving the court, Arthur trudged to the police station at Regent Street, Broadway, and asked to be locked up:

> I said to the sergeant, 'Sergeant, put me away. I'm no good and I haven't been sober for eight years. Give me a chance and put me away.'
>
> The sergeant sniffed and said, 'You stink of metho. Get out!'[12]

Arthur thought to himself: 'When I don't want them to put me in, they do it; now, when I want them to put me in, they shut me out.'[13]

It was winter by then, a dismal one for many people in the depressed and divided Sydney of 1930. Thousands of families had been evicted from their homes and several shanty settlements had formed: there was a big one at the Domain, an old haunt of Arthur's. Among the few bright spots for all Sydneysiders was the ongoing construction of the Harbour Bridge. The two mighty half-arches were first joined in the centre during August 1930,[14] and coincidentally, that was also the month in which Arthur's life was transformed.

The vital day was 6 August 1930, a Wednesday. This may have been the very day that Arthur was sent packing by the sergeant at Regent Street police station.[15] At any rate, on the evening of 6 August, he fronted up with a few of his derelict mates to one of R.B.S. Hammond's weekly Men's Meetings at St Barnabas' on Broadway. The attraction?

It had nothing to do with 'religion'. Rather, word had got around that after these meetings, every man got a cup of tea and a rock cake. As Arthur told the story years later:

> In those days you had to know when things like that were on to stay alive. At St Barnabas' Church we went around the back to the School Hall where Archdeacon Hammond used to preach for about an hour before the cuppa tea came on.
>
> There were 300 of us down and outs in the hall, and six people on the front seat, all decent and clean and dressed properly.
>
> I said to the bloke next to me, 'Who are they?'
>
> He said, 'They're Christians.'
>
> I said: 'Well, look at them and look at us. I'm having a go at what they've got.'[16]

9.1. St Barnabas', Broadway, the church at which R.B.S. Hammond served as rector from 1918 to 1943. During the 1930s, St Barnabas' was the base from which Hammond organised an extraordinary range of charitable services for Sydney's poor.

It seems, then, that Arthur was inclined to give Christianity 'a go' even before Hammond began speaking. There is no record of the subject of the talk that night, but it is fair to assume that Hammond preached the gospel in his usual way – compellingly and winsomely. He was an orator of world class, a burly and avuncular figure with 'a natural gift of incisive, compelling and arresting speech.'[17] He also knew how to pitch his message to suit a given audience.

9.2. R.B.S. Hammond, 1930s.

Seated before him that evening were many down-and-outs and ne'er-do-wells, perhaps 300 in all. Some, like Arthur, would have known little or nothing about Christianity. Hammond truly *loved* needy men such as these. They were his reason for being.

No doubt Hammond got their attention quickly with a couple of pithy anecdotes from contemporary life. His serious message, one imagines, would have been simple and direct.[18] However low your station, however big your handicaps, however bad the things you have done, *God loves you*. But you are a sinner. On your own you are helpless – and doomed. God sent Jesus to Earth to show you the way of salvation. Thanks to Jesus' death on the Cross, if you ask God for mercy with a penitent heart then all your sins will be forgiven – never counted against you again, in this life or the next.

Such meetings usually ended with an open invitation to all non-Christians present to 'go forward' to the front of the hall and 'receive Christ.' According to one of Arthur's closest friends, Hammond's plea that night was this: 'If any of you men are sick of the lives you are living, there is One who loves you who will set you free and His name is Jesus.'[19]

9.3. Wednesday Night Men's Meeting at St Barnabas' during the Great Depression. On 6 August 1930, a down-and-out Arthur Stace attended one of these meetings for 'a cuppa tea and a rock cake.' He heard a Hammond sermon on the saving power of the gospel and found the 'Rock of Ages.'

One can imagine Arthur's reaction. He was desperate. He was ashamed of his dark past and his dire present. He knew he needed love and forgiveness. He knew he needed the power to change. But he did not go forward at the meeting itself.

The moment of conversion – the taking of 'the Leap' – is ineffable and mysterious. Sometimes it is not consciously appreciated by the convert. Christians believe that it is God – the Holy Spirit – who brings it about. Arthur later said that he 'came under strong conviction of sin' and desired 'to be delivered from its bondage.' He also 'realised that Christ was stronger than strong drink.'[20] After drinking his tea and eating his rock cake, he left the hall alone, crossed Broadway, and walked into Victoria Park (adjacent to Sydney University). There, under a large fig tree, in the dark and out of sight, he knelt down and wept. Then he cried out a simple prayer: 'God, God be merciful to me a sinner!'[21] The choice of words suggests strongly[22] that, at some stage during the evening, Hammond had expounded the prayer of the repentant publican:* 'And the publican, standing afar off, would not lift up so much as *his* eyes unto heaven, but smote upon his breast, saying, God be merciful to me a sinner' (Luke 18:13).

9.4. Fig tree in Victoria Park, diagonally opposite St Barnabas', Broadway. Was this the tree under which Arthur Stace prayed on the night of Wednesday 6 August 1930: 'God, God be merciful to me a sinner'?

Arthur always insisted that from that night onward, he never touched a drop of alcohol. 'God really heard my cry that night!' he once declared. 'God really met me that night in the park! ... The desire to drink was taken away! I was a changed man!'[23] Although successful 'cold turkey' recoveries from addiction have always been rare, there is no good

* In other translations, including the NIV, the repentant sinner is a tax collector.

reason to doubt him. His famous catchcry – repeated countless times over the next 37 years – was that he 'went into the meeting for a rock cake and came out with the Rock of Ages.' Peace had come to his troubled soul.

§

Within a short time, quite possibly the very next day, Arthur returned to St Barnabas' and introduced himself to the Rev. Hammond. One imagines that Hammond greeted him warmly, elicited the basics of his story, and encouraged him to attend Sunday services and Wednesday night Men's Meetings on a regular basis. No doubt, also, Hammond offered some immediate practical help – a few solid meals, a fresh set of clothes, a warm place to sleep.

Arthur made rapid progress. Truly, he was born again. According to Lisle Thompson, 'in a little while after his conversion, [he] learnt what he call[ed] the two secrets of success in the Christian life.' These for him were prayer and obedience.[24]

Thompson described Arthur's daily prayer routine:

> Arthur Stace rises early to read the Bible and pray simple, sincere prayers. At midday hour he prays again and when evening falls prayer arises again, for cleansing and help. Much prayer, says, Arthur Stace, keeps the channel clean, keeps us in touch with God.[25]

As to obedience – that is, obedience to God's teaching as explained and exemplified by Jesus (John 14:23, 31) – Thompson wrote:

> To Arthur Stace God is the power. Arthur Stace, Arthur declares, is weak, unclean and powerless, but God has all power, so obey God in everything, small and great, and His Spirit will break sin's power and make the crooked Will straight.[26]

For Arthur, the clearest outward sign of his new life in Christ was the ability to give up the grog. He also stopped smoking and gambling, and refrained from swearing or blaspheming. And, in what seems to have been a conscious attempt to imitate the respectable-looking Christian men who had so impressed him at Hammond's Wednesday night meeting (the ones sitting up the front), he began dressing and grooming himself neatly. Thereafter he always wore a suit and tie, Homberg hat and shiny shoes.[27]

We may be sure that R.B.S. Hammond was deeply moved. In Arthur he had found walking, talking proof of his most fervent beliefs: the destructiveness of alcoholism, the possibility of reform, the desirability of abstinence, the fruits of Christian charity. And above all, the saving grace of God. Almost as soon as the changes in Arthur were manifest, Hammond put him in charge of a small five-bed hostel in Ultimo (43 Burlinson Street) for the rehabilitation of alcoholic men.[28] It proved an inspired decision, entrenching Arthur in his new calling. It also made Hammond another devoted, lifelong friend. As he had once written in *Grit*: 'A true friend is a diamond ... [Friends] are not always to be found among relations or those regarded as equals, but often from among those humble men who are loyal and grateful.'[29]

Arthur *was* grateful. And, understandably, he was also excited – perhaps a little proud. Around this time he visited Darlinghurst police station, one of the places at which he had often spent the night in a holding cell during his previous life. He told the sergeant that he had become a Christian and sworn off alcohol for good. They would never need to lock him up again! The sergeant scoffed: 'Knowing you, this will just be a short-term change. You'll soon be back in the gutter again – you'll see.'[30]

But Arthur was never back in the gutter. A few months later he was still on the straight and narrow and could not resist another visit to the sergeant. That time, the man was impressed.[31]

In due course Hammond gave Arthur more responsibility. As he regained his self-respect, he found that people were more decent to him. On top of his voluntary work, he eventually secured paid employment – a state government job as a labourer, one week on and one week off, levelling the sand hills at Maroubra. The pay was £3 a week.[32]

§

It is a feature of the *Eternity* story that Arthur Stace became associated with R.B.S. Hammond at the height of his fame and influence. Hammond was a respected figure in Church of England circles before the Great Depression, but by the time it was over he was a general household name.

Soon enough, Arthur must have realised that he had joined the inner circle of a major public figure. Hammond was appointed a canon of St Andrew's Cathedral in 1931 and his feats were reported regularly in the city's newspapers. He became a close personal friend of some highly distinguished men, including the Governor of New South Wales, Sir Philip Game, and the Lord Mayor of Sydney, Sir Samuel Walder. Both admired Hammond's work for the underprivileged and encouraged it at every turn.[33]

On 25 November 1930, Sir Philip Game opened the first of the so-called 'Hammond Hotels'. This building, in Blackfriars Street, Chippendale, provided emergency accommodation for up to 120 men. Next day the *Sydney Morning Herald* reported:

> This hotel (which possesses no bar) has been launched ... in order to allow single men to take advantage of the Government's issue of rations for the unemployed. Under the conditions laid down by the Government, single men may receive rations only provided they have some approved place in which the food may be cooked. The new premises fulfil this condition.[34]

But Hammond was just getting started. In May 1931, with another winter approaching, he set up a second Hammond Hotel, a shelter for 130 unemployed men in a converted four-storey warehouse in Buckland Street, Chippendale.[35] Again, Sir Philip Game presided at the official opening.[36]

Arthur may well have been at this function, watching on quietly.

By the end of 1932, Hammond was operating four Hotels in or near the inner city and a Poor Relief Department out of St Barnabas' itself.[37] He had also inaugurated his most ambitious project of all: a pioneer home scheme for unemployed and evicted families at a bushy site near Liverpool in south-western Sydney. Hammond bought the land by cashing in his own life insurance policy. The place came to be known as 'Hammondville'.[38] Today it is an established suburb of Sydney.

This, then, was the Christ-like example now set for Arthur Stace. It was a far cry from what he had grown up with and, during his first 45 years, become used to.

In the autumn of 1932, Arthur got a powerful reminder of the life he had left behind. His wayward older brother, William John Stace, was involved – if only indirectly and quite by chance. William was now living in Sydney and employed as an attendant at the Botanic Gardens. On 7 April 1932 he heard a gunshot close by and ran towards its source. Lying on the grass he found the dead body of a middle-aged man, a revolver still smoking in his hand. The dead man was J.T. Toohey, 57, a former director of Toohey's brewery. He had committed suicide.[39]

Arthur must have heard about this episode. It is safe to assume he was still in contact with his brother,[40] and the story reached the press. Why might it have given Arthur pause? Because J.T. Toohey, like him, had been gassed on the Western Front. Toohey had also felt keen bereavement: the death of a close family member the year before.[41] But perhaps most ironic of all was the fact that Toohey was one of the scions of the liquor industry. He had not survived his tribulations, but Arthur had.

10. Echoes of Eternity

For thus saith the high and lofty One that inhabiteth eternity, whose name is Holy; I dwell in the high and holy place, with him also that is of a contrite and humble spirit, to revive the spirit of the humble, and to revive the heart of the contrite ones.
Isaiah 57:15

There were two huge days in Arthur Stace's early Christian life. The first and most important was Wednesday 6 August 1930 – the day of his conversion. The second, utterly critical in the *Eternity* story and only slightly less important for Arthur, came two years later. Apart from Arthur himself, the central figure was John Gotch Ridley.

As we saw in Chapter 8, Ridley by the early 1930s had created a name for himself as a travelling evangelist. In due course his fame extended beyond the Baptist church to Protestant circles generally, and in early 1932 he appeared as a speaker at the 29th Annual Katoomba Christian Convention.[1] This was (and still is) a major event, crossing denominational lines. Even so, Ridley's loyalties always remained with the Baptists. And though he was not now a member of the congregation at Burton Street Tabernacle in Darlinghurst – the place of his own conversion back in 1915, in the days of William Lamb – he maintained a close association with it.

The resident pastor at Burton Street for 13 years from March 1927 was the Rev. Harold G. Hercus (1881–1943), another notable figure in the *Eternity* story. Like Lamb, he was a New Zealander by birth and a pre-millennialist in his theology. Though a 'gifted expositor'[2] in his own right, Hercus happily encouraged younger men of talent. In the late spring of 1932 he organised a 'Special Mission' at Burton Street, with Ridley as the guest speaker. It was a packed program, advertised not only in Baptist publications[3] but also the mainstream press. On Saturday 5 November 1932, the following ad appeared prominently in the *Sydney Morning Herald*:

> BURTON-STREET CITY TABERNACLE,
> DARLINGHURST
> Eight days' Evangelistic Campaign
>
> ---
>
> Preacher: EVANGELIST John G. Ridley
> 7 p.m. First Evening Service of an eight days' series ...
> Subject – 'Few There Be That Find It – Why?'
> These services will be continued nightly at 7.30 o'clock[4]

There was follow-up ad a week later on Saturday 12 November for the last three days of the Campaign.[5]

It is possible that Arthur Stace saw these advertisements or had them pointed out to him by someone at St Barnabas'. Perhaps he already knew of Ridley by reputation – his mentor, R.B.S. Hammond, certainly would have. Whatever the case, Arthur turned up at Burton Street Tabernacle on the penultimate night of the campaign, Monday 14 November 1932.

Let us set the context. For Sydney generally, the Great Depression was still biting hard. It was eight months since the opening of the

Harbour Bridge and five months since the dismissal of Jack Lang by the NSW governor. Conservative governments were back in power in both Canberra and Macquarie Street, trying to steady the economic ship. A keenly awaited Ashes series was about to commence, featuring Australia's batting prodigy Don Bradman, then 24. It was hoped that the cricket would cheer people up, but it was not to be. The visiting English side had a ruthless captain, Douglas Jardine, and a bevy of fast bowlers.[6]

10.1. Dole queue in Sydney during the height of the Great Depression, January 1932.

For Arthur Stace, life was still not a bed of roses – but it now had meaning and purpose. He was a reformed man, always sober and decently turned out, working for the Rev. Hammond and participating in church life at St Barnabas'. He was thirsty for Christian knowledge. Perhaps he smiled to himself that November evening as he made his way to the Tabernacle through the streets of Darlinghurst. These were familiar streets, after all – the ones in which, in the 1920s, he had often lolled about stinking drunk.

10.2. The Burton Street Baptist Tabernacle in Darlinghurst, to which Arthur Stace came on 14 November 1932 to hear John Ridley's sermon, 'Echoes of Eternity.' Ridley himself had been converted at the Tabernacle as an 18-year-old, in mid-1915.

There was a large crowd at Burton Street that night – perhaps 400 or 450 people. As Arthur probably knew in advance, Ridley took as his theme 'Echoes of Eternity.'[7] He spoke for an hour or so, and Arthur listened spellbound.[8]

A record survives of the notes that Ridley used,[9] so the content of the service can be reconstructed with confidence and in detail. Ridley began by quoting the Old Testament text on which it was based, Isaiah 57:15.[10] Then, in his strong, earnest voice, he let rip:

> Eternity! Like a solitary mountain peak jutting far up above its fellows and standing in stately isolation. So this word appeals to us tonight. The Mt. Everest of Scripture.
>
> Eternity! I hear it coming out of the past gathering strength like a roll of thunder and bursting with a loud clap in the present, go sweeping on with incessant rolls and rumblings into the unknown future. Surely among all the subjects that face the preacher today, there can be none more momentous than Eternity!

Ridley's conception of eternity was the biblical one. It encompassed the notion of timelessness – 'it has no beginning ... no ending ... no boundaries' – but was not, thereby, woolly or indefinite. Eternity, he said, was the 'lifetime of God.' It was the domain of the necessary Supreme Being, the Creator, the one true God who had always existed and would always exist. For human beings, Ridley went on, eternity meant 'the life to come', the 'endless future' after physical death – and the nature of that eternity, terrible or sublime, would be determined by God for each individual. 'You have got to face it; you have got to face it,' he thundered.

It was an artfully structured talk. Ridley pointed to three aspects of the world 'which have and are echoing Eternity.'

The first was creation – that is, the physical universe itself. After an eloquent riff on the abundant glories of nature, he drew upon two episodes from his own life. One was the drowning of a man at Manly beach in Sydney which he had witnessed as a child; he recalled his own feelings at evening: 'Where was he? In Eternity? Oh heed the message of the mighty deep!' The other episode was from his days as a jackeroo:

> Is there no echo of Eternity to that stockman who has ridden 12 hours over wide, lonely plain and expanses that speak of wider expanses and now at night, with his saddle as his pillow, he lays down to rest and gazes at the twinkling stars – the stars which told Abraham of his Children of promise – the stars that were David's companions in his shepherd days – surely they echo of greater regions than those he has been riding through – regions of Eternity?

Such ruminations were to be contrasted, Ridley argued, with the banal thoughts of most people most of the time. He gave some examples, one of which surely produced a wry nod from ex-alcoholic Arthur: the manual worker who dreams of 'the spree he intends having at knock-off time.' Perhaps Arthur recalled his very first spree at the Mt Kembla pub.

Ridley's second echo of eternity was 'the Christian' – the individual believer who had battled through life and might still be doing so.

'Eternity will reveal,' he insisted, 'why you are buffeted by pains and persecution.'

10.3. Ridley in preaching mode.

Here, one imagines, Arthur lent forward in his seat. Like Ridley himself – they were fellow survivors of the Western Front – Arthur had experienced more than his share of suffering. Ridley was encouraging him to persist in his faith, even if it brought *more* suffering in this world, because suffering that was endured in the name of Christ had precious value. 'That is God's guarantee to you brother and sister – God's consolation in the conflicts of life – Eternity,' Ridley said.

Thirdly, he concluded, 'the Cross echoes Eternity.' What he called the 'greatest monument of all time' was, at the simplest level, a reminder of mortality: 'Men and women, *death* is the doorway to Eternity and *you* must die. Yes, it is an individual journey. You *must* die.'

There followed an orthodox Reformed explanation of the meaning of the Cross – of each person's need to respond to Jesus in this life, to make a decision whether or not to rely on his sacrifice of atonement for the sins of the world (1 Peter 3:18). Arthur had made his own personal decision back on 6 August 1930, under the fig tree, and must have felt joyful and thankful as Ridley hammered the message home.

'The whole of your endless future depends on what you do with Him,' Ridley explained, for it was *Jesus* who 'governs Eternity.' This was a neat way of expressing a core gospel teaching: it is Christ – not

God the Father – who will judge each human being (John 5:22, 26–27), while also acting as an 'advocate' for those who have placed their faith in him (1 John 2:1).

Ridley's final plea that night was unscripted – not reflected in his notes. He raised his loud voice even louder and cried:

> Eternity! Eternity! I wish that I could sound, or shout, that word to everyone on the streets of Sydney. Eternity! Friends, you have got to meet it. Where will you spend Eternity?[11]

That final rhetorical question – 'Where will you spend Eternity?' – was not original. Decades earlier, it had been posed by one of the most esteemed Baptist preachers of all time, Charles H. Spurgeon (1834–92).[12] Some in the audience at Burton Street must have recognised it as such, but probably not Arthur. Spurgeon's question would have been all the more piercing if heard for the first time by a recent convert.

Arthur left the Tabernacle inspired. In his words, this is what happened next:

> Eternity went ringing through my brain and suddenly I began crying and felt a powerful call from the Lord to write 'Eternity'. I had a piece of chalk in my pocket and, outside the church, I bent down right there and wrote it.[13]

To Arthur's astonishment, the word came out smoothly in perfect copperplate: *Eternity*. Though he was *not* illiterate,[14] he had always struggled with writing and spelling.[15] Yet this single word, which meant so much, looked so good. It must have seemed to Arthur like a gift of God. Many Christians would insist that it was – if not an out-and-out miracle, then a providential sign and the genesis of a divinely ordained mission. The Apostle Paul insisted that 'it is God who works in you to will and to act in order to fulfil his good purpose' (Philippians 2:13, NIV).

Or, as Arthur put it, 'That was the moment that decided me to start writing "Eternity" on the footpaths and I've been doing it ever since.'[16]

10.4. Immediately after Ridley's 'Echoes of Eternity' sermon, Arthur felt a powerful call from the Lord to write 'Eternity'. He did so there and then, on the pavement outside the Tabernacle, using a piece of chalk he found in his pocket.

DAVID LEVER, *ENLIGHTENMENT*, OIL ON BOARD, 2000/01.

His practice was to rise each morning at 4am and pray for an hour. Then, after a light breakfast, he made his way on foot or by public transport to the suburb he had decided to visit that day. He usually spent at least two hours at work in the streets – often up to four or five hours, depending on his other commitments[17] – writing the word in a prominent place every few hundred yards.[18] In a typical session he would do it as many as 50 times.[19]

In the words of May Thompson, Arthur was a 'pavement pastor' who acted with 'confidence in the knowledge he was doing the will of his God.' His approach was methodical:

> Wherever people walked, he chalked ... Wherever transport commenced and terminated – at railway barriers, subway entrances, bus depots and quay turnstiles. Along the main streets of the city, the congested inner city area, the harbour foreshores, the beach suburbs, the Art Gallery, University entrances, on steps leading into courthouses, schools, churches and especially Kings Cross, [which] was his special parish.[20]

§

The organisers of the Special Campaign at Burton Street judged it a success. A fortnight later, in the 29 November 1932 issue of the *Australian Baptist*, one 'J.M.' reported:

> The ten days mission from November 6 to 16th, with Mr. John Ridley as missioner, was launched with much prayer and from the start a very marked and hearty response by large audiences was the result. The open-air campaign, supported by the Gospel Vans was well maintained every evening of the mission. Numbers yielded to the call of the Gospel and decided for Christ and some for baptism. We trust the influence of these special services will remain, bearing much fruit to the Master's glory.[21]

Mark that last sentence! 'We trust the influence of these special services will remain, bearing much fruit to the Master's glory.' As we shall see, no one could possibly have envisaged just how much.

11. Rivers in the desert

Be the change that you wish to see in the world.
Mahatma Gandhi

Arthur spent the remainder of the 1930s building himself up in a Christian way of life. There were two main aspects to this: the visible aspect, seen by the world and traceable through the historical record, and the invisible aspect, the things he did alone or which went on inside his head. The beginning of his *Eternity* mission fell somewhere in between.

First, the incontestable facts. From 1933 Arthur was living on site at the Hammond hostel at 43 Burlinson Street, Ultimo,[1] and working intermittently as a labourer. His life centred around the weekly activities at St Barnabas', Broadway – services, prayer meetings, Bible study – and the Rev. R.B.S. Hammond's myriad charitable works. General economic conditions had begun slowly to improve, but there was still widespread deprivation in inner Sydney through the rest of the decade. Hammond's Hotels provided a vital service.

Hammond conducted an overseas mission tour in mid-1933, to Hawaii. On his arrival back home to Sydney in August, he was accorded a big public welcome in the chapter house next to St Andrew's Cathedral. It was attended in person or in spirit by many of the state's most powerful men – secular and religious. One, the Rev. S. Varcoe Cocks, a prominent Methodist, sent a telegram: 'I hold him to be Sydney's greatest citizen.'[2]

If Arthur was not there himself that night, he would certainly have read and heard all about it. Perhaps his mentor's return was a stimulus, for shortly afterwards Arthur made what may have been his first public appearance as an evangelist.

On Saturday 21 October 1933, the *Sydney Morning Herald* carried an advertisement for a Gospel Service ('the Captivating Jesus') to be held next day at the YMCA's premises in the city. The principal speaker was a Mr W.B. Ogden, but there was also a supporting act:

> TESTIMONIES by Ranji Burns, ex-pugilist, Jack O'Keefe, Arthur Stace.[3]

It seems probable that Hammond – or someone in his wide network of contacts – had encouraged Arthur to tell his story publicly and made the necessary arrangements on his behalf.

Y.M.C.A., 325 PITT-STREET. Mr. W. B. OGDEN. 7.15 P.M., GOSPEL SERVICE. OPEN TO ALL. SUBJECT, "THE CAPTIVATING JESUS." TESTIMONIES by Ranji Burns, ex-pugilist, Jack O'Keefe, Arthur Stace. Stirring singing.

11.1. Notice in the *Sydney Morning Herald*, 21 October 1933. This was probably Arthur's first advertised public speaking appearance.

It also seems probable that the YMCA appearance was the first (or among the first) of several made by Arthur around this time.[4] During the 1930s, Hammond often spoke at large Christian meetings in Sydney conducted outside the auspices of the Church of England. These included the United Intercessory Service in the Lower Town Hall and the City Men's Bible Class – both founded in the 1920s by William 'Cairo' Bradley (1870–1945), another notable Sydney evangelist of that era[5] – as well as regular gatherings at Paddy's Markets and Dalrymple's bookshop. Bradley also conducted many 'tent missions' throughout Sydney.

There is every likelihood that Hammond or Bradley, or both, took Arthur along to these events occasionally and that Arthur watched and learned. Sooner or later he would have been invited to speak. To be sure, by the end of the 1930s, he had developed a knack for informal preaching – both indoors and in the open air.

In late 1934 or early 1935,[6] Hammond took over from the Salvation Army the operation of a men's shelter in Buckland Street at the former factory premises of John Danks & Son. This was a considerably bigger

11.2. Promotional booklet about the Hotel Hammond in Buckland Street, Chippendale, at which Arthur worked from early 1937.

establishment than the Hotel in Buckland Street which Hammond had opened in 1931. In fact, it was a sprawling collection of buildings and sheds covering more than an acre of ground. There were several dormitories and a large communal dining hall, as well as showers, toilets, and washing and ironing facilities. A cinema screen, a wireless set and a piano were provided in the dining hall for entertainment. In all, this Hammond Hotel could accommodate up to 325 unemployed men each night. Its slogan was 'Where Need Is the Latchkey.'[7]

In the first half of 1937, Arthur was appointed by Hammond to take charge of the so-called Emergency Depot,[8] a place at Buckland Street 'where needy men could come to have essential sewing done, to have their boots repaired, to shave themselves and to secure an item of clothing.' In addition, items including writing material, stamps, cotton and needles were given away, and, where necessary, train fares provided.[9] A Furniture Department was also set up, at which second-hand pieces were sold cheaply or gifted away. Arthur worked there too.[10]

A wonderful photograph survives from this time showing Arthur seated at a desk at the Emergency Depot. He is gazing into the distance, while, behind him, five unemployed men are shaving. Two Christian banners adorn the walls: 'What Must I Do to be Saved? Believe on the Lord Jesus Christ' and 'The Coming of the Lord Draweth Nigh.'[11]

In this new position, Arthur had found another calling. Surely he felt honoured to be part of a Sydney institution that was helping so many desperate men.

There is a rousing passage in *He That Doeth* in which a former guest of the Hammond Hotel at Buckland Street – an English gentleman educated at Harrow, who had fallen on hard times – describes his week's stay. Arriving in a sullen mood, he was soon disarmed and ultimately won over. What impressed him were not only the amenities – 'spotlessly clean' dormitories, 'good food', an 'extensive library'– but

11.3. Arthur (seated, left) supervises the Emergency Depot at the Hotel Hammond in Buckland Street.

the friendliness, intelligence and sobriety of the guests. He attributed their 'perfect discipline' to the courtesy and non-judgmentalism of the staff, and above all to the 'courage and vitality of Canon Hammond'.[12]

His overall verdict was this:

> Truly this is Christianity, and the Canon and all his staff are endeavouring to live up to the precepts and teachings of the Christ they follow. A most practical bulwark against Communism and discontent, and a pillar of light in a city of greed.[13]

Many influential people thought the same. On 31 December 1935, the Sydney commercial radio station 2UE had broadcast its New Year's Eve program from the Hotel in Buckland Street. The special guest speaker was a former prime minister, Billy Hughes – the 'Little Digger' himself.[14] Arthur may have been there to hear and see Hughes, in his capacity as a friend of Hammond or a staff member at the Ultimo hostel in Burlinson Street.

Once Arthur began working at Buckland Street in 1937, there is evidence that he lived on site or slept there occasionally.[15] The English gentleman quoted above described various men in the dormitory during his stay, including one in the next bed:

> On my left was a little man, irresistibly like Charlie Chaplin, who was deeply engrossed in a learned work on the chemical formation and manufacture of coal gas. He was very secretive over his reason for this technical study, and I noticed later that whenever he stopped reading the work he locked it carefully away in a little bag.[16]

In due course Arthur became renowned for using a lump of coal as a prop during his evangelistic talks – he had, of course, once worked in a coal mine.[17] So we may be sure that this 'little man' was him (many years before he became famous).

The episode described by the Hammond Hotel guest is further indirect proof, not only of Arthur's early efforts in or towards evangelism, but of his level of literacy. In that regard, it is also worth noting that, around this time, he wrote another letter to the AIF:

> Dear Sir
>
> Could you kindly forward on a Duplicate discharge as the State Labour exchange will not accknowledge [sic.] any other writing from the Repatriation & it has put me in a very difficult situation both for work & the Dole, as I have lost my discharge. I will be very grateful to you if you can forward something in that line from Head quarters.[18]

A few days later, Arthur swore a statutory declaration explaining the circumstances in which the discharge had been lost: 'I lost it some years ago in shifting from one place to another & burned in the rubbish in mistake as far as I can think.'[19]

During the 1930s, Arthur became involved in more charitable and evangelistic work. The exact starting dates are uncertain, but there is no doubt that he began making regular visits to at least three places in Sydney that housed lonely, hopeless-seeming men of the sort he had once been. He kept up this work for many years – in some cases into the early 1960s.[20]

On Wednesday evenings, it became his habit to visit a hostel for derelicts and alcoholics in Francis Street, East Sydney. Part of the Central Methodist Mission, later known as 'Francis Street Annexe' or the 'Sydney Night Refuge', it could house up to 100 men.[21] Arthur chatted to them, listened to their stories and told them his. He adopted a similar approach during visits to an inmate of the mental asylum at Callan Park – the place he had narrowly escaped entering himself back in the late 1920s – and the Leper Lazaret at Little Bay.[22] The Lazaret was a hospital and quarantine station established in the 1880s, initially for the treatment of infectious Chinese immigrants.[23] Later, and until the mid-1960s, it operated as an offshoot of Prince Henry hospital, completely enclosed by a tall fence to isolate those inside from the rest of the hospital patients.[24]

In ministering to men such as these – truly the despised and rejected of Sydney – Arthur was living out the gospel (cf. Matthew 25:36; Hebrews 13:3). What is more, he did it skilfully and unobtrusively, drawing upon his own experience. Those who knew him best believed he 'brought cheer and hope to desperate cases.'[25]

He did not succeed with his own closest family, however. Clara excepted, all his siblings would die as drunkards[26] – and, as far as these things can ever be known for sure, *not* as followers of Jesus.

Arthur must have tried to convince them. In the years immediately following his conversion he would have been at his keenest, and all of them except Sam[27] were living close by in inner Sydney.[28] But it was not to be. Minnie's body and spirit gave up first: on 10 May 1936, at the age of 56, she died of bronchopneumonia in Newington State Hospital, Lidcombe, and was buried two days later in Rookwood cemetery.[29] She was still married to Alexander Campbell when she died, but no notices of her death or funeral were published in any of Sydney's major newspapers. The two official witnesses to her burial were not family members.

Arthur had joined a new family at St Barnabas'. During the 1930s he made several friends there, including a teenage boy named Bernard Judd[30] who would later become a Church of England minister and another significant actor in the *Eternity* story. Arthur owed a great deal to St Barnabas', and his reverence for R.B.S. Hammond never diminished. Yet by the end of the decade he had found a new spiritual home – the Burton Street Baptist Tabernacle in Darlinghurst. Arthur's name appeared on the membership roll there for the first time in 1939.[31]

When – and why – did he decide to make the move? His reasons can safely be inferred.

For a start, Burton Street was the place where John Ridley had delivered the 'Echoes of Eternity' sermon in 1932. It had moved Arthur profoundly and inspired the most important project of his life. More generally, by the late 1930s, his Christian outlook had evolved. The charitable work which had occupied him with Hammond was no longer quite so pressing: the worst of the Depression was over by 1938 or thereabouts, and the Buckland Street Hotel was forced to close in mid-1939 when the owners sold the property.[32] Hammond was nearing retirement age.

Meanwhile, Arthur, though past 50, strained with the zeal of a recent convert. He had become a fired-up evangelical, and while there were some of those in Sydney Anglican circles, the Baptists positively abounded with them. The minister at Burton Street until March 1940, Harold Hercus, was in that mould, and the legendary William Lamb also maintained connections there. (For some months in 1940, Lamb came out of retirement to serve as the interim pastor.[33]) Other probable attractions for Arthur were the Baptists' emphasis on open-air mission and the 'all day Sunday' character of Burton Street worship.[34]

He must have undergone a 'believer's baptism' in 1939.[35] The method used at Burton Street was full body immersion: there was a tiled baptistery at the Tabernacle, with steps going in and out, big enough to fit two people at a time.[36] The person being baptised wore white clothes (shorts and T-shirt for men, a dress for women). Arthur's ceremony would have been a sight to see.

§

There is a school of thought that Arthur did not begin his *Eternity* mission – the daily chalking or crayoning of the word on Sydney footpaths – until a few years *after* he moved to Burton Street.[37]

It is true that references to the *Eternity* phenomenon did not appear in Sydney newspapers until the 1940s. It is also true that once, during a radio interview with 2GB's Jim Waugh in 1964, Arthur gave an estimate of the length of his mission ('twenty years') suggestive of a start considerably later than 1932.[38] But that remark was exceptional, easily explainable in its context and by Arthur's advanced age when he made it.

Quite possibly his routine became more regimented as the years went by. But the heavy weight of evidence supports the traditional version of events: Arthur began his mission on the night of Ridley's sermon at Burton Street on 14 November 1932. 'That was the moment that decided me to start writing 'Eternity' on the footpaths, *and I've been doing it ever since,*' he told the Sydney journalist who broke the story to the general public in 1956.[39]

That was the clear understanding of Ridley himself[40] – who came to know Arthur intimately – and of the Rev. Lisle Thompson, the man who persuaded Arthur to 'go public.'[41]

It was also what Arthur said in the Jim Waugh radio interview itself. Notwithstanding the 'twenty year' remark, he told Waugh that he began writing *Eternity* immediately after hearing John Ridley's sermon[42] – and the date of that sermon, 14 November 1932, is absolutely certain.

There is also strong corroborative evidence from an independent third party, never before published. The late Ron Barker (c. 1922–2016) served as an RAAF navigator in 1941–45[43] and was a long-time resident of Sydney. During his final years, he lived in the southern suburb of Gymea. In a signed statement provided to Elizabeth Meyers in 2009, Barker attested to having seen a 'nondescript' man 'neatly attired in suit and felt hat' chalking the word *Eternity* on Sydney pavements several times *before* World War II, when he (Barker) was still a teenager. In his words:

> I saw him several times back in those days. It was about 1937 or 1938. Who or what he was, was not a question at the time, but it was a fascination to see him pause at this particular spot.
>
> Sydney was a city emerging from the depression period. The city streets were the site of the occasional pavement artist seeking a few coins as appreciation of the chalk art being portrayed on the asphalt surface. One such place was in George Street almost at the corner of Martin Place. The MLC building was an old and imposing background for chalk art and the pavement here was often in use.
>
> He paused as [if] he was attracted to the spot and quietly, without any demonstration, bent down and wrote in beautiful script

> letters, just one word – Eternity – then continued on his way. Those passing by didn't seem to take much notice of his effort. Except the occasional one who paused and read.
>
> And on several other occasions around that time, I saw him repeat that effort. I remember stopping for several moments and gazing at his message, at that young age, not being aware of the importance of the word. But it left a lasting impression ...

Then the clincher:

> ... for within a year I had faced up to the question of my Eternity and made a decision to accept Jesus Christ as Lord of my life, a decision that has lasted over seventy years.[44]

No Christian forgets the circumstances of their conversion. And Barker's were especially conducive to accurate memory: he had the tail end of the Great Depression and the onset of World War II as markers. All the details ring true. These are the earliest known sightings of *Eternity* chalkings written by Arthur Stace.

12. More precious than rubies

There is no more lovely, friendly or charming relationship, communion or company, than a good marriage.
Martin Luther

By the early 1940s Arthur Stace had got his life in order. He was a committed Christian and a decent citizen, with a growing circle of friends. Through Baptist circles he even got to know John Ridley himself, who came to call him (affectionately) 'little Stace'.[1]

For Arthur, meeting the man who had delivered the 'Echoes of Eternity' sermon[2] was surely a thrill, perhaps a bit daunting. Ridley had become an ordained minister of the Baptist Church in 1934,[3] and his reputation as an evangelist continued to grow. He was of upper-middle-class background, eleven years younger than Arthur, and happily married. He was also the father of a sweet little daughter (Ruth, born in April 1936). On the face of it, there was little to draw him to a single working-class battler like Arthur. Even so, in due course, the two men must have realised they had a big thing in common, over and above their shared Baptist faith – service on the Western Front in World War I. Though Ridley had come back with a Military Cross, he, just like Arthur, had struggled mightily with poor health and readjustment to civilian life.

(Ridley continued to suffer indifferent health throughout his life[4] and in 1934 was forced to cope with a very public family scandal. His worldly father-in-law, Professor H.G. Chapman, died suddenly in May of that year: it soon emerged that he had committed suicide by taking poison. Investigations revealed not only his unorthodox personal life, but the fact he had embezzled large sums of money entrusted to his care. Much of it had been spent on extravagant gifts for his mistress. His estate was bankrupt.[5])

One of the keys to Ridley's success was the help he received from Dorothy, his wife of 50 years. In the words of H.E. Evans, 'their marriage was a love-match, sealed by their mutual devotion to the Christ of Calvary and cemented by a united desire to reach out and win others to the Saviour.'[6] In short, they were kindred spirits. Dorothy Ridley was not only an affectionate wife and a wise and devoted mother;[7] she was a talented evangelist in her own right.

A Christian wife was the one thing that Arthur still lacked.

§

Ellen Esther Pearl Dawson – known always as 'Pearl' – was a no-nonsense spinster in her forties when she met Arthur Stace. They were fellow volunteers at a city soup kitchen.[8] Further details of their courtship are sparse – times, dates, places[9] – but we know Pearl had already been living in Sydney for about a decade, working as a housekeeper for a doctor and his family in Chatswood.[10] In that role she was very fondly regarded: the doctor's wife once remarked to one of Pearl's nieces that her aunt was suitably named, because she was 'indeed a pearl.'[11] Her own family thought so too. Among other acts of kindness, Pearl regularly sent home second-hand clothes (cast-offs from the doctor's children) for her younger relations.

12.1. The Dawson family of Millthorpe, New South Wales, early 1900s. Pearl Dawson, Arthur's future wife, is the girl lying propped on her elbow at front left.

Pearl's back story is worth recounting. Like Arthur, she had not had an easy life, but her upbringing was much more stable and respectable than his. William and Sophy Dawson, her parents, were solid citizens of the town of Millthorpe in central west New South Wales (not far from Orange). They were God-fearing people – William a Methodist, Sophy an Anglican – who raised no less than eleven children in a frugal but tight-knit home.[12] (Another four children died in infancy.)

Pearl was the eighth-born of the eleven children who lived to adulthood. As a little girl she had suffered from a serious illness, acrodynia (or 'Pink disease'). Now known to have been caused by mercury poisoning from babies' teething powder, and long since eradicated, it made Pearl's skin extremely painful to the touch. For a time her mother carried her around on a pillow.[13] But she recovered in due course and was able to attend school, where she learned to read and write to a decent level. At home she helped with the chores and the care of her three younger siblings. It appears that, by the time she entered adulthood, her main attributes were set in stone: a handsome and statuesque, if rather severe, appearance;[14] a reserved, sometimes abrupt manner; formidable domestic skills, especially as a cook; deep religious faith; a heart of gold.[15]

Next to nothing is known of Pearl's early adult years in Millthorpe, which ran in parallel with Arthur's stint in the AIF and the 'wilderness' period that followed. She came to Sydney in the late 1920s in search of paid work[16] and found it with the doctor and his family in Chatswood. Her arrival in 'the big smoke' thus coincided with the absolute nadir of Arthur's life – his addiction to metho, his near-committal to an asylum, his rebuke by a magistrate ('don't you know I have the power?'), and his failed attempt to have himself locked up in a police cell. (See Chapter 9.) She had not been in Sydney long when Arthur was converted to Christianity in August 1930.

12.2. Pearl as a young woman, many years before she met Arthur.

It is not known where Pearl worshipped during the 1930s, but it was probably at one of the Anglican churches on Sydney's North Shore. That is where she lived.[17] And it would have been a natural step from an Anglican congregation to volunteer work at one of R.B.S. Hammond's Hotels in the city.

Pearl's first impressions of Arthur are not difficult to imagine. By the time they came into contact he was a thoroughly admirable man – not physically imposing, but neat and tidy, diligent and unfailingly polite. Though poorly educated he had a sharp mind, and could recite passages of Scripture with alacrity.[18] He also had a keen sense of humour, an indispensable arrow in any suitor's quiver. During conversation at the soup kitchen he doubtless exhibited these traits. He may also have discussed some of his other voluntary work and, after a while, shared some of his life story. At least one of Pearl's brothers had served with the AIF in France during World War I,[19] so that was another point of common interest.

Probably Arthur harboured no serious hopes of wooing Pearl. She was ten years younger than him, a lady from a different world: he must have felt conscious of his unprepossessing appearance and sordid, grog-addled past. He may also have doubted his ability to provide for a wife on his meagre income. Once, at an open-air meeting at Paddy's Markets in Haymarket, an interjector yelled out: 'Why don't you get married, Arthur?' He shot back: 'She'd see a lot more dinner times than dinners!'[20]

But perhaps, with Pearl, a lack of conscious 'trying' worked in Arthur's favour. Candour and humility are often appealing qualities.

At any rate, by 1941, he and Pearl were friends, at ease in each other's company. They were in a prayer group together which met regularly at the city premises of Cairo Bradley's Campaigners for Christ.[21]

§

By 1941[22] Arthur had also begun missioning in the open air on the corner of Bathurst and George Streets in the city. He made this his weekly practice every Saturday night for many years, no doubt inspired by masters of the art such as Hammond, Ridley and Bradley. Open-air speaking was an especially popular method of evangelism in all Protestant churches of that era.

Arthur's style was as homespun as it got. In the company of one or two helpers from the Burton Street Tabernacle, usually women, he walked from the church to his regular spot (a distance of a mile and a half) and set up a portal organ and a street light.[23] A few hymns would be sung and then Arthur got cracking. According to one eyewitness:

> He had a novel way of starting ... He would put his Bible on the footpath and place his hat on top of it and walk around it yelling out, 'It's alive! It's alive!' When a crowd gathered, he would lift his hat and hold up his Bible and yell, 'It's alive – it's the Word of God, it's sharper than any two-edged sword and it knows all about you![24]

What followed often depended on the reaction of the crowd. Arthur responded to interjectors skillfully, with a blend of humour and earnestness.[25] His use of the Australian vernacular was winning – he had a regular line about the 'bumpers' (dead cigarette butts) that he used to scavenge as a drunk, the 'big bumpers' being saved for 'visitors' – and he bounced and moved around with enthusiasm.[26] When people showed genuine interest, he or his companions would offer them a Christian tract – they always brought along a good supply.

Did Pearl Dawson go along to watch Arthur in action? Did he tell her about his various Christian endeavours? The latter, at least, seems likely. What is certain is that late in the year 1941, *Pearl proposed to Arthur*! 'Why don't we get married?' were her exact words.[27] She must have realised they were compatible, and that it made no sense for them to live separately, but that Arthur might never dare to ask her. In the 1940s it was a brave thing for a woman to be so forward. Pearl's family disliked the story being told.[28]

Many years later, May Thompson fondly pictured the scene:

> The middle-aged kindly Christian gentleman who had known no home life, meeting the homely housekeeper Pearl. Eating her lovely scones, sampling her delicious pies, while he expressed admiration

> for her culinary arts, melting her soft heart with his stories of the difference between her cooking and restaurant [meals] ... his shining admiring eyes looking into her brown kindly ones ... and her saying 'why don't we get married?'[29]

Once the ice was broken, Arthur wasted no time. He bought a wedding ring for Pearl and made the necessary arrangements, asking Archdeacon[30] R.B.S. Hammond to marry them at St Barnabas'. This happened on 22 January 1942 in circumstances of the utmost simplicity: just the two (legally required) witnesses were present.[31] On the marriage certificate, Arthur recorded his occupation as 'missioner'.

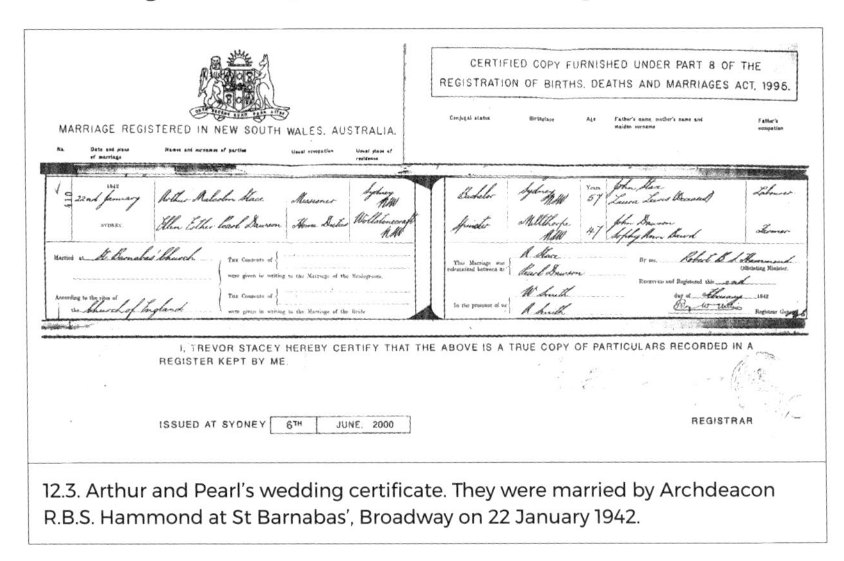
MARRIAGE REGISTERED IN NEW SOUTH WALES, AUSTRALIA.

CERTIFIED COPY FURNISHED UNDER PART 8 OF THE REGISTRATION OF BIRTHS, DEATHS AND MARRIAGES ACT, 1995.

No.	Date and place of marriage	Names and surnames of parties	Usual occupation	Usual place of residence	Conjugal status	Birthplace	Age	Father's name, mother's name and maiden surname	Father's occupation
410	1942 22nd January SYDNEY	Arthur Malcolm Stace	Missioner	Sydney NSW	Bachelor	Sydney NSW	Years 57	John Stace / Laura Lewis [illegible]	Labourer
		Ellen Esther Pearl Dawson	Home Duties	Wollstonecraft NSW	Spinster	[illegible] NSW	47	John Dawson / Sophy Ann [illegible]	Farmer

Married at St Barnabas' Church According to the rites of the Church of England

The Consents of .... were given in writing to the Marriage of the Bridegroom.
The Consents of .... were given in writing to the Marriage of the Bride.

This Marriage was solemnized between us: A. Stace, Pearl Dawson
In the presence of us: W. Smith, A. Smith
By me, Robert B. S. Hammond, Officiating Minister.
Received and Registered this 2nd day of February 1942 [illegible] Registrar General

I, TREVOR STACEY HEREBY CERTIFY THAT THE ABOVE IS A TRUE COPY OF PARTICULARS RECORDED IN A REGISTER KEPT BY ME.

ISSUED AT SYDNEY 6TH JUNE, 2000

REGISTRAR

12.3. Arthur and Pearl's wedding certificate. They were married by Archdeacon R.B.S. Hammond at St Barnabas', Broadway on 22 January 1942.

Afterwards Arthur enquired of Hammond about the cost. The grand old man shook his head, took his wallet from his pocket and extracted a five-pound note. He handed it to Arthur. 'For the honour,' he said.[32]

§

Pearl gave up her job as a housekeeper with the doctor's family in Chatswood. Probably straight away, but certainly by 1943, she and Arthur moved in to a modest little terrace house at 12 Bulwara Road, Pyrmont.[33] That would be their marital home for another 18 years.

If he had not done so already, Arthur must then have told her about his *Eternity* mission. For the rest of their married life, Pearl's contribution was to lay out his clothes the night before – three-piece suit, white shirt, tie, Homberg hat, shiny shoes. They were always immaculate and became another of his trademarks.[34]

The newlyweds soon paid a joint visit to Millthorpe so that Arthur could be introduced to Pearl's relatives. If any of them had harboured concerns that he was an ex-alcoholic, he soon won them over. And Pearl's own contentedness was obvious to all. One of her sisters pulled her aside when Arthur was out of earshot and asked point blank: 'How are things going?'

Pearl replied: 'Happy as Larry!'[35]

13. Growing in faith

I know your deeds, your love and faith, your service and perseverance, and that you are now doing more than you did at first.
Revelation 2:19 (NIV)

Arthur and Pearl Stace soon became a well-known couple at the Burton Street Baptist Tabernacle in Darlinghurst. It is unclear whether Pearl had already begun attending services there before she married Arthur in January 1942, but thereafter they always worshipped together. What is more, both threw themselves keenly into service.

Arthur continued his open-air missioning in George Street on Saturday nights. Pearl began working in the Tabernacle's basement kitchen: she was responsible, among other things, for cooking a hot dinner on Wednesday evenings for those in the congregation who attended the mid-week prayer and Bible study meeting. She also helped out as required on Sundays and made 'many cuppas' for all and sundry.[1]

Together, Arthur and Pearl met newcomers at the door on Sundays and made them feel welcome.[2] They also maintained involvement in Christian activities outside Burton Street, such as Cairo Bradley's Bligh Street prayer group and other special events. It is a safe bet they were at Central Baptist Church in George Street on Saturday 16 May

1942 for the Annual Meeting of the Sydney Evangelistic Crusade – R.B.S. Hammond and John Ridley were speakers on the same platform,[3] possibly for the last time.

Selfless workers such as Arthur and Pearl were crucial for the Tabernacle in and from the transition year of 1942. Few may have realised it at the time, but for various demographic reasons, numbers there had peaked before the outbreak of World War II.[4]

In June 1942 a new minister arrived, the Rev. R.M. (Bob) Leghorn. He was another pre-millennialist in the mould of Lamb, Hercus and Ridley.[5] Energetic and ambitious, always looking to add to his flock, he instituted a Sunday school scholar drive and open-air Sunday schools in local suburbs. During the war years, he also had some success in attracting American servicemen to listen to his sermons (sailors especially were often in the vicinity of Woolloomooloo).[6]

In at least one instance, Leghorn was responsible for inviting a new person to the Tabernacle who became a very dear friend of Arthur and Pearl Stace (and an important source for this book).

Edith Summergreene was a young bride of 20 or so when she began attending Cairo Bradley's prayer meetings at Bligh Street in the city. It was there, in the latter half of 1941, that she had first met Arthur and Pearl. Edith was lonely: her husband was overseas serving in the armed forces. In the spring of 1942, a few months after his arrival at Burton Street, Bob Leghorn was the guest speaker at one of the Bligh Street prayer meetings. He heard Edith give her testimony (she had been 'born again' only the year before) and, evidently, was impressed by her.[7]

As Edith told the story many years later:

> Twice in the next couple of months he [Leghorn] invited me to his church – the second time was to be his guest at the Christmas dinner. I plucked up the courage to go and who should be at the door but Pearl and Arthur Stace. From that day on they were my

> mentors and constant companions. They took me with them to Open Air in the parks and streets around Darlinghurst and Railway Park ... And Pearl kept her eye on me when I was very young and unwise in the ways of the world.[8]

A close bond quickly formed. A little later in the 1940s Arthur and Pearl visited Edith's family in the country – there is a photo of the two of them sitting together on a riverbank in the sun, looking happy and contented.

§

World War II had a marked effect on the Christian scene in inner Sydney generally and at Burton Street Tabernacle in particular. It was a mixed bag. On the one hand, all congregations suffered from the absence of Australian servicemen and women overseas.[9] And petrol rationing made it more difficult for families living in the suburbs to come into the city to attend services on Sundays – a trend that continued after the war.[10]

On the other hand, the war opened up new opportunities for evangelism. Sydney was a busy place, and many people lived with the spectre of sudden death hanging over them.

Frank ('Bones') Jenner (1903–77) was another famous street missioner in Sydney who came into his own during World War II. English-born, an ex-sailor and ex-gambler, he had been converted in 1937 at an open-air meeting in Collins Street, Melbourne, and thereafter devoted his life to spreading the gospel message. His approach was direct – and, as it later emerged, at times successful.[11] Stationing himself somewhere on George Street during busy periods, he addressed passers-by along these lines: 'Do you mind if I ask you a question, Sir, – just one question? If you died within twenty-four hours, where would you be in Eternity, Heaven or hell? Just think about it, Sir.'[12]

Most people continued on their way. But a few stopped and talked. If anyone showed interest, they were directed to an appropriate church or gospel meeting. Jenner later estimated that he asked his question about 100,000 times.

There were obvious similarities with Arthur's *Eternity* campaign. Indeed, it is likely that Jenner and Arthur sometimes crossed paths – they worked within a few blocks of each other when Arthur came to George Street on Saturday nights to conduct his open-air street missions. Jenner was also well known to R.B.S. Hammond, John Ridley and Bob Leghorn,[13] and attended numerous Christian gatherings in Sydney, so he and Arthur may even have been formally introduced.

At the least they had a mutual friend. A South Australian serviceman named Murray Wilkes encountered Jenner one night on George Street in February 1944. Soon afterwards – as a direct result of pondering Jenner's standard question – Wilkes converted to evangelical Christianity. Within no time, he was working with Arthur on George Street in open-air missioning.[14]

13.1. The Burton Street Tabernacle's first 'gospel waggon', a converted baker's van acquired in 1944.

In 1944, the Burton Street Tabernacle purchased its first 'gospel waggon', an old Bedford baker's van converted for the purpose. The side and rear panels on the left-hand side were built to open out, in order to form a platform and awning for kerbside meetings, and the text of a Bible verse was painted on the right-hand side.[15] It was another variation on the *Eternity* theme:

> GOD HAS APPOINTED A DAY
> IN WHICH HE WILL JUDGE THE
> WORLD IN ALL RIGHTEOUSNESS
> Acts 17:31
> ARE YOU READY?

Arthur and others at Burton Street began using this vehicle for open-air missioning on Sunday afternoons and evenings, in Taylor Square. Bruce Leghorn remembers Arthur calling him up to give his testimony – without warning – when he was a boy of 13.[16]

Despite everyone's best efforts, attendance at the Tabernacle itself gradually declined during and after the war. The basic problem was that more and more families were moving out into the suburbs, away from places like Darlinghurst, and those who still wished to worship preferred churches near their homes. This trend continued for decades and affected all Christian denominations, for good and ill. Nevertheless, invaluable missionary and charitable work continued in the inner city and adjacent working-class areas.[17] The success or otherwise of such work can never be measured by church membership numbers alone.

§

For Arthur Stace, the five years following World War II were extremely active. Overall, he must have felt a fulfilled and happy man. Yet there were also times of grief – intense reminders of his sad past.

On 12 May 1946, Archdeacon R.B.S. Hammond died at the age of 75. He had been retired two and half years, but very few Sydneysiders had forgotten him. All the city's newspapers carried long and laudatory tributes. At the funeral service two days later, a huge crowd overflowed from St Andrew's Cathedral into the grounds surrounding it, and many of those present were obviously moved. The archbishop's text was Daniel 10:19: 'O man greatly beloved.' One aged man standing in the southern transept was overheard to utter: 'No one ever cared for us as much as he did.'[18]

Arthur's thoughts must have been similar. The following Sunday, at a special memorial service at St Barnabas', he was one of just a few people accorded the privilege of speaking to the congregation in appreciation of the late, great man.[19] He also attended a third service on 26 May 1946, at St Anne's, Hammondville: a church register

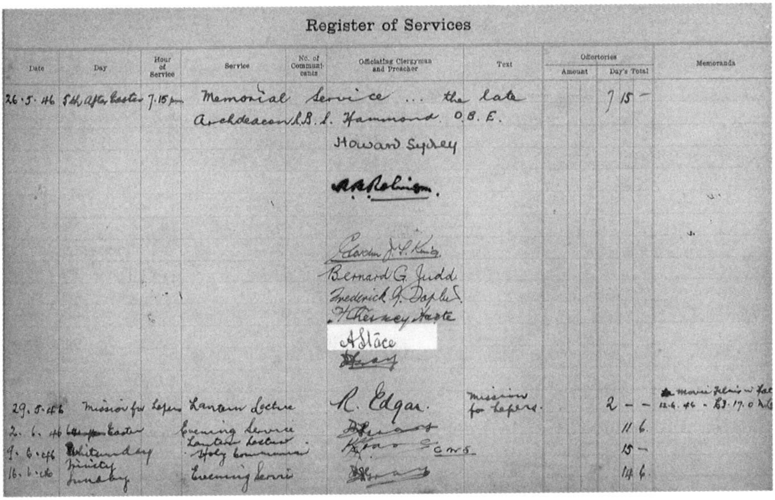
Register of Services

Date	Day	Hour of Service	Service	No. of Communicants	Officiating Clergyman and Preacher	Text	Offertories Amount	Offertories Day's Total	Memoranda
26.5.46	5th after Easter	7.15 pm	Memorial Service … the late Archdeacon R.B.S. Hammond O.B.E.		Howard Sydney			7 15 –	
29.5.46	Mission for Lepers		Lantern Lecture		R. Edgar	Mission for Lepers		2 – –	
2.6.46			Evening Service					11 6	
9.6.46	Whitsunday		Lantern Lecture / Holy Communion					15 –	
16.6.46	Trinity Sunday		Evening Service					14 6	

13.2. Register of St Anne's, Hammondville, listing attendees at a memorial service for Hammond on 26 May 1946. Arthur's signature ('A. Stace') appears with that of the Anglican Archbishop of Sydney, the Most Rev. H.W.K. Mowll ('Howard, Sydney').

survives in which Arthur's signature ('A. Stace') appears below that of such luminaries as the Archbishop of Sydney.[20]

Hammond, in life, had never paid heed to flattery, even if sincerely meant. But he would have been proud of Arthur's faith-motivated *deeds*. We know that Arthur became close to one of Hammond's main protégés, the Rev. Bernard G. Judd (1918–99). Arthur had met Judd at St Barnabas' in the 1930s when he was just a teenager, and the two must have come into contact again around the time of Hammond's death. By then Judd had been ordained, and during the following year, 1947, he was appointed the rector of St Peter's, East Sydney. St Peter's was within walking distance of the Burton Street Tabernacle, and the physical proximity of their respective churches was no doubt a factor in the pair keeping in touch.

Judd, like Hammond, was a hard taskmaster. Yet he came to regard Arthur as a 'trophy of grace.'[21] By the late 1940s there was plenty of objective evidence to justify that opinion. Let us count the ways.

First and foremost, there was Arthur's reverence for the Bible. Everywhere he went he carried in his pocket a well-thumbed copy of *The New Testament*. It was an Oxford University Press edition, printed for the British and Foreign Bible Society. Many passages were underlined, and on the inside front cover Arthur kept a list of his favourite hymns. Most telling of all: next to his name and address (12 Bulwara Road) he had written: 'If lost, finder rewarded.'[22]

There was also Arthur's service at the Tabernacle. Within the church's own circles, he was much admired.

Bruce Leghorn highlighted his spruce appearance ('when the Lord cleans up the inside of a man's life, he also cleans up the outside', Arthur once told him) and, more important, his passionate enthusiasm. 'During prayer time at the Wednesday night meetings,' Leghorn recalled, 'Arthur would invariably be the first on his feet and would always commence his prayer with the words, "Bless the Lord, O my soul, and all that is within me, bless His holy name!'" (cf. Psalm 103).[23] Leghorn also remembered Arthur's talk to the Young People's Bible Class in which he drew analogies between the salvation experience and the properties of coal. This was the talk in which Arthur utilised a lump of coal as a prop.[24]

Edith Summergreene held up Arthur as a role model for her young husband, who returned from the war in 1946 with a serious drinking problem. '[He] was a 16-pint a day man. But my cry to the Lord was "Lord, you did it for Arthur in Jesus' name, do it for my Vincent."' In time, her prayer was answered.[25]

13.3. During the mid-1940s, not long into their marriage, Arthur and Pearl holidayed with their friend Edith Summergreene in country New South Wales. In this shot, taken by a riverbank, they still look a picture of happiness.

Denis Padgett was a wide-eyed 17-year-old when he arrived at Burton Street in 1946. 'I was very impressed with Arthur,' he recalled many years later,

> hearing his testimony, hearing him pray at church prayer meetings, getting to know about his Christian witnessing, CBD open-air meetings and bright, joyful guest-speaking. Meeting him initially [he struck me] as a little, humble, fairly insignificant-looking man

> ... I soon realised he was a wonderful spiritual 'giant', always 'full of the Lord' and ready to talk about Him in ordinary conversation.[26]

(Padgett – like many others[27] – was rather scared of Pearl. By then she had a reputation as a 'dragon lady', at least among the younger members at the Tabernacle. But most people also recognised her softer side. In Padgett's words, 'she had a real "heart of gold" in serving others, [she was] always out to oblige others.' Even so, he always called her 'Mrs Stace'.[28])

Arthur's third main sphere of influence was by way of open-air missioning and other forms of oral evangelism.

He had developed an 'inimitable' style and was much sought-after as a guest speaker. And he was prepared to travel. For example, in July 1948 he preached by invitation at several events in central west New South Wales (at Dubbo, Yeovil, Bournewood and Wellington). One local newspaper heralded his arrival in florid terms – 'Domain "Deadbeat" to Preacher'[29] – and was glowing in its praise a fortnight later. 'Splendid congregations,' it reported, 'listened with amazement to his telling testimony. His visit to the district will not soon be forgotten.'[30]

Another time Arthur made a trip to Goulburn to give his testimony at the local Baptist church.[31] One wonders whether he told anyone that he had lived in the town in the 1890s as a foster child. (See Chapter 3.) At the least, he must have been moved – even spooked – by the experience of returning there.

He was also effective in his Saturday night missioning in the Sydney CBD. One evening in 1948, a teenage lad named Les Nixon was in the city with his mates when one of them directed Nixon's gaze towards the corner of George and Goulburn Streets, near the old Anthony Hordern building. The centre of attention was a man pointing up at the sky. Nixon remembered them all walking over to investigate:

> [Lo] and behold, it was a neat and wiry man in a hat warning the people. 'Look up, look up!' he cried. When a crowd gathered, he bravely announced, 'That's where the Lord Jesus Christ will come again!' and proceeded to describe the dramatics of Jesus' return to Earth. I was hooked, and went out of my way to watch his street meetings ... from then on.[32]

Nixon went on to become a prominent Baptist minister. He was the founder in 1961 of Australia's Outback Patrol, a Christian community service organisation dedicated to propagating the gospel in remote rural areas. After decades of experience, Nixon paid this tribute to Arthur Stace: 'I think I owe [him] a great deal of gratitude ... as he helped me understand the value of ... following the "Jesus" example – capture attention first, to relay the message of the gospel.'[33]

A year or so later, Arthur began yet another missioning activity – this one conducted in broad daylight. From August 1949, he worked as a part-time cleaner and lift operator at the city offices of the Australian Red Cross.[34] He was an exemplary employee, well-respected by other staff members.[35] But he attracted attention each lunch time when he left the office carrying a suitcase. It was his practice to walk to the corner of Jamieson and Clarence Streets.[36] There he sat on the pavement with his back to the wall, the suitcase placed open beside him. On the inside lid he had inscribed an Old Testament verse: 'Be sure your sin will find you out' (Numbers 32:23).

Arthur kept this up for six years. According to one source, 'many fruitful conversations resulted.'[37] He handed out a good number of tracts.

On top of all this, the *Eternity* mission continued every morning for at least a few hours. Always seeking God's guidance as to where to go, he visited some new suburbs in Sydney – Ashfield was one, Mosman another.[38] But it was the 'battler' suburbs within a few miles of the CBD that he frequented most often. In Balmain during the mid-to-late 1940s, an introverted little girl named Joan Graham several times saw Arthur in the act of chalking *Eternity* in the vicinity of her parents' home in Trouton Street (near Mort Bay). Now 80, Mrs Joan Reilly vividly recalls Arthur's trim, neat demeanour – even down to the act of slipping the piece of chalk back into his suit pocket.[39]

13.4. Petty's Hotel (right), later the Sydney offices of the Australian Red Cross. Arthur worked in this building as a cleaner and lift operator in the period 1950–55, missioning during his lunchtimes at the corner of Jamieson and Clarence Streets.

Even when he was on trips to the country with Pearl to see her relatives, Arthur did not rest. One of Pearl's nieces, Stella Hesse, once saw *Eternity* chalked on the trunk of a tree, 20 feet up, on the side of a road near Mandurama. It stayed there for many years.[40]

At some stage Arthur began using a capital '*E*' at the beginning rather than a small '*e*': a wag had started to follow him around writing '*M*' in front of his '*eternity*'.[41] He also switched to using packer's crayon instead of chalk, because it was waterproof and lasted longer.

He preferred the yellow colour because he felt it stood out better on asphalt, but used white if that was all he could get.[42] The crayons cost him 'six bob a dozen', and he went through that many in a week when he was 'running hot.'[43] By then he had added two more slogans to his repertoire – 'Obey God' and 'God or Sin'[44] – though neither ever captured the public's imagination like his original did. In due course, Arthur realised that *Eternity* had more impact and he reverted to that word alone.

There was, and still is, something gloriously evocative about that one word: *Eternity*. It has inspired to serious thinking many sorts of people, not just those of 'religious' bent.

In February 1948, John Ridley became chairman of the editorial committee of a fortnightly Baptist newspaper, *The Herald of Hope*. It was aimed, like Arthur's writings, at directing people's thoughts to the afterlife.[45] The contributors to its pages were learned theologians who may well have impressed Arthur himself. But there is no question that, in the long run, Arthur reached many, many more people.

By this time, mentions of the *Eternity* phenomenon had begun to appear in the Sydney press. In September 1947 the *Sun* referred on its front page to 'the fellow who chalks "Eternity" on walls and pavements.'[46] A few months later, in January 1948, the official newspaper of the Australian Communist Party, the *Tribune*, weighed in for its own purposes:

> Look at Sydney's walls and footpaths any morning. Chalked on them are such refinements as 'Kill the Jews,' 'Hang the Tykes,' 'Kill Commos,' etc. Here and there somebody chalks 'Jesus Saves,' and somebody else chalks 'Obey God' or 'Eternity'. All this chalking is not done by men who ride in limousines, but by working men. The boss divides and rules ...[47]

It is to be emphasised that all this time Arthur was conducting his *Eternity* campaign anonymously. He wanted attention to be focused on the message, not the messenger. Apart from Pearl, only a handful of Burton Street members were in the know.[48] Edith Summergreene was one;[49] another was a Mrs Betty Pickering (nee Smith), who once spotted Arthur in action, crayon in hand. Like Edith, she was sworn never to blab. 'You won't tell anyone, will you?' was one of Arthur's signature lines.[50]

It mattered much less if he was seen by people who did not know who he was. Inevitably, this happened on occasions. Policemen questioned him periodically, around 20 times in all. They were concerned he was 'defacing the footpaths', but eventually let him be.[51] The police's only recourse was to report him to the city council. 'After a while they got to find out my back life,' Arthur once explained, 'and ... the [council] inspector said: "Isn't it better to see him doing this than you fellas chasing him through the lanes and streets of Sydney?"'[52]

No doubt it helped a lot that Arthur's writing was in chalk or crayon – an ephemeral medium – rather than, say, paint. But strictly he was in breach of the law, and, thankfully, someone at the Council exercised their discretion in his favour. (It was not until 2014 that the New South Wales parliament passed legislation explicitly permitting the marking of public footpaths or pavements in chalk.[53])

There were other notable sightings. In or about 1949, a young Dorothy Hewett – the Australian author-to-be – observed Arthur at work outside the Oxford Street ice works. The incident stuck in her memory, and she utilised it nine years later when writing her breakthrough novel *Bobbin Up*.[54]

§

The 1940s had been an exciting decade for Arthur, but it ended on a sombre note. Both his older brothers had come to the end of their lives.

Samuel Seaward Stace, 67, was the first to die. Bizarrely, his passing in June 1949 was front-page news. He was one of several victims of major flooding across New South Wales. A widower by then, living alone in a 'hut' or 'shack' on the property of a Mrs Makin, his body was found in a creek at Geard's Hill on the outskirts of Wollongong. According to the *Sydney Morning Herald*, 'it is thought he was returning on Saturday night after spending the day in Wollongong, and in the darkness did not notice that the bridge was covered in several feet of water.'[55] Had he been drunk? The local newspaper used a time-worn phrase to describe him: 'a well-known local identity.'[56]

At least Sam left three adult children behind him, two of whom mourned his death publicly.[57] His funeral was well attended.[58] By contrast, William John Stace, the oldest of the three brothers, never married and appears to have lived out his last days at a sanatorium on the south coast, at Waterfall, which specialised in the treatment of tuberculosis.[59] Even his exact date of death is unknown.

14. As iron sharpens iron

Think where man's glory most begins and ends
And say my glory was I had such friends
W.B. Yeats[1]

Three extraordinary Christian ministers played vital roles in the life of Arthur Stace. The first two were R.B.S. Hammond and John Gotch Ridley, both, in their day, household names. The third, the Rev. Lisle M. Thompson, was never so well known. But he deserves to be remembered and honoured.

It was Thompson who persuaded Arthur to 'go public' and reveal himself to the people of Sydney as Mr Eternity. But for Thompson, there would probably be no legend. Moreover, he and his wife May became – Pearl aside – the closest and most loyal friends that Arthur ever had. Their backstory is another interesting tale.[2]

§

Lisle Thompson was born in Ulverstone, Tasmania, on 2 April 1910. While he was still a small child, his parents, Edward and Annie Thompson, bought a dairy farm in Lismore, in northern New South

Wales, using the proceeds of Annie's inheritance from her adoptive father. In Tasmania both Edward and Annie had been officers of the Salvation Army (they were married in uniform), but in Lismore they became foundation members of the town's Baptist church.

One of Lisle's most vivid memories from boyhood was of a visit made to his family's Lismore home by the superintendent of the NSW Home Mission Society, Dr A.J. Waldock (1873–1961).* Arguably 'the best known leader in the Baptist denomination across Australia in the first half of the twentieth century',[3] Waldock singled out Lisle for early praise. Placing his hand on the lad's head, he pronounced with confidence: 'I feel you will make a fine minister of the gospel.' It proved an accurate prophecy.

The Thompsons made a success of their dairy farm and sold it for a handsome sum. By the early 1920s – while Arthur Stace was mired in habitual drunkenness and John Ridley was recovering from his nervous breakdown – they had moved to Sydney, making their home in the tranquil north-western suburb of Eastwood. Lisle shone academically at the local state primary school and in due course won scholarships to Hurlstone Agricultural Continuation School (1924–26) and Hawkesbury Agricultural College (1927–28). He graduated dux of the latter, with first class honours, while also excelling in a number of sports (first-grade rugby and cricket, as well as tennis, golf and boxing).

By the time he completed his studies, Lisle was a believing Baptist. As a teenager he was inspired by an up-and-coming itinerant preacher, English-born Wilfred Jarvis (a friend and contemporary of Ridley and, at least theologically, very much in the same mould[4]). Nevertheless, Lisle did not immediately feel a call to ministry. He had valuable secular

* At a Canberra Sunday school in the mid-1920s, Dr Waldock once discussed the biblical account of creation with an impudent boy named Gough Whitlam. Whitlam's parents were staunch Baptists.

qualifications and, in 1929, accepted an offer of work in Grafton as foreman of a butter factory.

He toiled in that post for six years before deciding to train for the ministry. The call came suddenly and forcefully, on 18 July 1933 (a Tuesday). As Lisle later described it,

> I met my God at 1.30 pm ... and claimed all my share of Pentecost. I had shared in the blood of Calvary years before, but had lived a life worldly, selfish and careless ... A process of God's dealing with me came to a crisis ... and I was immediately conscious of a call to service in the Kingdom of Christ. It became an irresistible urge.[5]

In February 1934 he came to Sydney and entered the Baptist Theological College at Ashfield. There, under the stewardship of long-time principal George Henry Morling (1891–1974) – another giant among Australian Baptists[6] – he studied hard. Not everything came easily, especially the rules of grammar in Hebrew and Greek, but Lisle persisted. He also learned the ropes as a student pastor during stints in Cessnock and Merrylands.[7]

At the end of 1938 he graduated dux of his year, carrying away many special prizes.[8] In addition, he earned a diploma from the Melbourne College of Divinity, a Licentiate of Theology (L Th), which was conferred upon him in absentia the following year.[9]

Lisle Thompson had a bright, capacious mind, but as we shall see, he also possessed a becoming generosity of spirit and a soft gentleness of soul. R.B.S. Hammond was a saint, but he exhibited a curt, impatient streak in dealings with those who worked with him day to day.[10] (Much the same was said of Mother Teresa.) John Ridley was brave and true, but also, one senses, somewhat highly strung. He was an evangelist, pure and simple. Of the three big men in Arthur Stace's life, Lisle was the most rounded human being.

As we have seen, it was in 1939 that Arthur, 64, switched from the Anglican fold at St Barnabas' to the Baptist Tabernacle in Darlinghurst. Early that same year, the Rev. Lisle Thompson, 29, took up his first full-time posting as a Baptist minister, at Bankstown in Sydney's outer-western suburbs. It proved a momentous step in more ways than one. By December he had met, wooed and married a vivacious local woman.

14.1. Lisle and May Thompson in Hyde Park, Sydney, on the day of their engagement, June 1939.

(The story of how Lisle Thompson found his wife is instructive, and not only for the light that it sheds on his character. It is a nice example of the biblical theme that following a righteous path may, unexpectedly, lead to great worldly blessings (cf. Proverbs 4:18; Matthew 6:33). Within a few months of his arrival at Bankstown, Lisle was keen to increase his flock. He was told about a middle-aged woman, Margaret Phillips, then worshipping in an Anglican congregation in the nearby suburb of Yagoona where she lived. Mrs Phillips' husband William had been involved in the building of the Bankstown Baptist Church; she herself had been raised as a Baptist in England. Why had she left? Lisle decided to visit her and find out – and perhaps persuade her to come back. Mrs Phillips was soon won over. Indeed, so completely was she won over that she marked out the handsome, engaging young pastor as a suitable match for her daughter – a

24-year-old beauty named May. Several dinner invitations followed, and blossoming love did the rest.)

Lisle and May Thompson served at Bankstown until 1942 and thereafter for four years at Manly, on Sydney's northern beaches. They lived in the manse attached to each church while raising three infant children, Elizabeth (b. 1941), Paul (b. 1943) and Helen (b. 1945). Lisle also served a long term as secretary of the Social Questions Committee of the Baptist Union of New South Wales, in which capacity he built 'a reputation for straight talking to all sections of the community.'[11]

Then came a major change of pace.

14.2. The Thompson family in the late 1940s, during Lisle's period as State Evangelist in New South Wales. From left: Lisle, Paul, Elizabeth, Helen, May.

In 1946, Lisle left his comfortable appointment at Manly to become the Baptists' official state evangelist in New South Wales. It was an onerous post requiring a huge amount of travel, but he still needed to provide a home for his wife and children. Scraping together the money for a deposit, he and May bought a ramshackle old house at 25 Empire Street, Haberfield (a disused property attached to the local Baptist church). The family moved in. It was a happy household, but, for Lisle over the next five years, little more than a base camp. For weeks at a time he would leave Haberfield in a 1935 Chevrolet gospel wagon and journey to different parts of the state, preaching the gospel, displaying films and distributing Christian literature.[12] After each trip his wife and children welcomed him back home excitedly, only to wave him away again a week or so later.

To give the flavour, over the course of a fortnight at Molong in September 1950, Lisle preached a different sermon each night from Wednesday to Sunday. His topics included 'Can I Be Sure There Is a God?', 'Some Good News You Cannot Afford to Miss', 'Prophecy and Christ's Return – Is It Near?' and 'God's Blockade on the Road to Hell.'[13] Lisle's regular companion on these trips was a song leader and piano accordionist, Bill Thitchener, who became 'Uncle Bill' to the Thompson children.

Contemporary reports speak in the highest terms of Lisle's earnest and effective ministry.[14] He invariably won many new converts while also providing acute analysis of the strengths and weaknesses of the churches he visited. But the hectic lifestyle was unsustainable in the long term, and after five years of it, Lisle was finally convinced to do something else. Now 40, he was offered a role that would enable him not only to utilise his talents fully but also to live at home full-time and share in the upbringing of his young family. His wife May had been a sole parent to their three children for too long.

The new role was 'co-pastor' at the Burton Street Tabernacle in Darlinghurst, alongside the incumbent of nine years, the Rev. R.M. (Bob) Leghorn. Lisle's brief was to evangelise the eastern suburbs of Sydney, focusing on open-air work. He started in March 1951 and there met Arthur Stace.

§

Darlinghurst was a forbidding environment for the Thompson family. Lisle understood the harsher side of humanity. May did too, though she had seen less of it. But for all of them it was a new world. The infamous Tilly Devine still lived in Darlinghurst in 1951, one block back from the Tabernacle, in Palmer Street. There were also many run-of-the-mill working-class battlers, still prevalent in the Darlinghurst of the 1950s.

The children had led sheltered lives, rarely if ever encountering the sad types who now confronted them in the streets and alleys near the Tabernacle: prostitutes, drunks, brawlers, derelicts, drug addicts, flashers. As to the last: Elizabeth Thompson, nine when she first came to Darlinghurst, once convinced her mother to let her take her younger brother Paul to a milk bar on Oxford Street. While they were slurping their shakes at the front counter, dressed in their Sunday best, a fellow customer opened his coat to Elizabeth and revealed all. She grabbed Paul's hand, fled back to the church and did not tell her mother.

The Tabernacle was a haven, and the Thompsons soon got to know the regular worshippers there. One man stood out: Arthur Stace.

Lisle and Arthur quickly formed a close bond. Lisle was taken by Arthur's service ethic ('a shining example of a balanced and bright Christian'[15]) and Arthur by Lisle's genuine concern for the needy and helpless. The new pastor arranged meals and shelter where he could, talked to drunkards, attended at the local courthouse and helped some men find jobs. These were new priorities at the Tabernacle. In its previous history 'there was little place for social justice, or community care ... little practical assistance was ever offered.'[16] The overwhelming focus was personal salvation. Lisle, in a Hammond-like way, sought to blend the two.

Lisle and Arthur also shared a love of open-air mission and were as thrilled as each other when, soon after Lisle's arrival, the Tabernacle acquired a brand new gospel wagon. It was a 1951 two-ton Austin, specially tailored to the church's needs by Starr Brothers of Newtown and 'one of the best purpose-built examples of [its type].'[17] Much larger and more comfortable than the Bedford baker's van it replaced, it was equipped with an AWA public address system and a 35mm film strip projector.[18] There were Bible texts painted on both the right- and left-hand sides: 'The wages of sin is death, but the gift of God is eternal life. Romans 6:23' and 'Repent ye and believe the Gospel. Mark 1:15.'

14.3. The Burton Street Tabernacle's first purpose-built gospel wagon, acquired early in 1951. Both Rev. Lisle Thompson and Arthur Stace used this vehicle extensively in their open-air missioning activities. In this shot, Lisle (at right) stands beside Rev. R.M. (Bob) Leghorn.

Arthur began using the van on Saturday nights for his open-air preaching at the corner of George and Bathurst Streets. A long-time worshipper at the Tabernacle, Rex Beaver, usually drove him there. Arthur never learned to drive for the simple reason he never had enough money to buy a car.

One Saturday night later in 1951, Lisle went along to watch. Positioning himself among other onlookers around the gospel van, he heard Arthur tell a potted version of his life story. It astounded him. Not so much the story itself – the basics of which he probably already knew – but the passion of Arthur's delivery and his skill in dealing with interjectors. The quiet, humble man who Lisle had come to know at the Tabernacle was transformed. After Arthur described his conversion experience at St Barnabas', a voice cried from the crowd: 'How long ago was that, mate?' Arthur shot back: '21 years ago last August 6th, 1930! 21 years God has saved me from drink, 21 years no gambling, 21 years without thieving, 21 years without lying and cursing.'[19]

As Lisle recalled six years later: 'With my eyes moist with tears I moved back to my car and sped home thanking God for [Arthur's] delivery from his awful life.'[20]

The next day, Sunday, was a vital one in Arthur's story. It is to be stressed that until then, Lisle had no inkling that Arthur was the person writing the word *Eternity* on the pavements of Sydney. Like most other Sydneysiders he had seen examples of it and was aware of press speculation as to the possible motives and identity of the culprit. This is Lisle's version of what happened that Sunday:

> At 3 o'clock the keen-ites were all aboard the Gospel Van and I drove it deep into Sydney's slum area. The meeting started and while another brother was preaching I followed a few steps behind the Church cleaner [Arthur] around the corner and out of sight. I came around the corner just in time to see his hand slip into his outside coat pocket and out came a yellow crayon. He stopped and like a flash spelled out the letters '*Eternity*'. No one else could write it just like that with such speed except someone who had done it many times.
> 'So you're Mr Eternity, Arthur,' I said.
> 'Guilty, your honour,' 66 year old Arthur Stace chuckled. 'But you won't tell anyone, will you?'
> 'Not without your permission,' I guardedly replied.[21]

From that moment, Lisle knew that he had a potentially huge story on his hands. The question was how to get Arthur to agree to let him tell it.

§

Lisle did not press Arthur at first. Instead, he got to know him better, teasing out fuller details of his life story and gaining his trust and confidence. Gradually Arthur opened up, taking Lisle to some of his 'old haunts' in Sydney and revealing 'intimate details of his early life, youth and manhood.'[22]

At the end of 1951, the Rev. Bernard Judd published a book-length biography of R.B.S. Hammond, *He That Doeth*. It received favourable

The Sydney Harbour Bridge, New Year's Day 2000, around 12.30am Australian Eastern Standard Time. This image was seen on television by billions of people around the world.

COURTESY WARREN CARDWELL, ETERNITY PRODUCTION AND DESIGN. PHOTO BY COLIN KIRTON - WORLDWIDE PHOTOS.

Arthur Stace never tired of saying that he came to St Barnabas' on the night of 6 August 1930 for 'a cuppa tea and a rock cake', but came out with the Rock of Ages. Like all the other 'down-and-outs' in the hall, Arthur had to listen to a sermon from R.B.S. Hammond before he got his supper.

DAVID LEVER, *TEA AND ROCK CAKES AT BARNEYS*, AUGUST 1930, OIL ON BOARD, 2000/01.

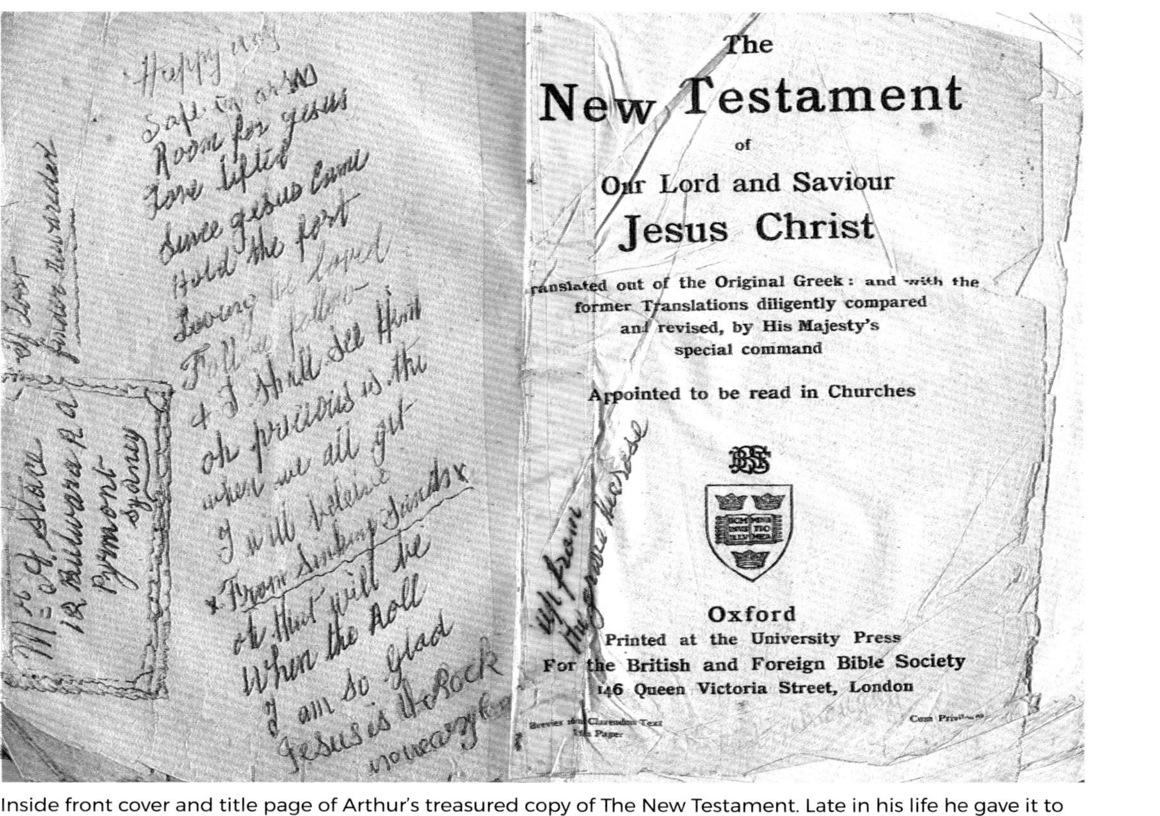

Inside front cover and title page of Arthur's treasured copy of The New Testament. Late in his life he gave it to May Thompson.

IMAGE COURTESY OF ELIZABETH MEYERS.

I am a boy. I am walking down the street where I live, there is a word written on the pavement in yellow chalk. "Eternity" what does it mean? Why is it there? who wrote it?

as I grew up I saw that word often on the streets of Sydney ... Colin Anderson sung his sensational tribute to "Mr. Eternity", ARTHUR STACE, in the Sydney University Revue "FIRST, NO PINKY" in 1965. I began to use the word "Eternity" in my artwork... Ross Campbell introduced me to a poem about Arthur Stace (by McCauley, Stewart or Hope?). In 1983 for Christmas, my Aunt Elizabeth gave me a book, "Ratbags" by KEITH DUNSTAN, in it was the story of ARTHUR STACE, so I learnt the story of the author of the word that puzzled me all those years ago...

E-ter′ni-ty (-tў), *n.*; *pl.* ETERNITIES (-tĭz). [F. *éternité*, L. *aeternitas*, fr. *aeternus*. See ETERN.] **1.** Infinite duration, without beginning in the past or end in the future; also, duration without end in the future; endless time.

The high and lofty One, that inhabiteth *eternity*. *Is.* lvii. 15.

2. Condition which begins at death; immortality.

Thou know'st 't is common; all that lives must die,
Passing through nature to *eternity*. *Shak.*

Letter by Martin Sharp, 17 October 1990.

One Monday morning in November 1963, workmen responsible for reconstruction of the GPO clock tower in Sydney's Martin Place made an amazing discovery: a chalked Eternity inside the main bell. No one knows exactly when or how Arthur managed it, but it is still there.

DAVID LEVER, *THE BELL*, OIL ON BOARD, 2000/01.

Hammondville
Homes
Via Liverpool
Dec 1965

Dear Mrs Thompson
I have taken a long while
to tell you how much I thank for your help
in many ways to me since I have known
you, even right up to 4 months when you said
the house & cleaned up the place when I was
quite unable to lace my boots & then again for
you coming up to see me & the nice refreshments
you brought, with enough to satisfy us all.
I am very grateful, I had a bad time with
the ulcers & it has just only taken up a lot
to what it was, if it gets better I may be able
to get down to Burton St. now & again.
I have had a lot of visitors here to
see me & thank the Dear Lord for all the way
He has led me. I have 4 of these men here
coming to church & many have heard the Gospel.
Thank you for your prayers. May the Lord Continue
to use you in His service
Till He Come Stand fast in the LORD
Yours
in His Name Arthur

Letter from Arthur to May Thompson, written from Hammondville in December 1965.

IMAGE COURTESY OF ELIZABETH MEYERS.

Eternity, 2 x 3.9 m, wool and cotton, designed by Martin Sharp, woven at the Australian Tapestry Workshop by Cheryl Thornton, Georgina Barker, Merrill Dumbrell, Katia Takla, Laura Mar. The text of Isaiah 57:15 appears in the background.

Celebrations 2001, 2 x 3.54 m, wool and cotton, designed by Murray Walker, artist: Martin Sharp, incorporating 'Ngak Ngak in Limmen Bight River country' by Ginger Riley and text by Patrick White (Riders in the Chariot), woven at the Australian Tapestry Workshop by Grazyna Bleja, Merrill Dumbrell, Milena Paplinska and Cheryl Thornton.

Martin Sharp's screen print poster *Eternity Haymarket!* (1977).

USED WITH THE PERMISSION OF THE NATIONAL GALLERY OF AUSTRALIA.

FREE at your church or bookshop
W: eternitynews.com.au
F: eternitynews
T: @eternitynews
Number 81, June 2017
ISSN 1837-8447
Brought to you by the Bible Society

Eternity

Here's Lucy!

How Senator Lucy Gichuhi learnt to pray and really read the Bible

Being a single mother gets you killed

Survey: genuine faith a real winner

Refugees really need friends

Bible Society Australia's monthly newspaper, *Eternity*, was launched in 2009.

attention in the Sydney press and was advertised as 'an ideal Christmas present.'[23] Lisle almost certainly read it; if so, the passages about Arthur can only have increased the esteem in which Lisle held him.

Perhaps this acted as a spur. The following year, 1952, Lisle arranged for Arthur to speak at a major Christian rally at Molong; it was hailed as a triumph.[24] Lisle also wrote an eight-page tract about Arthur's journey from sin to redemption. Entitled *The Crooked Made Straight*, based on notes handwritten by Arthur, it held up Arthur as a 'modern miracle' – living proof of the saving power of the gospel over the 'evil companions' of heredity and environment.[25] It was Arthur who chose the title:[26] he considered himself a once-crooked man who had become straight.[27] (Cf. Isaiah 40:4, Luke 3:5.)

Tucked away near the end was this paragraph:

> Very few people in the city of Sydney know that the famous footpath message ETERNITY is written by Arthur Stace. This one-word sermon has challenged thousands and thousands.[28]

Despite the work that had gone into it, Arthur was hesitant to allow publication. And here an extremely interesting question arises: *why?*

It cannot have been shame about his own drunken, criminal past, given the candour with which he always told his story at open-air meetings.[29] True, the revelations in *The Crooked Made Straight* would be in writing, in permanent form, but Bernard Judd had published some of them in *He That Doeth*. Just possibly, Arthur was concerned about his youngest sister Dora. Minnie was long gone and Clara Go-Hing had died in December 1951,[30] but Dora was still alive. Arthur may have been nervous about her being labelled in print as a prostitute. (Judd had not mentioned this.)

There are two much likelier explanations. One is that Arthur baulked at the prospect of wider fame. The inclusion of the paragraph about *Eternity* would hamper his efforts to remain anonymous.

Another explanation (not mutually exclusive) is that there was at least one aspect of Arthur's past that he did not want publicly revealed: his six years in foster care in Goulburn, described in Chapter 3. We will return to this issue in the next chapter.

Whatever the case, he withheld his consent for the time being. And, importantly, Lisle Thompson respected his wishes.

§

During 1952 and early 1953, a nasty internal schism wracked the Burton Street Baptist Tabernacle. The co-pastoring arrangement between the Rev. Bob Leghorn and Lisle came under strain. At one stage in 1952 Leghorn resigned, only to be persuaded to return. The matter simmered for a while, but the underlying problems remained unresolved. In February 1953 Leghorn resigned again, this time for good.[31]

The full circumstances need not concern us. In due course the two ministers were reconciled – both were generous enough to let bygones be bygones. And to this day, their respective families remain on friendly terms. Even so, the incident is highly relevant to the *Eternity* story because, in the short term, the church split. A sizeable number of people left the Tabernacle and eventually formed a new congregation under Leghorn's pastorship.[32]

Arthur and Pearl Stace faced a critical choice. Should they follow Leghorn or stay at Burton Street under Lisle Thompson? They stayed.

In Lisle Thompson, Arthur recognised a kindred spirit. Lisle empathised with the 'no-hopers', just as Arthur did. In February 1953 the choice was easy. In retrospect, if Arthur had decided the other way, his identity as Mr Eternity would probably have remained a mystery.

15. Knock and it will be opened

It is one of the most remarkable stories of a comeback from the edge of Hell ever printed.
Tom Farrell, *Sunday Telegraph* (Sydney), 24 June 1956, on Arthur Stace

---

After the split of February 1953, life at the Burton Street Tabernacle settled into a pattern. Despite the exodus by followers of Bob Leghorn, there were still about 150 members on the roll. The Sunday morning service attracted something of the order of 100 worshippers; the evening service about 70.[1] The faithful core group – perhaps 20 or 30 stalwarts – was extremely tight-knit.

Soon after Lisle Thompson became sole pastor, Arthur and Pearl Stace began to be paid for their work as the church's cleaners and caretakers. In that capacity, they were the first to arrive each Sunday. Years later, May Thompson recalled:

> Arthur was always punctual to open the doors – and pleasantly attentive to every worshipper. My first impression was how immaculately attired he was, respectful in his manner to his pastor

> and family, hastening to the car as it moved up ... at the side church door. Opening the driver's door first then the others, removing any article from the boot that needed transferring into the sanctuary, flowers, typewriter, overcoats, food – nothing was too much trouble. His warm handshake and pleasant smile preceded every greeting.[2]

May also admired the thorough way in which Arthur and Pearl went about their job as the Tabernacle's cleaners. 'The hours they spent in its care were far in excess of the remuneration they received.'[3]

Eleven-year-old Elizabeth had also taken a shine to Arthur by now. During services, she noticed the way he sang in a loud, exultant voice and banged his hymn book against his leg in time to the music. It emerged years later that Arthur went through many hymn books – he utilised a supply of 20 otherwise disused *Redemption Songs* books stored in a cupboard at the back of the Tabernacle. He liked them because the print size was bigger in the old edition and thus easier for him to read. When one of these books became unusable from long, exuberant use – he broke one into quarters – Arthur simply selected another.[4]

For the Thompson family – and hard workers such as Arthur and Pearl – church on Sundays was an all-day affair. They would leave home not long after 8am[5] in order to arrive at the Tabernacle by 9am. Sunday school for children began at 9.30am and the main service at 11am, followed by a communal lunch to which everyone brought their own food. Once the cleaning up was done, people were free to spend their time as they chose (Arthur's custom was to retire to the vestry for an hour of private prayer[6]). Children in the 10–15 years age bracket attended Christian Endeavour at 3pm. Then preparation began in earnest for the evening activities.

At 5pm everyone reassembled for 'Sunday tea', a light meal prepared by Pearl which invariably consisted of Sao biscuits with cheese and tomato and scones with jam and cream. Those whom Lisle Thompson dubbed the 'keen-ites' then departed to conduct an open-air meeting at 6pm on the corner of Oxford and Burton Streets. Others – mostly older ladies – stayed for a prayer meeting at the Tabernacle, which Arthur led with vim and vigour. The evening service was at 7pm.[7]

Usually Arthur did not stay for the evening service, but not because he wanted to go home and rest. He managed to operate on only two hours' sleep a night.[8] His Sunday nights were spent at refuges, visiting 'no hopers' – there was a place he often went to not far from the Tabernacle in Commonwealth Street, Surry Hills, run by a non-denominational Christian organisation called the Sydney Rescue Work Society (now Integricare).[9] He also ministered to homeless people on the streets. Some of them were old friends and acquaintances from his wilderness years.

By coincidence, one of Arthur's old buddies lived in Empire Street, Haberfield – the same street as the Thompson family. Elizabeth Meyers recalls Arthur dropping in at their house on occasion (presumably after visiting his friend) and being invited by her mother to stay for lunch. Once, after one of these lunches, May saw *Eternity* chalked at one end of Empire Street and 'Obey God' at the other.

§

More and more Sydneysiders were taking serious notice of Arthur's writings. During the first half of the 1950s, there were at least two confirmed sightings of *Eternity* in the city's rich eastern suburbs. Both were made by boys who would grow up to be famous men.

In or about 1953, seven-year-old Simon Townsend – later a conscientious objector to the Vietnam War, and later still a popular children's television presenter – saw the word written on the pavement in front of his childhood home in Russell Street, Watsons Bay, opposite St Peter's Anglican church. It was a 'neck-prickling discovery'[10] because, even at age seven, young Simon was intensely curious about God, life and death. Decades later, a sadder, middle-aged Townsend recalled:

> I knew about Mr Eternity and how this word would appear all over Sydney. And one day I went down to get the milk and when I got to our front gate I saw outside on the footpath, outside our place was written 'Eternity'. And I thought this was like a blessed event. I ran upstairs, alerted my parents. Everyone came downstairs and had a look. 'Eternity' had appeared at our doorstep. It was like nothing was ever going to change. Everything was going to stay the same and just as happy, just forever. For Eternity. And of course life doesn't turn out to be like that.[11]

In the twenty-first century, Townsend was still pondering *Eternity*.

Even more consequential was the sighting made in 1955 by a thirteen-year-old lad named Martin Sharp. He was walking along Cranbrook Road in Rose Bay, near his home, and had never seen anything written on the street before. He thought to himself 'Wow, what's that?' and wondered about it.[12] Sharp grew up to become a distinguished Australian artist with a decidedly spiritual side. In that capacity – as we shall see in Chapters 19 and 20 – he made a major contribution to the *Eternity* legend.

These and countless other individual sightings went unrecorded at the time. But by the early 1950s there were frequent references to the *Eternity* phenomenon in the Sydney press. Arthur joked about these sometimes with Edith Summergreene, one of his closest confidantes at Burton Street. 'We are in the paper again, Edith,' he would say brightly. Especially amusing was the speculation as to Mr Eternity's identity. 'Yes, we are a retired schoolteacher now!' he once chuckled. In Edith's words: 'It was a great joke because we knew the truth.'[13]

One prominent theory was that the writer must be a commercial artist, so perfect was the copperplate lettering; another held that it was done with a stencil or template.[14] A few other examples will give a sense of the fun that journalists and pranksters had.

In June 1953, the *Sun*'s popular columnist Jim Macdougall quipped: 'The joker who writes ETERNITY is now using yellow chalk. Must be getting hotter.'[15] A few months later, in September, Macdougall followed up with this gem:

> Columbia are showing shortly the screen version of the controversial, highly provocative book, *From Here To Eternity*. Tom Dole, Columbia's sales promotion boy, looking for new sales angles, is anxious to contact the bloke who writes Eternity on pavements and walls.[16]

Arthur did not take the bait, though within days Mr Dole received four crank calls from an anonymous man who intoned in a lifeless voice: 'repent or perish.'[17] And a little later in the year, someone from Columbia began chalking 'From here to' on the streets of Sydney. Another popular newspaper columnist, the *Sun Herald*'s Gilbert Mant, speculated that 'the expectation is that the fellow who chalks "Eternity" will oblige with a postscript and thus advertise the screen version of James Jones' war novel.'[18]

On 1 November 1953, the *Sun-Herald* reported the experience of a Mosman woman, Mrs G.R. Scott, on the Sydney Harbour Bridge. Mrs Scott had encountered 'a fairly young, country-type of woman ... fiery and enthusiastic,' who 'spoke to her for a long time about the transience of earthly life and the importance of the hereafter.' As this woman spoke, a male companion – 'quieter, ascetic, rather cultured looking' – carefully chalked a word on the footpath. Mrs Scott concluded: 'From what they said to me, I'm sure they must be the people who write "Eternity" around Sydney.'[19]

The man cannot have been Arthur, who always worked alone (and could not credibly have been described as 'cultured-looking'). Rather unhelpfully, Mrs Scott did not specify the word she had seen the man chalking – either that, or the reporter failed to mention it. The fact that this story was run at all is indicative of *Eternity*'s growing fame.

There were several other press mentions in 1954. Gilbert Mant referred to 'the mystery man who chalks "Eternity" in ... copperplate writing on Sydney's pavements.'[20] The *Farmer and Settler* ran a story about a 'magnificent tabby cat' – well-known in the CBD – who had been spotted sleeping on the pavement outside the old Dalgety's building:

> Between the fore and hind legs of the cat could be seen the copperplate handwriting in chalk of that enthusiast who continually warns the motley inhabitants of Sydney of the imminence of death and of the life to come – 'ETERNITY'.[21]

(In March 1955, the same newspaper reported the feline's sad passing, with suitable puns about the next world.[22])

§

Arthur turned 70 on 9 February 1955 and just eight days later Pearl turned 60. The reaching of these landmarks seems to have prompted Arthur to take stock of his situation. He told Pearl that he wanted to retire from his job at the Red Cross and devote more time to writing *Eternity* on Sydney streets.

Pearl's initial reaction was to worry, for Arthur's repatriation pension was modest indeed. 'How will we live?' she asked him. 'The Lord will help us,' Arthur told her.

Her doubts were not immediately assuaged. Soon afterwards she confided in May Thompson while they were working in the Tabernacle's kitchen. 'Art says it's a mission to him, like the pastor's job is to [Lisle] and our thirteen missionaries' work is to them. What should I do?' May's response was simple: 'Well Mrs Stace, pray about it.'

According to May, this is what happened next:

> [Pearl] smiled gently – she was a devout, good, honest and kindly woman – and turned to her preparation of the Wednesday evening meal. On the Sunday after she drew me aside [and said], 'I told Art to do what he wants. We won't be able to give as much, but we will continue with the church cleaning. We don't know how much good it does but he was guided to do it and I won't stand in his way.'[23]

She added: 'We'll both go on the pension.'[24]

15.1. *The Crooked Made Straight*, Lisle Thompson's tract about Arthur, first published in 1955. Such was Arthur's modesty, it had taken Thompson some years to persuade Arthur to allow him to publish it.

Pearl had considered the lilies of the field[25] and relented. It was an important decision, enabling Arthur to retire from the Red Cross on 3 June 1955.[26] He could now spend whole days writing *Eternity*, rather than, as previously, just a few early morning hours. He began to travel farther afield, taking trains to outer Sydney suburbs such as Camden.[27] He went to Cessnock, Newcastle, the Blue Mountains, Wellington – even to Melbourne.[28]

By then he had added a fourth slogan to his repertoire, 'God 1st',[29] but he did not keep that up for long. *Eternity* remained far and away his and the public's favourite.

Arthur made a second big decision in 1955. Finally he gave Lisle Thompson permission to publish *The Crooked Made Straight*. Dora's death in late 1953 may have been a contributing factor: there was no one left in the Stace family with sensibilities to offend. That, and Arthur's ever-increasing trust in the wisdom of his pastor.

As a condition of allowing publication, however, Arthur insisted that 'only certain information should be revealed in his lifetime.'[30] The information withheld can only have been that pertaining to his six years in foster care in Goulburn, since every other aspect of his life was covered in candid detail. Evidently, for Arthur, the memory of being abandoned by his mother at age seven remained extremely painful. This explains a sentence in all editions of *The Crooked Made Straight* that is now known to be inaccurate, or at any rate ambiguous: 'Arthur Stace was hardly schooled at all by 12 years of age, and was taken from his irresponsible parents and made a State ward.'[31] As we saw in Chapter 3, Arthur was made a State ward at seven, not twelve, and it was Laura's decision to give up the four older children (they were not taken from her). She had chosen to keep Dora.

Many sections of the tract have already been referred to in this book. But it is worth quoting the conclusion in full:

> *Reader,* the *power* of God can make a bad man good, overcome the *power* of inborn heredity and environment, evil companions, and habits. Yes, the *power* of God can make a crooked man straight. You may not (and we hope not) have gone down the downward path like Arthur Stace *but we have all sinned*. Will you repent of your sins, and call upon God to save you and then cling to God in earnest prayer and obedience? This gospel is true for it works. Behold a modern miracle in the life of Arthur Stace and take heart, for the God that can save Arthur Stace can save you, too.[32]

Thompson had been confident that the tract would be an excellent evangelistic tool, and so it proved. Many copies were distributed by open-air missioners and in Baptist and other Protestant Christian circles. Even so, for another year or more, most members of the general public did not make the link between Arthur Stace and Mr

Eternity. The tract had not yet found its way into the hands of the mainstream press, and much to Lisle Thompson's irritation, erroneous theories continued to be circulated. At one stage a tall ginger-headed man wrote *Eternity* around Sydney streets for three months, claimed responsibility at the *Herald*'s offices, and got his photo published.[33]

It took an extraordinary set of circumstances before the truth became common knowledge.

§

Elizabeth Thompson turned 15 on 13 April 1956. Her parents had promised her a special birthday party and the date was fixed for Saturday 5 May. Invitations were sent out and preparations began; Lisle's main contribution was to repaint much of the Haberfield house to spruce it up for the big day. As dawn broke on the morning of the party all seemed in readiness. But at 7am, just as Lisle got up, a severe pain struck him across the chest. It was a heart attack – a bad one.

Lisle later wrote: 'For some hours I peeped through the thin curtain which separates time and Eternity. I felt at peace with God but regretted the thought of leaving my dear wife and three lovely children ... it was not to be.'[34]

The immediate crisis passed. Later that day Lisle's condition stabilised (and the party went ahead). A cardiograph revealed that this was, in fact, his *second* coronary occlusion. The first one, two years earlier, had been wrongly diagnosed as rheumatic pain. On that occasion, Lisle had resumed his full program after a mere week's break, but this time around it was different. He was told to stay at home in bed for three months.[35] Visitors were forbidden, and for a long time none came.

For a man of Lisle Thompson's drive and energy, three months' enforced inaction and isolation must have been frustrating in the extreme. But there was a vital side benefit for the *Eternity* story. As he recuperated, Lisle read many newspapers. And after a month or so, at May's instigation, he received one special visitor – Arthur Stace.[36]

On the day that Arthur came to see him, Lisle took the opportunity to raise – yet again – the question of his revealing to the general public his identity as Mr Eternity. This time Lisle took the bull by the horns. Annoyed and disturbed by the ongoing press speculation – there had been a snippet in the *Daily Telegraph*'s 'Town Talk' column as recently as 15 June[37] – he begged Arthur to allow him to 'clear things up.' The proper course now, he insisted, was to send to the press a copy of *The Crooked Made Straight*, the tract he had prepared about Arthur's life story. He emphasised the good it might do: learning about Arthur's identity – and how far he had come – could 'widen the blessing to needy people like he [Arthur] had been.'[38]

Arthur Stace had avoided public notoriety for many years. He was an unusually humble man. But he was also a loyal mate and an obedient Christian. Whether moved by Lisle's predicament or persuaded by his arguments, he gave in. 'Yes, all right, pastor,' he said. 'Go ahead.'[39]

Ill as he was, Lisle wasted no time. He dictated a letter to the editor of the *Sunday Telegraph*, outlining the basics. May saw to it that the letter was typed and sent, along with a copy of *The Crooked Made Straight*. Within days the *Sunday Telegraph* had assigned to the story one of its best reporters, a 39-year-old star in the Frank Packer stable named Tom Farrell. Farrell interviewed Arthur on Saturday 23 June[40] and the story ran the next day as a full-page spread.

The headline proclaimed:

> THE MAN THAT SYDNEY'S WONDERED ABOUT ...
> EVERY DAWN HE CHALKS A PAVEMENT CHALLENGE

There were two photos, one of Arthur in action, crayon in hand, the other of him and Pearl standing together smiling. Drawing heavily on *The Crooked Made Straight*, Farrell related the gist of Arthur's life story

SUNDAY TELEGRAPH, JUNE 24, 1956 5

THE MAN THAT SYDNEY'S WONDERED ABOUT ...

EVERY DAWN HE CHALKS A PAVEMENT CHALLENGE

FOR 25 years puzzled Sydney people have stared at a one-word sermon — "Eternity"— chalked in yellow on footpaths and walls.

Since 1930, the writer with the yellow crayon has kept his identity secret except from a few close friends.

By TOM FARRELL

But now the Sunday Telegraph introduces "Mr. Eternity"—72-year-old Arthur Stace, of Bulwarra Road, Pyrmont.

Over the years, many people have guessed wrongly about the man with the yellow crayon.

Some newspapers have depicted him as a crank.

One man went to a newspaper and claimed falsely that he was the Eternity man.

But now Arthur Stace has been persuaded by the Reverend L. M. Thompson, of Burton Street Baptist Tabernacle, to tell his story—and it is one of the most remarkable stories of a comeback from the edge of Hell ever printed.

The fine, firm handwriting that millions of people have read on Sydney's footpaths wasn't learned at school.

Arthur Stace had little schooling.

He was born in a small slummy place in Balmain.

His father and mother were both drunkards.

Two sisters and two brothers also became drunkards.

So did Arthur.

"I recall the time when we all of us sat around a table crying because there was nothing to drink and no money left to go out and buy it," he said yesterday.

His father, mother, sisters, and brothers died drunkards and derelicts.

All of them were in and out of jail many times.

Both sisters ran houses of ill-fame for many years.

One of them was ordered out of the State three times.

The police took out a liquor prohibition order against Arthur's brother Sam, but abandoned it when Sam said, "I'll get it and drink it until I die."

As a child Arthur Stace slept under bags under the old house.

Waking in the mornings, he crept out to steal milk from verandahs because there was no breakfast when father and mother were on the drink.

He learned to live on his wits, stealing bread, cakes and lollies from shops and bakers' carts and even picking scraps out of garbage cans.

By his twelfth birthday [illegible]

Arthur Stace had had little schooling.

He was taken from his drunken, irresponsible parents and made a State ward.

At 14 he went to work in a south coast coalmine.

He was slightly built and never grew taller than 5ft. 3in.

The work in the mine was hard.

With his first week's pay he hurried to a hotel and ordered the first beer he had ever bought with his own money.

STACE
This is the man who writes ↓

Within a year, when he was only 15, he was carted to jail and charged with drunkenness.

He stumbled from job to job, town to town and jail to jail in a fog of alcohol.

In his early twenties he moved back to the city, where he fell naturally into the sort of life in which he'd been brought up.

AROUND Surry Hills he found a job as tout for a local pub, carrying liquor from the pub to brothels, including one run by his sister.

In an upstairs room of [illegible] was a [illegible] Arthur also ran grog supplies.

He said yesterday: "I worked a fair bit as a cockatoo, or lookout man, for the pubs and two-up schools and houses of evil around that part."

He drifted in and out of burgling teams which, because of his small stature, used him chiefly as a lookout.

When World War I broke out, he enlisted in the 19th Battalion, and became a side-drummer in the band.

In France, the band put away their instruments and became stretcher-bearers.

He contracted pleurisy, and was on his way to the doctor's tent one day when a gas shell landed a few yards away.

The blast lifted Arthur off his feet, and the gas half-blinded him in one eye, an injury he still carries.

Back in Australia, he says, "I fell in with the same sorts I'd been with before.

"When we were broke, we waited for the next shipload of soldiers to come in and lived on them until they were broke.

"So it went on for years—always drunk, always broke, I was just one of a bunch of no-good derelicts.

"I started drinking beer, then wine, then spirits, and finally I was drinking methylated spirit."

His frail body, ill-nourished through childhood and adolescence, began to give up under the battering Arthur was giving it.

His mind started to go.

He knew his mind was going but he couldn't get away from the grog that was eating into it.

The police picked him up for the umpteenth time one day in 1930.

The depression had begun to strangle Australia.

Arthur Stace was one of the thousands of men who wandered the streets sounding the "No Men Wanted" signs outside every factory.

But dirty, ill-clad, a metho addict, he had even less chance than the rest of getting a job.

Every sixpenny handout went for another bottle of metho.

AS Arthur stood in the dock at Central the magistrate said, "Don't you know I have the POWER to put you in Long Bay or the POWER to set you free?"

"Yes, sir," said Arthur.

That day, he remembers, he signed the pledge.

He had signed the no-grog pledge before, but this time, he resolved, it would be different.

He said yesterday: "The magistrate talked about 'Power.'

"I knew what I wanted was power—power to give the stuff up.

"I went to Regent Street police station and said to the sergeant, 'Sergeant, put me away. I'm no good, and I haven't been sober for eight years. Give me a chance and put me away.'

"THE sergeant sniffed and said, 'You stink of metho, get out.'

"Outside the police station I ran into a mob that was going along Broadway.

"One of them said, 'Come on. There's a cuppa tea and something to eat at the Church hall.'

"In those days you had to know when things like that were on to stay alive.

"At St. Barnabas' Church we went round the back to the school hall, where Archdeacon Hammond used to preach for about an hour before the cuppa tea came on.

Arthur Stace, 72, and his wife look cheerfully out on a world he wants to reform.

"There were 300 of us down and outs in the hall, and six people on the front seat, all decent and clean and dressed properly.

"I said to the bloke next to me, 'Who are they?'

"He said, 'They're Christians.'

"I said, 'Well, look at them, and look at us. I'm having a go at what they've got,' and I got down and prayed for God to be merciful to me.

"That night, a sinner was saved.

"With God to help me, I found it possible to lay off the drink.

"As I got back my self-respect, people were more decent to me.

"At last I got a job on the dole on the sandhills at Maroubra, one week on and one week off at about £3 a week.

"I had a special little mate, Tibby, a good football referee, who started to take drink to the boot factory where he worked.

"He dropped dead at his bench one day and they found 25 empty rum bottles under it.

"Peter, a mate I went to the war with, started to drink after he came back.

"He'd been a choir boy at St. Mary's.

"He went to jail for begging alms and being drunk and today he has over 200 convictions.

"He's one of the nicest little blokes you'll ever meet when he's sober—very well brought up.

"When he sees me now, he cries.

"I met him in Pitt Street last week and he had tears on his face and he said, 'Why can't I be like you, Arthur?' and I said, 'You can be, boy.'"

The day that Arthur Stace became a Christian was August 6, 1930.

It was some time after that when he heard the Reverend John Ridley, a Military Cross winner of the First World War, and one of Australia's best known evangelists, preaching in Sydney.

"Mr. Ridley said, 'Oh, that I could go out into the streets of Sydney and say to the people, **"Eternity! Eternity!"**'

"That was the moment that decided me to start writing **'Eternity'** on the footpaths, and I've been doing it ever since.

"I must have written it hundreds of thousands of times.

"After eight or nine years I added a new one, **'Obey God,'** and five years later I began using **'God or Sin'** as well.

"Then I added **'God 1st,'** and now I use all four at different times."

ARTHUR STACE'S method of work is simple and inflexible.

He rises about 4 a.m., prays for an hour, has a bite of breakfast and sets out for the suburb he has chosen the night before, usually arriving about dawn.

Then, with his thick yellow crayon ("Six bob a dozen, they've just gone up") he writes "Eternity" in the clear, firm script that has become famous.

Walking briskly, he stops to write every couple of hundred yards, avoiding other people, but always writing where he thinks it will be best seen.

By 10 a.m. he is home again.

He prays again at midday, then sets off on a round of good works to missions, rescue societies, or perhaps an asylum.

On Saturday nights, at the corner of Bathurst and George Streets, he leads the gospel meeting he has led for 24 years—started just after he was saved from a metho drinker's death in St. Barnabas' school hall.

In the old days Arthur Stace preached the Gospel from the gutter, but now he has a fine van, electric lighting, and an amplifier.

On Wednesday nights he goes to the Methodist hostel in Francis Street to preach to the derelicts who seek a bed for the night.

The Rev. Thompson, one of the few men who have shared Arthur Stace's secret, said yesterday:

"Arthur's one-word sermon has challenged many thousands.

"No one will ever know how many lives it has influenced, perhaps as dramatically as Arthur Stace's own life was influenced on August 6, 1930."

15.2. Tom Farrell's *Sunday Telegraph* article of 24 June 1956, which 'unmasked' Arthur to the Sydney public as Mr Eternity. The article was engineered by Lisle Thompson from his sick bed.

in suitably racy prose. He included a couple of nice extra anecdotes, relayed by Arthur during his interview the day before. These shed further light on the world from which Arthur had come:

> I had a special little mate, Tibby, a good football referee, who started to take drink to the boot factory where he worked.
> He dropped dead at his bench one day and they found 25 empty rum bottles under it.
> Peter, a mate I went to the war with, started to drink after he came back.
> He'd been a choir boy at St Mary's.
> He went to jail for begging alms and being drunk and today he has over 200 convictions.
> He's one of the nicest little blokes you'll ever meet when he's sober – very well brought up.
> When he sees me now, he cries.
> I met him in Pitt Street last week and he had tears on his face and he said, 'Why can't I be like you, Arthur?' And I said: 'You can be, my boy.'

Farrell ended his piece with a quote from Lisle Thompson, whom he had also interviewed the previous day:

> Arthur's one-word sermon has challenged many thousands. No one will ever know how many lives it has influenced, perhaps as dramatically as Arthur Stace's own life was influenced on August 6, 1930.[41]

In those days, the *Sunday Telegraph* had a huge circulation. People who had not read the story themselves were very quickly told about it. Among those who got a surprise were one of Pearl's sisters ('The man who writes "Eternity" is Pearl's husband!' she exclaimed proudly to a niece[42]) and several of Arthur's former colleagues at the Red Cross ('It's Mr Stace!').[43] It is probable that John Ridley himself first learned of his key role in Arthur's mission as a result of Tom Farrell's article.[44]

Arthur's popularity as a speaker spiked. His address at Pyrmont had been included in the first edition of *The Crooked Made Straight*, but in subsequent editions it was left out. After the Tom Farrell story, he and Pearl were besieged by an unmanageable number of callers.[45]

For 15-year-old Elizabeth Thompson, Arthur assumed hero status. Her abiding memory of the episode is of seeing her father sitting up in bed, a grin on his face, reading the Tom Farrell piece. Thereafter his health seemed to improve, and early in August he returned to work at the Tabernacle.[46]

As for Tom Farrell, he resumed his busy journalistic career, having played an important role in our story. But in the interests of historical accuracy it seems necessary to make two points. First, it would be a big stretch to say that Farrell 'solved' the *Eternity* mystery – an achievement routinely attributed to him for the rest of his life, and even in death.[47] His June 1956 piece for the *Sunday Telegraph* was always regarded as among the highlights of his career, but unlike some of his other scoops, this one was handed to him on a plate.

The second point that needs making is this. In his dealings with the *Sunday Telegraph* in 1956, Lisle Thompson neither sought, nor received, any money in return – for the Burton Street Tabernacle or himself. In 1994 Tom Farrell suggested that Lisle 'was probably looking for a donation' and that 'there must have been some arrangement which had been made by somebody else on the paper.'[48] This was not so.

§

The improvement in Lisle Thompson's health proved a false dawn. After a mere three weeks back on the job, he suffered another heart attack. It struck at 5.30pm on Tuesday 28 August 1956 and was even more severe than the one on 5 May. As Lisle later recalled:

> [The pain] was worse than before, deep and paralysing. All through the night it continued resisting pethidine and morphia injections

> given by a kindly doctor who came at 7pm, 11pm, 3am, and 6am. I opened the door of death and looked squarely into the face of God and my conscience and then closed the door again to survive and return to the land of the living.[49]

That day, 29 August, Lisle was admitted to the Western Suburbs Hospital at Croydon. He remained there for many weeks, his blood thinned down with heparin and dynamin (the standard medical treatment for coronaries in those days).[50] Apart from medical staff, only May was permitted to see him. Lisle became so pale and weak that fears were held for his life, and eventually May decided that a visit from Arthur might help. One evening she brought him along.[51]

May's selection of Arthur is telling. She could have called upon any of the worshippers at the Burton Street Tabernacle, including deacons and other officeholders, or any of a number of pastors within the Baptist Church. That she picked Arthur shows the esteem in which the Thompsons held him. Arthur was not only a dear friend: he was respected as a man of God. May considered him a 'fine Bible student' who had 'sat under the ministry of some of the finest Bible preachers of his day.'[52]

An officious nursing sister at the hospital objected to Arthur, a non-family member, entering Lisle's room. May explained that he was a prayer leader at the Tabernacle and that his visit could only do good. The woman relented, but added brusquely: 'Be quick about it.'[53]

Arthur came in and greeted Lisle warmly. With considerable fervour he said a prayer for his pastor's life to be spared, and for his full recovery. But, conscious of the nursing sister's warning, he kept it short and quickly said his goodbyes.[54] Even so, May 'could feel the Divine Presence'[55] and Lisle's spirits were raised. Neither he nor May ever forgot Arthur's visit that evening, and after some months, Lisle *did* recover. Not fully: the tissue in his heart had been permanently scarred. Nevertheless, late in 1956, he was able to return to work at the Tabernacle.

There were several chapters yet to be written in the *Eternity* story.

16. Fruits of the Spirit

And that which should accompany old age,
As honour, love, obedience, troops of friends
Macbeth, Act 5, Scene 3

Arthur Stace was a celebrity now. Reluctant he may have been to assume that status, but once it happened he responded with alacrity. On Christmas Eve 1956, for example, he was invited by the Hamilton Baptist Church to be special guest speaker at its annual service of carols and films in Gregson Park, Newcastle. The church's secretary reported that he gave 'a very fine testimony' of his conversion to Christianity.[1]

One imagines that the next few years – his early to mid-70s – were among the happiest of Arthur's life. He still had his health and, unlike Macbeth, was blessed with most of the benefits that should accompany old age. One was fulfilment. So devoted had he become to his various missions that he was reluctant to take even a few days' holiday. After Edith Summergreene returned to Tamworth in 1953, she often invited Arthur and Pearl to visit her. While Pearl went several times, Arthur never did. But Edith never held it against him, as she knew his motives were good: 'some old mate might need help or need to be told about Jesus.'[2]

Another benefit of Arthur's old age was friendship. The revelation of Arthur's identity as Mr Eternity drew him closer to the man who had inspired it all, John Gotch Ridley. Modest and unselfconscious as he was, even Ridley must have felt a measure of pride. Now 60, he had attained lofty heights in the Baptist church. But this was something else again: it is every evangelist's dream to inspire another person to greater feats for God's glory. He and Arthur formed an 'unbreakable bond.'[3]

16.1. John Starr, a newcomer to the Burton Street Tabernacle in 1957, seen here in CMF uniform. Starr came to know Arthur intimately and later served a 30-year stint as the Tabernacle's secretary.

In this gorgeous twilight of his life, Arthur also formed a bond, unexpectedly, with two important new actors in the *Eternity* story.

The first was a 21-year-old trainee engineer, John Starr. In late April 1957, at the invitation of a Baptist mate, he had attended a Christian camp at Minnamurra where the guest speaker was none other than Ridley. Starr was 'shaken up', and the following Sunday presented himself at the Burton Street Tabernacle in Darlinghurst. Over ensuing years, he was built up in the faith by Lisle and May Thompson ('I owe all that I am to Pastor and his wife'[4]) and ultimately served a 30-year term as the Tabernacle's secretary.

Arthur Stace was one of the first people whom Starr met when he arrived at Burton Street in May 1957. Arthur's 'grin and welcome put the new chum at ease',[5] and despite – or perhaps because of – the large difference in their ages, the two men hit it off. Starr was fascinated and impressed by the 'white-haired little chap', and in the manner of inquisitive youth, he asked lots of questions. His detailed recollections are invaluable. Some have already been used in this book; others add a further layer of understanding to the man that Arthur was.

Among other things, Starr recalls some of Arthur's favourite sayings. Apart from those already mentioned – for example, 'You won't tell anybody, will you?' – Starr highlights three others.

After it had rained, Arthur often asked: 'Have you noticed that the gutters are lovely and clean?' It was not really a question but an observation, a lead-in to what was invariably his next line: 'God has saved me from the guttermost to the uttermost!' This was, of course, an allusion to his alcoholic past. He also quoted two Bible verses with regularity. One was Job 5:7: 'Yet man is born unto trouble, as the sparks fly upward.'[6] Another was a variation on Numbers 32:23 (the verse he wrote on the inside of his suitcase during his street mission near the Red Cross building in the city from 1949–55). Arthur's quip was this: 'Be sure your sin will find you in!' He meant *in gaol*.[7]

One of Starr's firmest memories is that Arthur was troubled by a black patch on the right of his lower lip, a legacy of his metho-drinking days. According to Starr, Arthur prayed earnestly for many years that God might remove it – 'following his marvellous salvation and enjoying the wonders of new life in Christ he fully expected that the obvious sign of his past would be taken away.' It never happened, and it is easy to understand why God would have wanted it that way. Arthur's success as a missioner to drunkards and derelicts was attributable in no small way to his ability to relate to them – and them to him. Eventually, recalls Starr, Arthur 'had peace about it.'[8]

Starr also recalls becoming aware as time passed that Arthur never went up to the Communion table with the deacons, 'other aged heads like A.A. Cobben or V.R. Byrne.' It seemed to Starr that Arthur – white-haired, well dressed, highly respected – was 'altogether Deacon material.' One day Starr asked the question straight out: 'Why aren't you a deacon, Arthur?' The reply was enigmatic. 'Aaaah ... the deacons – they're the men ... That's not for me.' He smiled and chuckled as he moved off.[9]

In due course, Starr came to realise that Arthur was just not interested in formal office. He loved to serve, but 'obscurity and secrecy was the rule.'[10] Having been 'outed' as Mr Eternity, he could no longer avoid a certain amount of public attention, but he never invited it himself. The message was everything.

Another realisation gradually dawned upon Starr: that Arthur was no slouch intellectually. Though poorly educated, he was quick on the uptake. And there was no hint of inverse snobbery in his nature: he greatly admired *qualified* men from whom he could learn, like Hammond, Ridley and Thompson.

Another such man was Dr Charles Jubilee Rolls (b. 1887), a descendant of the founder of Rolls-Royce. Educated at Cambridge, Rolls came to prominence as a Baptist missionary in the years after World War I, serving in India, New Zealand, Missouri and Abyssinia. He earned honorary doctorates in law, medicine and theology and was renowned for an erudite yet florid style of preaching that 'had some folks reaching for the dictionary.'[11] In short, to adopt a Shakespearean phrase, he was caviar to the general.

In September 1937 Rolls took up an appointment in Sydney as dean of the Sydney Missionary and Bible College, Croydon.[12] During a twelve-year stay in Sydney he became a well-known preacher and Bible study leader, including at the Burton Street Tabernacle. Arthur heard him speak many times.

Rolls' books had been important in the early Christian formation of John Starr. One Sunday lunchtime at the Tabernacle, probably in the late 1950s, a discussion began in Starr's presence about the ministers and other evangelists who had been most influential in peoples' lives. Starr mentioned C.J. Rolls and asked Arthur what he had thought of him. In Starr's words:

> I was not prepared for his response and I am ashamed to admit that I expected a quick brush off – 'he was way over my head', or some such reply. But instead to my astonishment his face lit up immediately in a wonderful smile [and] with such obvious joy and pleasure at the memory of that great scholar [he] said: 'That man was a fountain of knowledge, saying most wonderful things. I could listen to him all day.'[13]

§

Around this time there were several more sightings of Arthur's work by Sydney children who grew up to be famous. As we shall see in Chapters 19 and 20, some of them would make significant contributions to the *Eternity* legend.

Jim Low was a boy living in North Sydney in the 1950s when, quite regularly, he saw *Eternity* written on the streets there. Decades later he recalled that

> there was something special about its appearance in your own suburb. It also seemed very special when you saw the word on your own or when it looked like it had just been written and the chalk had not yet faded. I find that the word has a certain power to trigger other childhood memories.

He added: 'You were introduced to a concept of time which was hard for any young mind to understand without some sense of anxiety.'[14]

Low grew up to be a renowned country and western singer. In 1993, after a visit to his childhood haunts in North Sydney, he wrote a song dedicated to Arthur and his *Eternity* mission.[15] It begins:

> When I was a child walking down the street
> I'd see this strange word written, written at my feet
> Eternity was what it read, I asked my Dad just what it said
> And it meant forever, and ever and ever
> Always, always
>
> Chorus:
> And Mr Eternity
> The man whom we never see
> In the early light of day
> With his chalk he'd write away
> Eternity, Eternity.

Garrick Fay (b. 1948) – a rugby union international for Australia in the 1970s – was a boy of about eight when he spotted Arthur one day in the city, at the corner of George and Bridge Streets. It was outside his father's pub. To this day, Fay recalls not only seeing Arthur chalking *Eternity* on the pavement, but having a brief conversation with him.[16]

Actress Jacki Weaver (b. 1947) is another to have been impressed by *Eternity* as a child in the 1950s. She saw the chalked version often around Sydney and, once, during a visit to the city with her mother, also spotted Arthur in action. He was outside the old Bebarfald's department store, opposite Town Hall, on the corner of George and Park Streets. Weaver's mother cried out suddenly: 'Look Jac, it's the Eternity Man!' Writing in 2005, Weaver recalled that at the time of this incident Arthur Stace 'was already a legend.'[17]

Weaver's girlhood memory gels with the historical record.[18] In May 1958 the *Sydney Morning Herald* ran a long feature by Gavin Souter entitled 'Sydney is rich in characters.'[19] Arthur was held up as someone 'whose work is known from one end of the city to the other.' He was compared in that respect with another renowned street orator, Bea Miles (1902–73),[20] and depicted in a nicely drawn cartoon. Souter had asked Arthur how he decided where to go each day: 'It may just be Martin Place,' Arthur explained, 'or it may be Parramatta. [God] always tells me.'

Souter observed that 'Mr Stace probably has a larger readership than most advertising agencies.' This proved a prescient remark, for a year later Arthur was approached by the Red Cross to become a medium for their advertising for prospective blood donors. Arthur was agreeable, but at the last minute the deal fell through. He explained to a 'staff correspondent' from the *Herald*:

> They wanted me to write 'Blood Is Life – Enrol' every time I wrote 'Eternity'. My writing on the footy is the best-read advertisement in Sydney, they said. Then after a while they told me they couldn't get permission from the Lord Mayor. I wasn't sorry in a sense because I thought it might have upset my own business.[21]

In the same interview, Arthur made some interesting remarks about his methods:

> I put 'Eternity' at one end of the street ... and 'Obey God' at the other. They can't get out of the street without reading it. It stays there for three months, if not six. A man told me the other day, he said: 'Near my place, Arthur, that Eternity's been there for 12 months.' Up in Surry Hills it was.

He also described his routine that day:

> This morning I went to Randwick. The Lord leads me in different places. Five Dock after lunch. I just come home again now. I'd say I wrote it only 30 times today. Some of them concrete paths won't take it. Too light to show up.[22]

And he made a rare boast:

> I heard the other day about a young feller from Newcastle staying with his auntie near Grace Bros. One day, he saw 'Eternity' and he was convicted there and then. He went home and he didn't hardly touch his tea. His auntie said, 'What's wrong?' He let it out three days later. He said: 'It got me there and then.' He went back to Newcastle a different man.[23]

(Unfortunately, the identity of this man is unknown.)

The journalist was clearly won over. He called Arthur 'a reformed sinner ... [who] looks incapable of sin' and 'a hound of heaven, but a gentle one.'[24]

§

In 1958 another important newcomer came to the Burton Street Tabernacle, Dr C.K. (Cliff) Hemmingway. A kidney surgeon of 38 – tall, handsome and wealthy – he appeared to 'have it all.'

In fact, he was in the early stages of Parkinson's disease. His surgical career was in jeopardy (though he continued to work as a registrar at Auburn hospital) and his marriage had broken up. Having seen an advertisement for the Tabernacle's Sunday services in the *Sydney Morning Herald*, he arrived one morning seeking solace and direction. Lisle Thompson soon summed up his situation, later telling John Starr: 'It was easy to see what was wrong with him, he needed Christ!'[25]

In due course, Hemmingway did indeed find Christ. And as we shall see, he later became a great friend of Arthur's. But at least in the initial stages it was with the Rev. Lisle Thompson that he formed the closest connection. The two men were reasonably near in age – Hemmingway was ten years younger[26] – and had much in common. Aside from a shared passion for golf, both were learned, intelligent and charitable. By this time, in addition to his duties at the Tabernacle, Lisle Thompson was chaplain at two city hospitals and actively raising money for the purchase of a home near Centennial Park to accommodate elderly women in his congregation who lived in squalid one-room apartments.[27]

The arrival of Hemmingway and Starr at the Tabernacle coincided with a number of significant events and innovations. One was the legendary Billy Graham Crusade of February–May 1959, during which around 130,000 Australians 'came forward' for Christ.[28] The Rev. Graham was, of course, a Baptist – the most famous in the world – and Lisle Thompson encouraged involvement by his flock in the Crusade's Sydney activities at the Showground.[29] Arthur Stace almost certainly went along a few times – 'he would not have been able to stay away.'[30] The following year, as a direct result of the Crusade, the Tabernacle initiated an 'All Age Sunday School.' Arthur always attended and read from Scripture lustily when his turn came.

16.2. Men's Bible Study class at the Tabernacle, 1960. Arthur is seated at right.

Another noteworthy event that took place around this time was a visit to Arthur and Pearl's Bulwara Road home by a student at Moore

Theological College in Sydney, Peter Holland. Holland, then in his late 20s, had recently moved into the rectory attached to the old St Bartholomew's church at Pyrmont, as 'catechist-in-charge.' He was thus a near neighbor of the Staces. One day at college, a fellow student urged him to drop by and introduce himself to the now-famous Mr Eternity.

Soon afterwards, one afternoon just after lunch, Holland knocked on the door of 12 Bulwara Road. Pearl answered, and after Holland had explained who he was, she invited him inside. Holland ended up staying for two or three hours. He, Arthur and Pearl sat together in a small sitting room, chatting away animatedly about 'matters Christian.' At one stage Pearl made tea. During an interview in 2017 less than a fortnight before his death, Holland recalled that the house itself, while clean and tidy, was very sparely furnished. There was a view of railway sheds through the back window. But his hosts rose above their surrounds. Holland was struck by their friendliness, their contentedness together and the genuine interest they took in him. They 'poured out their hearts' and 'exuded a love for the Lord.'[31]

Early in 1961, the Rev. Lisle Thompson instituted a most valuable public service – a 'Clinic for Troubled People.' Based at the Tabernacle, and staffed by a team of qualified doctors and other expert and lay counsellors, it met every Friday night from 7.30 to 9.30 and every Sunday afternoon from 3 to 5. Its services were available free of charge to anyone, Christian or not, who had a problem that needed solving. The problems ranged from medical to legal to moral. Some just wanted a shoulder to cry on.[32] Cliff Hemmingway was one of the doctors who provided his services voluntarily.

Lisle and May Thompson appeared each Thursday evening at 9 o'clock on Sydney radio station 2CH to publicise the clinic's services. It was called the 'Burden Sharers Session' and attracted a lot of people to the Tabernacle – around 1,000 in three-and-a-half years.[33] Of course, some problems proved much harder to address than others. But the motives of all concerned were pure and there were many successes.

In an interview with *The Sun*'s Oliver Hogue, Lisle referred to a near-miraculous case – 'the most remarkable' he had encountered. It involved a professional woman who had been a hopeless drug addict; her husband had wanted to commit her to an asylum. At the clinic she was told about Christ, and the transformation was extraordinary:

> I'm not preaching a sermon on religion, because, as I've said, our clinic will help anyone with or without religion, but it is simply true that when the psychiatrist came to certify her the next day he was amazed. When he asked if she felt guilty and ashamed of herself she said she had the day before, but not now. She told him she had received forgiveness and would not touch a drug again.

The woman was true to her word. Thompson added:

> That was about 18 months ago. That woman has not touched a drug since – she won't even take an aspirin – and she's radiant. I'm proud to say she is one of our counsellors.[34]

There were clear parallels here with Arthur's own story. It is easy to understand why he insisted on offering his own services to the clinic – 'I'm not going to let you get all the plums!' he said cheekily one day to Lisle. 'What can I do to help?' In due course, it was decided that Arthur should come to the clinics and pray for those being counselled. This he did, most conscientiously, alone in the Tabernacle's prayer vestry. Often he did it for hours on end.[35] May Thompson recalled that he never asked about any of the details; he just implored God to grant the people the help they needed.

By this time Arthur revered Lisle Thompson. Again, it is easy to understand why. According to Oliver Hogue, Thompson had given an assurance that 'if any[one] needing help felt diffident about going to the clinic they could ring him or write to him at his home.'[36] This was typical of the man. Thompson had become a sort of living embodiment of the best qualities of Arthur's two other heroes, R.B.S. Hammond and John Gotch Ridley.

§

Let us end this chapter with a remarkable curiosity. Arthur probably never knew it, but by the early 1960s he had a kindred spirit in the United States, a man on another sort of religious mission whose writings had come to influence countless people. Incredibly, Walter Terence Stace (1886–1967)[37] was not merely a namesake and near-exact contemporary of Arthur's. He was a blood relation.[38]

After an elite English education and a long stint in the Ceylon civil service, W.T. Stace was employed in 1932 by Princeton University in New Jersey (one of the oldest of the American Ivy League colleges) as a lecturer in its Department of Philosophy. He had made a name for himself in the period 1920–32 by publishing a series of books on religious mysticism.[39]

At Princeton he was soon appointed Stuart Professor of Philosophy, a post he held for 20 years (1935–55). In his field – the philosophy of religion – he became a figure of genuine importance, publishing several more books for both the lay and specialist reader. Among the most influential were *The Concept of Morals* (1937), *Religion and the Modern Mind* (1952) and *Mysticism and Philosophy* (1960).[40]

And here is the kicker. Another of W.T. Stace's books – it was one of his most well-received – was called *Time and Eternity*. Published in 1952, its central thesis was that there are two orders of being: time (or the world) and Eternity (or God), and that these 'intersect' in the moment of mystic illumination:

> What is the meaning of the metaphor of intersection? This intersection means precisely what the eternal moment is experienced to be. It is one and the same human consciousness

which experiences both the temporal or natural world and that eternal and infinite order which is disclosed in mystical illumination.[41]

16.3. *Time and Eternity* by W.T. Stace (1886–1967), Stuart Professor of Philosophy at Princeton University and a blood relation of Arthur's. It is doubtful that the two cousins ever knew of each other's existence.

Make of that what you will. W.T. Stace's recondite ideas were a long way from the orthodox Protestantism of his Australian cousin. Even so, some fascinating questions arise.

For a start, did heredity and family influence play a greater part in Arthur Stace's religious make-up than has ever been supposed? Remember: Arthur's great-great grandfather, the Rev. Montagu John Wynyard, was chaplain to Queen Victoria. And Arthur's great uncle, the Rev. William Vincent, occupied the pulpit at a fashionable church in London.[42] W.T. Stace was just one of several eminent 'religious' ancestors. More thought-provoking still: of what might Arthur have been capable had he received a decent education? Did the cousins, on some conscious or unconscious level, communicate with each other? In another remarkable coincidence, W.T. Stace would die just three days after Arthur.[43]

17. The valley of the shadow of death

The death of a beloved is an amputation.
C.S. Lewis, *A Grief Observed*

At the beginning of 1960, Arthur turned 75 and Pearl 65. They also celebrated their eighteenth wedding anniversary. Ideally it would have been the start of a long, peaceful and happy twilight period in their lives. Sadly that was not to be. At some stage during 1960, Pearl was diagnosed with leukaemia.

Typically, she did not allow self-pity to chew her up. She remained an active worker at the Tabernacle right through that year and some way into the next. But it is possible that in her sick and weakened state her sharp temper grew more pronounced.

John Starr recalls an incident from 1960 when he was assigned by Lisle Thompson the job of cleaning up the Communion and Pastor's Vestry rooms. Deep in the Communion cupboard he found a shelf stuffed with loose, torn pages from old Bibles. They had accumulated over decades. Starr, a young buck in his early twenties, casually proposed to Pearl that the whole lot be tossed out.

Her reaction was fierce. 'Only the Devil would throw out the Word of God! How dare you suggest such a thing! What does that say about your view of the Word of God?' She told Starr that she would use them to make tracts, as was her custom.

Starr apologised and retreated, but later cleaned out the shelf anyway. He recalls the unexpected aftermath:

> Pastor Thompson was delighted with my efforts but I was in dread of facing Pearl when she discovered the empty shelf. [But] when I saw her she was genial and smiling ... My first thought was she could not have seen the empty shelf yet, but then she had been at work at the Church for days before I saw her. At the first chance I had I sneaked in and looked. The shelf was freshly papered and neatly packed with baptismal towels! I think she was actually grateful that she was relieved of that worry. Nor was it ever mentioned at any time in the future.[1]

The episode seems emblematic of Pearl: a (sometimes) gruff, diffident manner masked a spirit of love and devotion. Arthur referred to her as 'love' or (in male company only) 'the chief';[2] and the general consensus of those who knew them best is that Pearl called most of the shots in their day-to-day life. No doubt Arthur toed the line on small, unimportant things. But it is vital to remember that he had prevailed in the making of at least one really big decision: to leave his job at the Red Cross in 1955. She was *not* a tyrant. The opposite is closer to the truth.

Consider a second episode from 1960. Pearl's niece Stella Hesse was hospitalised in Sydney and twice received a visit from her aunt. Each time Pearl brought thoughtful gifts: 'some homemade pikelets, or biscuits; or small jar of jam; or a little vase with 3 or 4 bright flowers.' Stella recalled:

> [On] her second visit to me she did not seem very well. I remarked on this, and she replied, 'Oh, I will be all right tomorrow when I have the magic liquid'. [She meant] a blood transfusion! It was then I found out she had leukaemia.[3]

The illness got worse during 1961. Once Pearl was so stricken that she and Arthur decided to catch a taxi to the hospital. Pearl's nose was bleeding profusely, and the towels they had brought with them were not sufficient to contain the flow.[4]

These must have been the grimmest of times for both of them. It seems possible that Arthur's decision to throw himself into work at the Clinic for Troubled People (it started in early 1961) was motivated, in part, by a need for distraction.

Pearl died in hospital on Wednesday 12 July 1961.[5] Two days later, her funeral service was conducted by Lisle Thompson at the Burton Street Tabernacle and her remains interred at Botany cemetery.

§

Arthur, 76, was now a widower, living on his own at 12 Bulwara Road, Pyrmont. To outward appearances he adjusted calmly,[6] and, certainly, his *Eternity* mission continued. One day in November 1961, Peter Holland recognised Arthur at a tea tent near Katoomba Railway Station run by the Christian Missionary Society. He was in the company of another man (possibly Lisle Thompson) and Holland went over and joined them. During an hour-long conversation, Holland learned that Arthur had come to the Blue Mountains for the day to chalk *Eternity*. (The memory always remained vivid for Holland because he began work the next day as a 'deputationist' for the British and Foreign Bible Society.)[7]

So, Arthur kept busy. Even so, it must have been a difficult period of transition, and two people at the Burton Street Tabernacle were especially kind in helping him to get through it.

The first was May Thompson, who often prepared meals for him and assiduously asked after his welfare. Arthur trusted her so much that he gave her a key to his house. The understanding between them was that May could check up on him ('just in case') if ever he missed church. Arthur's own health was starting to fade by this time – his chronic bronchitis was worsening.[8]

The other Good Samaritan was Dr Cliff Hemmingway. Despite the big gap in their ages – some 35 years – the two men became close. Hemmingway treated Arthur to the purchase of a bespoke three-piece suit[9] and on Saturdays got into a routine of taking him out for lunch. After they had eaten, Hemmingway would drive them to some picturesque spot – Manly or Palm Beach, say. There, looking out at the ocean, they prayed and read the Bible together. Hemmingway came to know Arthur as 'a man of God who by the power of the Holy Spirit was dead to sin, self and the world'[10] (cf. Romans 6:11).

17.1. 12 Bulwara Road, Pyrmont, Arthur's home from 1942 to 1965, as it looks today.

In 1962 Hemmingway was responsible for an extraordinary act of charity. Arthur had confided that the lease was about to expire on his house at Bulwara Road: the owner wished to sell and had given him notice to vacate. Arthur began contemplating a move to a nursing home at Hammondville, and he had preliminary discussions on the subject with the Rev. Bernard Judd.[11] But Hemmingway forestalled him. Without even telling Arthur in advance, *he bought the Pyrmont property* and then presented his friend with the title deeds.[12]

Arthur's response is not recorded, but we may be sure that he thanked and praised God as well as his friend. Certainly, with his home base safe again, the next two years were most productive ones in his *Eternity* mission. Indeed, they would set the seal on his legacy.

17.2. The most famous photograph of Arthur, taken by Fairfax's Trevor Dallen in July 1963 and frequently reproduced.

The most famous photograph of Arthur is the one taken by a Fairfax staff photographer, Trevor Dallen, in early July 1963. In a special supplement published in the *Sydney Morning Herald* in 2008, it was ranked among the ten most iconic images of the century. Dallen once described the circumstances in which it was taken:

> The Melbourne *Herald*, which was also part of the Fairfax group, had a reporter based in our Broadway building [Paul Martin], and he got Stace in for an interview, and asked us to take a photo at the same time. Stace was a shadowy figure, and I was concerned that if we took him out into the street, I would turn my back and he would be gone. So we took him into the stairwell, and the journo got down below and I was up the top, and he was boxed in. I told him to write '*Eternity*' and then look up.[13]

17.3. A portrait photograph of Arthur taken by Trevor Dallen on the same day, never before published.

The photo accompanied a story by Paul Martin published in the Melbourne *Herald* on 13 July 1963. Martin approached his task by following Arthur around for a couple of hours in the early morning as he chalked *Eternity* on inner-Sydney pavements. Appearing under the headline 'A word in time from Mr Eternity', the story was nicely descriptive but broke little new ground. It did, however, contain this important (and strangely prophetic) sentence, proof positive of Arthur's notoriety:

> 'Eternity'... That one word has become a legend in Sydney and is almost as much part of the city as the Harbour Bridge.[14]

Three months later, on 22 September 1963, the *Sun-Herald* in Sydney ran its own feature story. Arthur had been admitted to Auburn Hospital for (unspecified) surgery – Cliff Hemmingway made the arrangements – and gave an interview from his bed. He hoped to be out and about 'in two or three weeks', he said, insisting he had 'a lot of work to do before I die.' He admitted, however, that he would not be making any more trips to the country. 'I think I'll concentrate on Sydney. There's plenty here to keep you on the move.'[15]

He was as good as his word. Not much more than a month later, he was back at it. Indeed, one of the very few *surviving* examples of *Eternity* was chalked not long afterwards.

On Sunday 3 November 1963, a key step was taken in the reconstruction of Sydney's imposing GPO clock tower in Martin Place. The main five-ton bell – the one that chimes each hour – was lifted by crane to the clock room, some 180 feet above ground level, while hundreds of spectators looked on.[16] Was Arthur one of those spectators? It seems he may have been. At any rate, the next morning, workers entering the clock room made a startling discovery. The bell now had *Eternity* chalked inside it! Three decades later, the quantity surveyor in charge of the operation, Sydney Davies, recalled receiving a phone call that Monday morning from his flabbergasted foreman.[17]

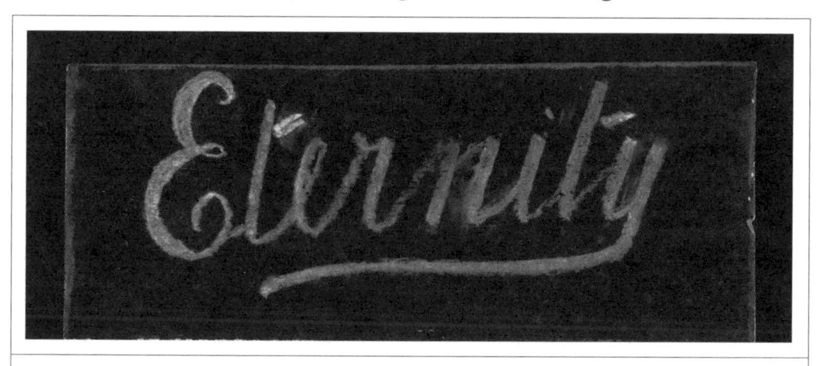

17.4. Chalked *Eternity* on black cardboard gifted by Arthur in or about 1964/5 to a fellow worshipper at the Tabernacle, Mrs Thelma Dodds. Since 2000 this item has been housed at the National Museum in Canberra.

To this day, no one knows quite how – or when – Arthur did it. But the chalking he made is still there. Only the '*i*' has faded.

A second surviving example of *Eternity* – held since 2000 at the National Museum in Canberra[18] – was also chalked by Arthur around this time. One Sunday lunchtime at the Burton Street Tabernacle, a fellow worshipper named Thelma Dodds produced a largish piece of cardboard (453mm x 180mm, about 18 inches by 7 inches) coated in blackboard paint. Mrs Dodds, a widow, was apparently very fond of Arthur and doted on him after Pearl's death. She wanted her very own example of *Eternity* as a keepsake, and Arthur did his best. But, as John Starr recalls, the exercise was not straightforward:

> Arthur tried to do it on the table but it just didn't work, he had to put it on the floor and even there I could see his arm just didn't have the proper freedom as the card was too small (the *Eternity* was less than half the size he usually did). Arthur told me afterwards he had terrible trouble with it ... it wasn't bad but you could tell it wasn't right. *Eternity* could only be done one way successfully and that was on the ground with freedom of movement for his writing arm.[19]

§

Early in 1964 Arthur's world was shattered by another premature death, that of Lisle Thompson. For the second time in less than three years, Arthur and the entire Burton Street congregation grieved the loss of a much-loved pastor and friend.

The circumstances of Thompson's death were tragic and sudden. Though only 54, the three coronaries he had suffered in the mid-1950s left his heart permanently damaged. On Saturday 18 January 1964 he was at home in Haberfield, up a ladder painting the side of the house, when another coronary struck him down. He lingered for half an hour before dying in his wife's arms.

May was left a widow at the age of 48. The following week she received a moving letter of condolence from John Ridley, now approaching 70. The grand old man sought to strike a balance between steely faith and natural human emotion:

> Dear May
>
> Little did I think when writing a line to you with Christmas greetings that within a few weeks a letter of deep sympathy should follow.
>
> Such is the unpredictability of life, that we know not what a day may bring forth. Tears filled mine eyes this morning [Sunday 19 January] as Bill Thitchener told me of the sudden call and, later, as I prayed before the congregation for the widow and family of a beloved fellow minister.
>
> My dear wife unites with me in sincere sympathy, and so would Ruth were she still with us (absent in N.Z. for a few weeks). We feel for you, indeed, and pray for His great grace to be granted in this grim season of sorrow and loss.
>
> Well I know you will not 'sorrow as those that have no hope', but human ties are very tender, and He, who wept at Bethany, knows the deep anguish of those whom death robs of a rich lover.
>
> Fear not, May: thy Saviour will comfort you and yours with the comfort of 'the God of all comfort'. Many of us will be praying for this very consolation.
>
> Lisle was a grand Bible scholar; an able evangelist; a good minister of Jesus Christ; a firm fundamentalist; and patient sufferer.
>
> He is now released from duty, and called by his Captain to 'a place prepared for him' in the Father's house:-
>
> 'O happy saint! For ever blest,
> At Jesus' feet how sweet your rest!'

Yours in His love,
John G. Ridley [20]

The funeral was held on Wednesday 22 January 1964 at the Burton Street Tabernacle. Some 500 people were packed inside, including many of the characters integral to the *Eternity* story: the whole Thompson family, of course, along with Arthur, Cliff Hemmingway and John Starr, among others. The service was conducted jointly by a group of eminent Baptist figures: G.H. Morling, President of the Baptist Union of Australia and Principal Emeritus of the Baptist Theological College of NSW; the Revs Alwin Le Claire (President of the Baptist Union of NSW), Alan H. Orr (minister of the Ashfield Baptist Church) and Bill Thitchener; and – who else? – John Gotch Ridley.

One and all must have been moved by the Rev. Orr's tribute:

> In personal work and pastoral care it would be difficult to estimate those who found Christ through his ministry, were baptised and are now members of the Church through the service of God's servant. In life and ministry he laid emphasis where it was needed. He was immensely practical, persistent and tireless to help all; no problem or need was disregarded as he served people of all ages. He was a model to any pastor.[21]

The next day, Thursday 23 January 1964, Bill Thitchener and May Thompson appeared on the Burden Sharers Session on 2CH to announce Lisle's death.

Over ensuing weeks the Thompson family received hundreds of cards and letters, many from people who had been brought to faith during Lisle's years as an evangelist or helped through the Clinic for Troubled People. The Clinic was forced to close soon afterwards, and sadly, Lisle's dream of a home for the elderly at Centennial Park was never realised. However, the money he had raised (some £30,000, including a government contribution) was donated by the Tabernacle to the Baptist Homes Trust, and a year later the 'Lisle M. Thompson Memorial Therapy Room' was opened at one of its nursing homes, 'Waldock' in Carlingford.

17.5. Lisle and May Thompson on 7 June 1963, at their daughter Elizabeth's wedding reception. Lisle had presided at the marriage ceremony earlier in the day at the Burton Street Tabernacle. He died of a heart attack less than a year later.

§

The Tabernacle was now without a minister. Arthur battled on through the rest of 1964, though his health was increasingly poor. In May there was a wistful mention of him in the *Canberra Times*; journalist Gavin Douglas, the paper's NSW correspondent, regretted the fact that Arthur 'no longer wanders as far afield as he once did in search of new pavements on which to inscribe 'Eternity'.'[22]

Arthur had slowed down but not stopped. Over the balance of 1964 there were two more notable events in the *Eternity* story.

One was an interview of Arthur by a radio journalist named Jim Waugh, broadcast on a program called *Monitor 64* on Sydney commercial station 2GB. A four-minute audio recording survives of the interview,[23] which is accessible on the internet.[24] It is a priceless record not only of Arthur's voice (surprisingly well-modulated) but of his personality as well. He comes across as bright and modest – and almost childlike in his enthusiasm.

Waugh began by asking him *why* he had spent so much of his life chalking *Eternity*. Arthur's reply was straightforward. 'I believe that we're in this world for two things,' he said, 'a help or a hindrance. I hope I'm helping other people to know that there's an Eternity to face [and that] to be living for it is a lovely thing to know!'

After explaining his original inspiration – John Ridley's 1932 sermon – he was asked by Waugh if his mission had done any good. Again the reply was clear and prompt.

'Yes, I could prove it in many cases,' Arthur said. 'Many cases where men have been turned from darkness into God's marvellous light. One of them done 17 years' jail and was turned and went back to his wife and now he's got a shop.' He added: 'And I could mention many others but it would sound like [a] boast ... I won't tell you about the others because soon you might think that I'm overdoing it or exaggerating.'

We will come back to this issue – the good done by Arthur's mission – in the final chapters. But, in that connection, it is worth mentioning one more episode from 1964.[25]

On a cold October night in that year, a 14-year-old schoolboy visiting Sydney from Newcastle, George Gittoes, encountered Arthur near Central Railway Station. Gittoes saw Arthur first in reflection, in a shop window, as he examined a movie poster. He turned around and observed an extremely frail old man bent over writing something in yellow chalk. The man had 'such an aura', Gittoes later recalled, though his shoes were too big and he had difficulty rising from his crouched position.

As the old man walked away, Gittoes examined the word on the pavement: *Eternity*. 'That one word seemed to be like a whole book of words,' he thought. 'It seemed to say everything.'[26]

Gittoes' recollection of Arthur's extreme frailty accords with the known facts. It was in late 1964 that Arthur finally made up his mind to enter a nursing home. He approached the Rev. Bernard Judd, who put in train the necessary arrangements to find him a place at Hammondville.[27] May Thompson, with the help of her new son-in-law, Lionel Meyers,* helped Arthur to clean out his house at Pyrmont in preparation for its sale. At Arthur's request, most of the furniture was given to a local Aboriginal family.

The sale went through in April 1965. When Arthur offered the proceeds to Cliff Hemmingway, the good doctor declined. In due course, as we shall see, the money went to charitable causes.

Finally, in mid-May 1965,[28] Arthur moved into a room at Hammondville and thus began the final chapter of his life.

* Elizabeth Thompson, 22, had married Lionel Meyers at the Burton Street Tabernacle on 7 June 1963. Her father Lisle Thompson conducted the service.

18. At home with the Lord

I don't expect to leave here under my own steam. But that doesn't worry me – I want to join the Lord.
Arthur Stace, Hammondville Nursing Home, June 1965[1]

Arthur was seriously ill when he entered Hammondville, but within a month he had responded to treatment. Medicine, regular meals and around-the-clock care soon saw him chipper as ever.

A reporter from the *Daily Telegraph* visited Hammondville in mid-June and found Arthur 'as neat as his own message.'[2] He was dressed in a trim, double-breasted navy-blue suit (the one Cliff Hemmingway had bought him) and was generally in fine form. After retelling the basics of his life story and demonstrating how he wrote *Eternity*, he was asked whether he still 'kept in practice.'

Arthur revealed that he had been out and about only the day before: 'I did a few in a beaut spot at the entrance to Liverpool station,' he said. Then his face lit up as another thought struck him: 'I've got to go to a foot specialist in town next Wednesday. I'll get some good ones in at Central. I always do all the barriers at Central. Nobody going anywhere by train can miss 'em then.'[3]

18.1. Rev. Bernard G. Judd, a protégé of R.B.S. Hammond and a friend of Arthur's from the 1930s. Judd arranged for Arthur to move into the Hammondville home for senior citizens in May 1965.

He was a much-loved figure by now, and not only in Tabernacle circles. In 1965 Gavin Souter published his wry, lucid book *Sydney*, which included several pages on Arthur Stace.[4] In the same year, the Sydney University Dramatic Society (SUDS) depicted him in a celebrated musical skit as part of its annual revue.[5] The role of Arthur was played by a young actor named Colin Anderson, whose performance was so popular that he was recognised by members of the public for the rest of his life. When he sang the chorus – 'Eternity! Eternity!/ From Bondi to Bennelong/Killara to the harbour/And Coogee to Kurrajong' – audiences clapped and cheered.[6]

Arthur had his share of visitors at Hammondville. One who came regularly was the new minister at the Burton Street Tabernacle, the Rev. Stewart Mitchell, who assumed the position in early 1965.[7] Mitchell once told John Starr that he felt God had called him to Burton Street to 'bury the saints.' He performed this service lovingly and patiently, on one occasion reassuring Arthur when he had become fearful that God 'wasn't talking to him.' At Mitchell's next visit Arthur was 'his old self again' – after two weeks of silence, Arthur said, God was talking to him again now.[8]

18.2. Arthur ministering to fellow residents of the Hammondville home for senior citizens in which he spent his last two years.

On another occasion Mitchell left with two envelopes stuffed with cash – generous donations by Arthur to the Tabernacle and the Australian Baptist Missionary Society.[9]

May Thompson (though no longer attending at Burton Street) also made the trip to see Arthur at Hammondville. In December 1965 she received the following letter:[10]

> Dear Mrs Thompson
>
> I have taken a long while to tell you how much I thank you for your help in many ways to me. Since I have known you, even right up to 4 months [ago] [sic.] when you sold the house and cleaned up the place when I was quite unable to lace my boots, then again for you coming up to see me & the nice refreshments you brought, with enough to satisfy us all. I am very grateful, I had a bad time with bronchitis & it has just only taken up [a lot] to what it was, if it gets

better I hope be able to get down to Burton St now & again. I have had a lot of visitors here to see me & thank the Dear Lord for all the ways He has led me. I have 4 of these men here coming to church & many have heard the Gospel. Thank you for your prayers. May the Lord continue to bless you in His service. Till He comes stand fast in the LORD.

Yours in His name

Arthur

Among several interesting aspects of this letter was the reference to Arthur's missioning activity inside Hammondville: 'I have 4 of these men here coming to church & many have heard the Gospel.'

It appears that, almost until the end, Arthur continued to make occasional public speaking appearances. In March 1966 he wrote to a Baptist pastor[11] who had invited him to a meeting:

Dear Brother

Just this small scribble to ask you to excuse me from the meeting on the 16th of April, some friends came up and told me that one of our missioners were come home [sic.] & would be at our church on that date [and] would like to see me. I hope I will be well enough to go to Sydney by then. I am getting a little better but very slow but must wait on the Lord's time. I hope & pray you & your wife & children are going along in better health. Thank you for all your hospitality to me and the help it has been.

Much prayer is going up for you by us here. May the Dear Lord richly bless all your labours for Him. So till we meet again and until He comes, farewell.

Yours in His Royal Service,

A Stace

Arthur had not forgotten Pearl, and Pearl's family had not forgotten him. Pearl's niece Dorothy Osborne visited Arthur at Hammondville at least once,[12] and Dorothy's mother and father wrote to him. On 1 December 1966 Arthur wrote back:[13]

> Dear Friends,
>
> Just this little note of thanks to you all for your very interesting letter I got this morning, yes we are nearing Christmas time which is a lovely thing to remember our Lords birthday and the kind things He did for us all in His earthly life. [He] never stops giving His Love and Compassion to help on our way each day. I thank Him many times a day for restoring me in many ways. I came here to die but have been able to warn many thousands more up here around Liverpool. The Dear Lord has given me some real good fruit for my labours which I little deserve. My eyes are better than they were & can read & get about pretty well. I hope & pray you all will have a lovely time together for the Christmas Season it may be our last we are a little nearer to [the] grave each day but how nice it is to be ready. May the Dear Lord give you all His richest blessings in all things now & Till He Comes, Be Strong in the Lord.
>
> Yours in His Royal Service, Arthur.

He added on a separate sheet of paper: 'Till we meet again if not here in *Eternity*.'

A few weeks later Arthur celebrated his last Christmas. He was in good spirits that day, attending the morning service conducted at the Hammondville chapel by the Rev. Bernard Judd, and the lunch that followed. The weather was hot, and Judd enquired politely whether, like most of the elderly residents, Arthur would retire for an afternoon slumber. 'No fear!' was his instant reply. He told Judd that he intended to travel into Parramatta to write *Eternity* in some prominent places on the footpaths there.[14] Early in 1967 he made his last known trip to Sydney, writing *Eternity* on the footpath in Forbes Street, Darlinghurst, just near St Peter's rectory.[15]

It may also have been on this trip (or another around the same time) that Arthur made one of his more remarkable chalkings. A nine-year-old girl named Jenny Turner was standing with her parents on the platform of Sydney's Museum underground railway station:

> [A] train stopped, the door opened, and for some reason so did the door on the opposite side of the train. This allowed me a view of the blackened and dirty railway station wall. Across the wall in elegant letters was the word 'Eternity'. The writing was high up and must have been done by Mr Stace whilst he was riding on a previous train. The open doors made the word look as if it was in a frame. The light colour of the chalk against the black and grimy wall made the word look like it was written with light.[16]

It was also around this time, during a visit by May Thompson to Hammondville in the last year of his life, that Arthur gave her a sheet of paper with *Eternity* written on it. May always treasured this item. When she died in 2002 she passed it on to her daughter Elizabeth, who still has it. It is a unique piece of Australian history because (unlike the other few surviving examples of *Eternity*) it also bears Arthur's signature.

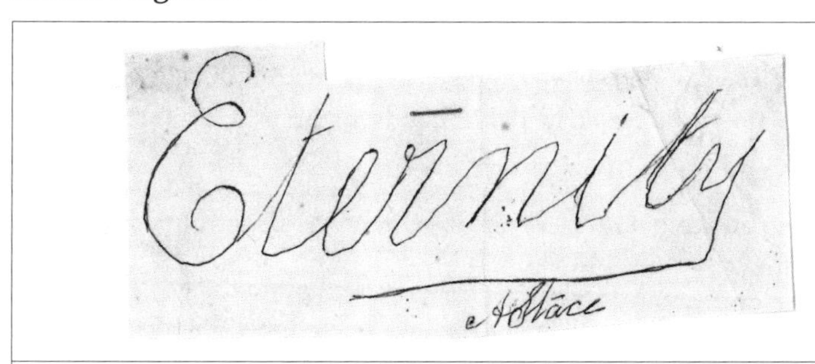

18.3. Handwritten *Eternity*, ink on paper, gifted by Arthur to May Thompson in December 1965.

During the last few months of Arthur's life, he was confined to bed at Hammondville. It appears that in or about April of 1967, he suffered a stroke.[17] He was still able to receive visitors, however, and just a few days before his death was well enough to speak to the Rev. Stewart Mitchell. According to Mitchell, Arthur said to him: 'Pastor, I am now ready and eager to go and meet my Lord and Saviour.' Mitchell demurred: 'Arthur, lad, we want you about for a long time yet.' But Arthur was serene, and he gently rebuked his pastor with a witticism: 'Well, a chap has to go sometime, you know.'[18]

Word spread in Baptist circles that their most famous son was fading fast. John Ridley came to Hammondville, accompanied by his chauffeur, Paddy Newnham. Ridley leant over the shrunken figure and whispered tenderly in his ear: 'Arthur, it's John – and Jesus is here.' But there was no response.[19]

On Saturday 29 July 1967, in the evening,[20] Edith Summergreene made her way out to Hammondville. By then in her mid-forties, she had not seen Arthur since 1953, the year she moved back to Tamworth, but had always remained deeply fond of him and Pearl for their kindnesses in the 1940s. (See Chapter 13.) Edith's account of what happened that evening is truly beautiful:

> I asked after Arthur. The matron told me that he was unconscious and would not know me. I said: 'May I see him?' He was in a cot with the sides up and I took his hand and said, 'Arthur, it is Edith.' There was no response. I held his hands in mine and started quoting John 14 ...

John 14 – in the King James Version, which was probably what Edith read to Arthur – begins thus:

> Let not your heart be troubled: ye believe in God, believe also in me. In my Father's house are many mansions: if it were not so, I would have told you. I go to prepare a place for you. And if I go and

> prepare a place for you, I will come again, and receive you unto myself; that where I am, there ye may be also. And whither I go ye know, and the way ye know. Thomas saith unto him, Lord, we know not whither thou goest; and how can we know the way? Jesus saith unto him, I am the way, the truth, and the life: no man cometh unto the Father, but by me.

Edith continued: 'I did not get through more than five or six verses and I looked at his dear face and there was a big fat teardrop ready to fall. PRAISE THE LORD.'[21]

The next day, Sunday 30 July 1967, Arthur breathed his last. He passed away in the evening and then – as Christians believe – saw God face-to-face.

§

The death of Arthur Malcolm Stace was big news. Over ensuing days, every radio and television station in Sydney carried the story. The newspapers of both Sydney and Melbourne also provided extensive coverage: the *Sydney Morning Herald* ran a front-page article under the headline 'Mr Eternity has written his last word.'[22] A piece in the *China Post* by Ian Pratt was read as far away as Taiwan. It began: 'Only a handful of Sydney's two million people knew Arthur Stace, but there is literally no one over the age of six to whom he has not preached the one-word sermon, "Eternity."'[23]

The funeral service for Arthur was held at the Burton Street Tabernacle on Tuesday 1 August 1967 at 2pm. The building was packed to overflowing, and a distinguished group of Baptist ministers conducted the proceedings jointly: the Rev. Stewart Mitchell, the incumbent, along with the Rev. Bob Leghorn (pastor at the Tabernacle from 1942–53), the Rev. Wilfred Jarvis (the man who had nourished Lisle Thompson's faith in the 1920s) and, of course, John Ridley.

Ridley had been reluctant to push himself forward, but Leghorn had felt it imperative that he speak and Mitchell had acceded graciously.[24]

The Rev. Bernard Judd – a direct, living link to R.B.S. Hammond – sent a heartfelt letter to Rev. Mitchell on the morning of the funeral. It began and ended thus:

> The monthly meeting of the New South Wales Council of Churches begins at 1.45p.m. today and this will prevent my attending the funeral service for Mr. Arthur Stace whom I have known for many years and esteemed as a personal friend. All who knew him recognised that he was a remarkable trophy of grace. His devotion to Jesus Christ and his tireless dedication to speak a word for Jesus were splendid to see.
>
> ...
>
> The last 37 years of his life were an outstanding example of the saving and keeping power of Jesus Christ.
>
> If you would be so kind as to associate me with the tributes to his memory at the Service today, I shall be most grateful.[25]

Similar sentiments were expressed by all speakers at the funeral service.

At the end of the funeral, Arthur's coffin was loaded into a hearse prior to being driven to the University of New South Wales. (He had left his body to science for research purposes.) John Starr recalled the scene outside the Tabernacle:

> [D]ear brother Ridley [was] standing off the footpath at the rear of the hearse somewhat on his own as the coffin passed because the footpath was full of people. He was rigidly at attention, that grand soldier's way of showing his utmost respect to dear Arthur. I was standing in the road alongside the hearse at this point but I must confess my eye was on brother Ridley. Suddenly brother Ridley became aware of my fixed gaze upon him, his eyes briefly flicked

> towards mine without any other part of him moving. He stiffened even more, lifted his head even higher, and arched his back a little further, to honour Arthur to the very best of his ability.

Ridley told Starr afterwards that 'nothing was too good for a saint like Arthur Stace'[26] and he (Ridley) himself later recalled:

> On the day of Arthur Stace's funeral service, Tuesday, 1st August 1967, this writer noticed, near the Burton Street Tabernacle ... a half-faded 'Eternity' in his copperplate with two lines drawn through it. Why crossed out? Perhaps to refer to the passing of 'Mr Eternity'; or, perhaps, to refute the royal truth of his one-word sermon to the city of Sydney.[27]

Let us hope it was the former.

Finally, on 13 August 1967, a service of thanksgiving for Arthur's life was held at the Tabernacle. Fittingly, for Arthur had always loved singing, there were four hymns, selected by May Thompson from among his favourites. Mrs Thompson chose well – collectively the hymns summed up the two essential aspects of Arthur's Christian life. The first two were about redemption ('Love lifted me! Love lifted me!/When no one but Christ could help' and 'What a wonderful change in my life has been wrought/Since Jesus came into my heart'). The other two were about evangelism ('Ho, my comrades! See the signal/Waving in the sky!' and 'Have you any room for Jesus?/He who bore your load of sin').[28]

The two readings from Scripture were also apt. The director of Campaigners for Christ, Alec Gilchrist, read from 1 Corinthians 1:18–31 – the famous passage beginning 'For the preaching of the cross is to them that perish foolishness; but unto us which are saved it is the power of God.' Even more appropriate was the reading by a Mr Markham from 2 Timothy 4:1–8, which includes Paul's exhortation to 'watch thou in all things, endure afflictions, do the work of an evangelist, make full proof of thy ministry.' It also contains Paul's immortal words of farewell: 'I have fought a good fight, I have finished my course.'

Arthur had indeed done the work of an evangelist and fought the good fight. Judgment – accountability in and for *Eternity* – held no terrors for him.

19. If what has been built survives

If you would not be forgotten as soon as you are dead, either write something worth reading or do something worth writing.
Benjamin Franklin

St Paul's first letter to the Corinthians contains a thought-provoking passage about the earthly legacy that every Christian will leave behind. Paul warns that

> fire will test the quality of each person's work. If what has been built survives, the builder will receive a reward. If it is burned up, the builder will suffer loss but yet will be saved – even though only as one escaping through the flames.[1]

In other words, a believing Christian who has left no worthwhile legacy will be saved – but only just. Paul made essentially the same point in his second letter to the Corinthians: 'For we must all appear before the judgment seat of Christ, so that each of us may receive what is due us for the things done while in the body, whether good or bad.'[2]

This is not salvation by works but judgment according to works – a very different thing.

It is time to assess the works of Arthur Stace. As we shall see, his legacy was far more substantial than that of most Christians. It emerged slowly at first, then snowballed into something quite extraordinary.

After Arthur's death in July 1967, there was a brief flurry of publicity. Apart from the stories in the secular media, mentioned in the previous chapter, John Ridley published a booklet about his life, *The Passing of Mr Eternity*,[3] and Sydney City Council considered a proposal for a bronze plaque to be erected in his memory at the north-western corner of King and George Streets. The plaque idea was stymied, however: first by the ruling Labor Party, in August 1967, and ultimately, in April 1968, by a group of Sydney city commissioners (the so-called 'Treatt troika' appointed by the Askin state Liberal government in late 1967 after the council was sacked).[4] As one newspaper columnist lamented, this was penny-pinching of a rather pathetic kind: 'A city should cherish its earnest eccentrics ... Stace made a ... unique contribution to the history of Sydney.' The cost of a plaque was 'trifling' by comparison.[5]

Arthur had not worried about storing up earthly treasures. On 3 June 1968 his estate was settled. The princely sum of $729.42 was distributed, half to the Burton Street Tabernacle and half to the Australian Baptist Mission Society. Dr Cliff Hemmingway accepted no fee in his capacity as executor.[6]

A better appreciation of Arthur's mission was exhibited in Christian journals. One admirer commented:

> A number of definite conversions are known to have resulted from people reading the word [*Eternity*] on a pavement and turning for help to someone who has pointed them to Christ. Typical is the story of the Jewish lady who had just stepped out of a shop in an extremely despondent mood. She saw the word on the pavement nearby and went away thinking about it. The thought of Eternity

> worried her until finally she fell on her knees and sought help from God. This was the turning point in her life as she later came into a full experience of Christ.[7]

The Jewish lady's conversion is another to add to the list of conversions precipitated by Arthur, along with those of Ron Barker (see Chapter 11), the youth from Newcastle (Chapter 16) and the married man who had served 17 years in gaol (Chapter 17). In the nature of things such stories are hard to verify, but they are heartwarming nonetheless. One suspects there may be quite a few more conversion stories concerning Arthur that, even now, have not been told. One emerged on 31 July 2017 after media coverage that day of the 50th anniversary of Arthur's death. The State Director and Evangelist at OAC Ministries Queensland, Josh Williamson, posted this comment online:

> There is an elderly man who attends Margate Baptist Church in Queensland who met Stace as he wrote the word, 'Eternity.' This man told me recently that as a young boy in Sydney, he found an older gentleman writing Eternity on the footpath. He asked the man what it meant; Stace then spoke to him briefly about the meaning. That young boy started to think and was later converted.[8]

In September 1968, a year or so after Arthur's death, May Thompson learned of another, similar case. It was not a conversion consequent upon an *Eternity* sighting – the lady who saw it was already a Christian – but it strengthened her resolve at a time of crisis. As May recalled:

> [W]hen flying to Orange with a party of Baptists to participate in a special gathering, I also fitted in a visit to Arthur's wife Pearl's family. As I revealed my ... mission [to] my seat companion [she] told me how at the entrance to [Campbelltown Court] she read the word Eternity in Arthur's copperplate writing. Her sad duty that day was to give testimony of a serious nature against her own brother for a criminal offence ... Her prayer for help for truthful

> wisdom went up at the sight of Eternity. Justice and help for the offender was the result.[9]

On 23 August 1969, the *Sydney Morning Herald* published a poem about Arthur[10] written by an extremely eminent man of Australian letters, Douglas Stewart (1913–85). Apart from being a most accomplished poet in his own right, Stewart had been literary editor of *The Bulletin* for over 20 years (1940–61) and was a hugely influential figure in publishing circles. In 1969 he was in the middle of a twelve-year stint with Angus & Robertson.[11]

As the decades went on, the cultural legacy inspired by Arthur Stace would grow exponentially. It had already begun during his lifetime – remember the passage in Dorothy Hewett's novel *Bobbin Up* (1959) and the popular Sydney University musical skit of 1965. But a poem by Douglas Stewart was something else again. And what a poem! The first and last stanzas have been quoted often:

> That shy mysterious poet Arthur Stace
> Whose work was just one single mighty word
> Walked in the utmost depths of time and space
> And there his word was spoken and he heard
> ETERNITY, ETERNITY, it banged him like a bell
> Dulcet from heaven sounding, sombre from hell.
>
> ...
>
> ETERNITY, it lades like morning dew,
> Like morning dew and he is lost in it;
> Yet one can say, as one can say of few,
> It was the greatest of all words he wrote
> And if it hardly changed this wicked city
> God rest his soul, his copperplate was pretty.

A little over a month after the publication of Stewart's poem, Cliff Hemmingway received notification from the University of New South

Wales that Arthur's remains were ready for burial.[12] It fell to May Thompson, with the help of the Rev. Stewart Mitchell, to ensure that the proper decencies were attended to. May arranged for Arthur to be buried with Pearl in the Botany cemetery. She notified the *Daily Telegraph* – which ran a nice story under the headline 'Mr. Eternity laid to rest'[13] – and attended with Rev. Mitchell at the burial service on Tuesday 7 October 1969. Both of them spoke eloquently.

Mitchell identified some especially apt gospel passages and even compared Arthur to Jesus himself:

> The change in Arthur's life was remarkable because Christ's saving love had lifted him up to the passion of selfless living for God and for his fellow man.
>
> What Christ said concerning Mary so long ago, was also true of Brother Arthur Stace when we review his life. Indeed, the Lucan passage[14] might well read in his case: 'His sins which are many are forgiven; for he loved much: but to whom little is forgiven, the same loveth little.'
>
> Arthur was forgiven a lot by Jesus, and He loved His Lord very much in return.
>
> You will recall the passage where John in his gospel[15] tells us: 'And again He stooped down, and wrote on the ground.'
>
> Half a million times Arthur Stace stooped down to write on the sidewalks his one-word sermon, 'Eternity.'

May's words were equally heartfelt. Recalling Arthur as 'gentle, patient, forgiving, wise [and] witty,' she expressed 'gratitude that he numbered me among his friends.' She also made a telling point about Arthur's popularity with journalists. It was because he was so 'completely natural and devoid of artifice,' May believed, that many accomplished newspapermen took to him. 'Their perceptive minds saw him as a dinkum Christian.'[16]

May, like the Rev. Mitchell, drew upon John's Gospel, noting that Arthur's story 'fulfill[ed] the marked verse in his own Bible':

> Ye have not chosen me, I have chosen you and ordained you, that ye should go forth and bring forth fruit, and that your fruit should remain; that whatsoever ye shall ask of the Father in my name, He may give it to you (John 15:16).

Finally, May used the occasion to renew her commitment to writing a full biography of Arthur, in order to meet Lisle's promise to Arthur during his lifetime. Lisle had promised Arthur that he would write such a biography after Arthur's death. But 'as Lisle predeceased [Arthur],' May said, 'to me was left the writing of the final chapter and the re-arranging of the material.'[17]

Soon afterwards, realising that John Ridley's 'Echoes of Eternity' sermon of 14 November 1932 had been a critical turning point, May wrote to Ridley asking whether he retained any notes of the occasion. He responded with a generous offer: to travel from his home in Bowral and redeliver the sermon in person at the Burton Street Tabernacle. This would enable May to include a full account of the sermon in her book. 'It is really for your book, dear May, that I am willing to repeat the message,' Ridley wrote.[18] A date and time was set – Sunday 1 February 1970 at 7pm. Invitations were issued and advertisements placed in three consecutive Saturday editions of the *Sydney Morning Herald*.[19] A huge audience attended on the night, including many representatives of the AIF for whom Ridley was a hero.

May Thompson had the foresight to ensure that Ridley's 1970 sermon was recorded on audiotape by the Christian Broadcasting Association. In the event, it was not an exact replica of his legendary effort of 1932[20] – 'the hour when Arthur caught flame'[21] – and Ridley himself opened in self-deprecating fashion:

> Thirty-seven and a half years ago I preached on 'The Echoes of Eternity' in this very pulpit with far more strength than I've got today, and with far more ability to remember things. But I trust that by the grace of God I will be able to present again to you those wonderful Echoes of Eternity.

He was indeed so able. Many who were present at the Tabernacle that February night in 1970, or who have listened to the recording since, would insist that Ridley was being too modest. Though well into his seventies and weakening in body, he still retained his great oratorical powers. At several points, he paid generous tribute to Arthur – 'we remember brave Arthur Stace tonight who wrote this tremendous word for all Sydney and other places to meditate on'; 'Dear Arthur Stace, he ... went out to relay [*Eternity*] far more than ever I could do, to relay it with his simple word all over the place until they couldn't ignore the little fellow.'

And, as ever, Ridley rammed home the key biblical message:

> Eternity, what a remarkable, uplifting, glorifying word once uttered, because there is only one Eternity and the eternal God is in command of it ... If anyone ever witnessed to Eternity it was Jesus, it was Jesus. And when the King comes and sits upon his throne he will divide the sheep from the goats, and he'll put the sheep on his right hand and the goats on his left. ... My Christian friends, are you fighting the Christian battle? Are you echoing? Eternity's got to come, friends, Eternity.

May Thompson and John Starr thought the sermon 'unforgettable' at the time,[22] and a veteran Baptist minister, the Rev. Dr Darcy Taplin, later described it to Elizabeth Meyers as 'one of the most amazing and powerful sermons I've heard preached.'

The sound recording is a priceless historical artefact (one of only two of Ridley's sermons that survives in audio format) and essential listening for any Christian.[23] The resonant timbre of Ridley's voice and his plaintive, ultra-sincere tone are highly evocative: one begins to imagine what the eighteenth- and nineteenth-century evangelical giants – Wesley, Whitefield, Spurgeon – must have sounded like.

It is easy to understand why Arthur Stace – a relatively recent convert in November 1932 – was so inspired by the original version.

More difficult for some to understand, perhaps, is that Ridley came to feel indebted to Arthur. That is the effect Arthur had on people. John Starr recalls Ridley becoming agitated one day in the early 1970s, during a conversation with Rev. Mitchell at the Tabernacle, because he (Ridley) had not gotten around to writing another tract about his late friend. Soon afterwards Ridley published a spirited six-pager called *Eternity! Where?* Arthur would have approved of its central point: 'Your attitude to God's Son decides your destiny.'[24]

§

The years passed. Then, in 1974, two further chapters were added to the *Eternity* story.

The first was quite intriguing. The word ARTHUR began appearing in chalk all around Sydney – on footpaths, walls and poles – printed in a blockline style. A newspaper columnist once claimed to have spotted the culprit, a little white-haired man in a black coat, but he escaped before being identified. Another newspaper called in a handwriting specialist. As it happened, no one ever discovered who was responsible.[25]

Was he (or she) an old friend of Arthur Stace? An admirer? It remains a mystery, intensified rather than solved by a sentence that appeared on a footpath one day:

ARTHUR IS JESUS' BROTHER AND IS THE POOR DEVIL WHO COPS THE LOT[26]

(There will always be scoffers and mockers, as the Bible repeatedly warns.[27])

Around the same time – mid-1974 – May Thompson made final arrangements in respect of Arthur and Pearl's grave in Botany cemetery. A handsome monument was made to order by Sydney stonemason John J. McDiarmid and erected at the site. McDiarmid, now in his late 80s, remembers well both the technicalities of the job and the 'graciousness' of May Thompson. While he explained certain aspects of the design to her, emphasising its solidity, May began singing an old hymn: 'Build on the Rock, the Rock that ever stands/Oh, build on the Rock, and not upon the sands.' McDiarmid had learned the hymn as a child and joined in the chorus.[28]

The headstone bears the following inscription:

In Loving Memory Of
ELLEN ESTHER PEARL
STACE
Died 12.7.1961. Age 66
ARTHUR MALCOLM (MR. ETERNITY)
STACE
Died 30.7.1967. Age 83*
REWARDED AND REJOICING
IN THE PRESENCE OF THEIR LORD

The inlaid '*Eternity*' on the grave's front step was hand-carved by McDiarmid in lead, to ensure it lasted for many years.[29]

May had been hoping to raise money to meet the cost of the monument from sales of the audio-recording of John Ridley's *Eternity*

* In fact, Arthur was 82 when he died. The headstone perpetuated an erroneous belief that he was born in 1884.

sermon of 1970. As it happened, she ended up bearing most of the cost herself with a little help from Pearl's relatives.[30] It had also been May's intention that Ridley compose the wording for the headstone. Back in 1970 he had said he was happy to try, but even then he was 'fearful of failing even in that' – 'my tide is running out,' he confessed.[31] By 1974 he was extremely frail and the task was beyond him.

19.1. Arthur and Pearl Stace's grave at Botany cemetery. Arthur's remains were buried there with Pearl's in 1969, but the monument itself was not installed until 1974. Commissioned and largely paid for by May Thompson, it was the work of Sydney stonemason John J. McDiarmid.

19.2. John J. McDiarmid and Elizabeth Meyers (née Thompson), August 2017.

Two years later, on 26 September 1976, John Gotch Ridley M.C. passed away. The *Sydney Morning Herald*'s Column 8 took suitable note, describing him as 'the Baptist minister who inspired the celebrated "Mr Eternity."'[32]

Ridley's death was a significant event in New South Wales Baptist circles. Stanmore Baptist Church in Sydney was full to overflowing for his funeral service, conducted by five Baptist ministers whom he had brought to faith. There was also a special service of thanksgiving and testimony held a month later at the Central Baptist Church in the city. Ridley was survived by Dorothy, his wife of 50 years – they had celebrated their golden wedding anniversary just a month before his death – and their only daughter Ruth.[33] Dorothy Ridley died in January 1994. Miss Ruth Ridley is still alive today, 81 years old but full of vim, living in Hobart, Tasmania.

§

Apparent coincidences abound in the *Eternity* story.

Less than a year after John Ridley's death, on 12 July 1977, an important memorial was unveiled in Sydney Square between St Andrew's Cathedral and the Town Hall. It is still there today, embossed in aluminium and embedded in the pavement adjacent to the waterfall – the single word *Eternity* in distinctive copperplate script, 21 cm (8 inches) high. In the words of Ridley's biographer, Harold E. Evans, 'this is a

19.3. *Eternity* plaque in wrought aluminium at Sydney Square, unveiled by architect Ridley Smith in 1977.

significant reminder of the ministries of *both* John Ridley and Arthur Stace.'[34] He might have added a third name, that of Archdeacon R.B.S. Hammond, who was also a canon of St Andrew's Cathedral.

The unveiling of the *Eternity* memorial in July 1977 was part of a major redevelopment of the whole Sydney Square site. The architect in charge, 40-year-old Ridley Smith, had been named after John Gotch Ridley himself.[35] When unveiling the memorial, Smith said:

> It is with a sense of very real privilege that I unveil this inscription and in doing so not only express the hope that all of us here will be able to say 'Meet you *in* Eternity' but that this spot may become more and more popular, causing people to say 'Meet you *at* Eternity.'[36]

The next day, the *Sydney Morning Herald*'s Column 8 wrote approvingly: 'The one-word sermon gleams in wrought aluminium. There's no undue prominence. No garish presentation. Merely the simple *Eternity* on pebbles as Arthur Stace would have wanted it.'[37]

It was also in 1977 that artist Martin Sharp produced one of his earliest pieces of work based on the *Eternity* motif. We saw in Chapter 15 that Sharp had been captivated as a teenage boy by an encounter with one of Arthur's chalkings in Cranbrook Road, Rose Bay. Sharp was also affected by the musical skit featuring Colin Anderson as Arthur in the Sydney University revue of 1965.[38] In 1975 he had incorporated *Eternity* in a huge portrait of his close friend Tiny Tim, commissioned by Macquarie University.[39] His 1977 work was a colourful screen print entitled *Eternity Haymarket!* A striking image – mainly in red, yellow and black – it was gifted to the National Gallery in Canberra in 1978 and has remained there ever since.[40]

The *Eternity* legend was gathering momentum. Before the decade was over, a man named Trevor Kelly noticed a block of hard cement in The Rocks imprinted with the word *Eternity* – it must have been written when the cement was still wet. Believing it to be the genuine article, Kelly cut out the block with an angle grinder and reset it, outside the Argyle Centre. A later attempt to authenticate it as Arthur's work was inconclusive.[41]

Finally, in 1979, well-known journalist and author Keith Dunstan (1925–2013) included a chapter about Arthur in his book *Ratbags,* a collection of character sketches. (The idea for the book was Barry Humphries', who wrote the foreword.) Although Dunstan perpetuated a few factual errors – as to the place and year of Arthur's birth and his supposed 'illiteracy' – it was a rousing, sympathetic portrait. A few years later Martin Sharp received a copy of *Ratbags* as a Christmas present from his aunt.

And there things rested for another decade, before a remarkable resurgence of interest in Arthur's story in the 1990s.

20. What do these stones mean?

I think of him like Patrick White. Patrick did it with a lot of words but Arthur did it with one.
Martin Sharp on Arthur Stace, 1994[1]

During the 1980s, little public attention was paid to Arthur Stace or his *Eternity* message. As Australia entered the last decade of the twentieth century, there was no indication of any burgeoning interest in him or his work. Yet within five years, his life would be the subject of an acclaimed documentary film and a general resurgence of media coverage – culminating, as we have seen, in the display of the word *Eternity* on the Harbour Bridge at Sydney's millennium celebrations.[2]

What sparked this? What was the tipping point? The vital month was November 1990.

Melbourne University Press published volume 12 of its indispensable magnum opus, the *Australian Dictionary of Biography*. Launched at Parliament House in Canberra on 7 November by the prime minister, Bob Hawke, this volume covered notable Australians with surnames beginning Smy–Z who had been prominent in the years 1891–1939. A new editor was in charge, Dr John D. Ritchie.

He pioneered a 'democratic' approach to the selection of subjects for inclusion, in order to make the *Dictionary* more representative of the experience of ordinary Australians.[3]

There was an entry for Arthur Stace.[4] The author was a young academic named Chris Cunneen (since 2015, Professor of Criminology in the Faculties of Arts and Social Sciences and Law at the University of New South Wales). His contribution was singled out by reviewers – favourably – as exemplifying the new editor's approach.[5]

This was a significant development. But it was not the chief reason for the explosion of interest in Arthur that soon followed.

20.1. A recent photograph of Remo Giuffre, the Sydney entrepreneur who sparked a surge of popular interest in Arthur's *Eternity* story during the 1990s.

In the same month, November 1990, the REMO General Store in Darlinghurst began using *Eternity* for merchandising purposes. REMO was, and still is, an ultra-trendy and highly successful commercial operation. Launched in 1988 by a young entrepreneur, Remo Giuffre, it now operates exclusively online; but until 1996, the business was run from a gracious Victorian building at the corner of Crown and Oxford Streets, Darlinghurst[6] – not far from the Burton Street Tabernacle. Earlier in 1990 Giuffre had commissioned artist Martin Sharp to produce a design. Giuffre, born in 1960, had seen Arthur's chalkings as a little boy (he recalls at least one sighting in the Haymarket district at the age of four or five); later, as a young adult, he had become aware of Sharp's use of *Eternity* in his artworks.[7] As discussed in earlier chapters, Sharp himself had become fascinated by the *Eternity* phenomenon during his boyhood in the 1950s. But in the intervening years another event had changed his life profoundly: the Ghost Train fire at Sydney's Luna Park on 9 June 1979. Henceforth Sharp saw 'the world ... as a struggle between the forces of light and the forces of darkness' and the Bible as a prophetic book.[8] In fits and starts, under the influence of his close friend Tiny Tim (who could recite the Bible chapter and verse), Sharp developed his Christian faith. As a consequence, Arthur's *Eternity* mission gripped his imagination more strongly.[9]

The result in 1990 was a striking piece of work for REMO – a five-metre painting on canvas featuring the word *Eternity* in rich sunflower yellow on a deep-blue background flecked with white stars. One hundred screen-print copies were produced, bordered in crimson and signed individually by Sharp in November 1990. (Copy 32/100 is now in the National Gallery in Canberra, having been donated by REMO in 1994.)[10]

20.2. Martin Sharp *Eternity* painting, commissioned by Remo Giuffre, about to be installed in his REMO store's Crown Street windows in November 1990.

REMO's marketing campaign was a hit. Sharp's original canvas was hung in the store's highly visible Crown Street windows and attracted a lot of interest. As Giuffre has recalled:

> People were very fond of our Crown Street windows, and they became an iconic addition to the culture and streetscape of Sydney. The most memorable window happened in November 1990 when we installed an original Martin Sharp *Eternity* mural, in memory of 'Mr Eternity' Arthur Stace.[11]

Giuffre has also written:

> Aside from Martin's mesmerising image, *Eternity* dovetailed perfectly with one of REMO's primary philosophies: the theme of anti-disposability '*Buy it once and own it forever.*', and our belief in the universal importance and value of commitment, perseverance and, most of all ... passion.[12]

The *Eternity* T-shirts sold like hot cakes. In 2016, they were still REMO's best-selling T-shirt for men and women.[13]

Christian purists might shudder. But the fact of the matter remains: Remo Giuffre was the man most responsible for rekindling interest in Arthur Stace. REMO's 1990 advertising catalogue included a reproduction of Trevor Dallen's iconic photo and some snappily presented biographical information. That catalogue, and Sharp's painting in the Crown Street windows, were noticed by several talented movers and shakers in Australian cultural circles.[14]

§

During the 1990s, the *Eternity* legend was revived and fostered in ways that Arthur could never have imagined.

ABC Radio National led the way in 1992 with an atmospheric production for *The Listening Room*, 'The Eternity Enigma.' Written and produced by Robyn Ravlich, it included readings from Douglas

Stewart's poem and interviews with writer Dorothy Hewett, actor Colin Anderson, architect Ridley Smith, and artists Martin Sharp and George Gittoes.[15] Gittoes (whom we met in Chapter 17 as a 14-year-old, when he encountered Arthur one cold October night in the city in 1964) won the Blake Prize for Religious Art later in 1992 for his painting *Ancient Prayer*.[16] The central, harrowing image combined Arthur's aged face with that of another man, Gittoes' friend Ronaldo Cameron, a dancer who had recently died of motor neurone disease.[17]

In 1993, country and western musician Jim Low visited North Sydney where he had grown up as a boy and seen *Eternity* chalked on the streets. He was inspired to write his haunting song 'Mr Eternity', a few lines from which were quoted in Chapter 16. The song received airtime in February 2000 on Ian ('Macca') McNamara's popular ABC Radio program *Australia All Over*.[18]

Then, in June 1994, came a major event: the premiere at the Sydney Film Festival of a 55-minute documentary about Arthur, *Eternity*, produced by Susan MacKinnon and directed by Lawrence Johnston.[19] The part of Arthur was played by a veteran Australian character actor, Les Foxcroft, himself a long-time resident of Darlinghurst.

With high production values and cinematography by Academy Award-winner Dion Beebe, it was an accomplished and stimulating work. It did justice to Arthur's motives without endorsing them, by presenting the views of a range of witnesses and commentators. In addition to the interviewees in Robyn Ravlich's 1992 radio program, listed above, MacKinnon and Johnston tracked down (among others) Rex Beaver, Trevor Dallen, Sydney Davies, Remo Giuffre, Rev. Bernard Judd, Paddy Newnham, Rev. George Rees, Ruth Ridley and May Thompson. The testimonies of Judd, Ruth Ridley and Mrs Thompson were especially important in conveying a proper sense of Arthur's true character and Christian motivations. Ruth Ridley – in a style reminiscent of her illustrious father – was particularly animated. All of the interviewees attended the premiere.

The film was released in commercial cinemas in October 1994 and screened on ABC television in May 1995. It was also shown at numerous venues overseas. It was widely praised ('remarkable and beautiful', 'addictive, surreal, elusive' were among the critical verdicts[20]) and seems to have stimulated a young Sydney woman to a burst of *Eternity* chalkings later in 1995 ('I just want people to think of what Eternity does mean,' she said, when spotted and questioned.[21]) Certainly, the film sparked a further wave of commentary about Arthur. Articles were run in publications as diverse as the *Catholic Weekly*,[22] the *Sydney Star Observer*,[23] *New Life*,[24] the *Daily Telegraph*[25] and *WHO Weekly*.[26] The *Sydney Morning Herald*'s religious affairs writer, Alan Gill, wrote a long piece,[27] as did its film reviewer, Doug Anderson.

Anderson's world-weary secularism was, however, a sign of the times. 'Johnston's film is, thankfully, not preoccupied with Stace's conversion and salvation,' he wrote, 'nor even the motives for his act of affirmation or redemption – or whatever.'[28]

The director himself, Lawrence Johnston, displayed similar ambivalence (as well as a misunderstanding of the gospel):

> Arthur Stace's message was really a warning in the Christian sense, about living a good life and you'll have eternal life. I'm not religious in a Christian sense – I didn't want to make a pro-religious film … I think of the film as an elegiac poem to the past.[29]

In another interview, Johnston revealed that Arthur had 'not really' interested him as a person. He was interested, rather, in Arthur's 'influence.' Johnson himself had been influenced by the death of four friends to AIDS. The film, he said, sprang from a 'sense of loss' – 'it's about holding on to history, holding on to the past.'[30]

Others were more laudatory of Arthur. In March 1995, in an explicitly Christian piece for the *Canberra Times*,[31] Richard Begbie bemoaned the excesses of the neo-liberal era, with its damaging and essentially phoney emphasis on consumer 'choice.' Arthur Stace, by contrast, 'lived out the joys of real choice.' Begbie concluded by posing a sharp rhetorical question: 'What could be worse than to choose an Eternity in which choice itself is relinquished?'

More cultural adaptations of *Eternity* followed.

In July 1995, the *London Review of Books* published a long poem about Arthur by Clive James, 'The Eternity Man.'[32]

In 1997 there was a scholarly article by Peter Kirkpatrick in the *Journal of Australian Studies*[33] and a striking sculpture of Arthur by Jan Mitchell made of old wharf piers. Some 2.5 metres high and weighing more than 200 kilograms, Mitchell's sculpture was one of six in an exhibition called 'Legends of Kings Cross' opened by the then premier of New South Wales, Bob Carr.[34] Arthur was depicted with a Bible under his arm.

In July 1998, a lengthy piece by David Dale about the ethics of graffiti appeared in the *Sydney Morning Herald*. It included a fond discussion of Arthur and was accompanied by the Trevor Dallen photo from 1963.[35] In December of the same year, George Miller's quirky animated feature film, *Babe – Pig in the City*, was released in Australia. The setting was the mythical city of 'Metropolis', an amalgam of many cities including Sydney. An *Eternity* sign was visible in the background.[36]

In mid-1999, a team of weavers from the Victorian Tapestry Workshop (now known as the Australian Tapestry Workshop) began work on a magnificent piece (200 x 390cm in dimensions) depicting *Eternity*. Based on a design by Martin Sharp, inspired directly by Arthur Stace and his mission, it included both the text of Isaiah 57:15 (in the background) and the first stanza of Douglas Stewart's poem (around the perimeter). The weaving job had begun in Melbourne but was completed in November/December at the Art Gallery of New South Wales in Sydney, where members of the public were able to watch the work in progress on a huge six-metre steel loom.[37]

This was the context in which Ignatius Jones decided to use *Eternity* on the Sydney Harbour Bridge for the millennium celebrations on New Year's Eve 1999. And he used it again just nine months later, in September 2000, at the opening ceremony of the Sydney Olympic Games. (Jones was co-creative director, with David Atkins, of both the opening and closing ceremonies.) The 'New Era and Eternity' segment ended with a mock-up of the Bridge.

Once again, Arthur Stace's magic word was seen by tens of thousands of Sydneysiders, and, on television, by billions of people worldwide. From a believing Christian's perspective, it was a staggering fulfilment of David's Old Testament injunction: 'Tell of His glory among the nations' (1 Chronicles 16:24).

§

The amazing response to *Eternity* has continued unabated in the twenty-first century.

In early January 2001, a renowned African-American gospel singer, Shirley Caesar, performed at the Sydney Festival in front of an *Eternity* backdrop. Soon afterwards, the then Lord Mayor of Sydney, Frank Sartor, announced that Sydney City Council would apply for a trademark in respect of the iconic yellow copperplate image. 'We believe it is a public asset and as such it needs to be protected,' he said.[38] In due course the Council approved the move and the trademark application was made and granted.[39]

Unsurprisingly, Sartor's intervention was unpopular in some quarters. A Uniting Church minister, the Rev. Harry Herbert, protested to the *Sydney Morning Herald*: 'It's so much against the intent of what Stace stood for.'[40]

Later in 2001 – the centenary of Federation – the National Museum of Australia was opened in Canberra. The prime minister, John Howard, did the honours on 11 March. In his official speech, Howard said:

> This is a unique museum. I remarked last night that in some respects it is very un-museum like. And that represents its challenge to the Australian people, and represents its special character. It has within its structures a recognition of the influence of Walter Burley Griffin on the establishment of Canberra. It also recognises that latterly acquired great Australian icon, Arthur Stace. The Eternity theme is a very important part of the museum.[41]

Eternity: Stories from the Emotional Heart of Australia was one of five permanent[42] exhibitions opened that day. Named in memory of Arthur and devoted to the broad theme of 'Australian people', it examined the lives of a wide variety of citizens, past and present, by reference to ten themes: chance, devotion, fear, hope, joy, loneliness, mystery, passion, separation and thrill.[43]

Arthur's life encompassed all ten of those emotions – and more. A key exhibit at the Museum was the piece of black cardboard on which he had chalked *Eternity* for Thelma Dodds back in the mid-1960s (see Chapter 17).

Six months later, on 6 September 2001 in Sydney, another exhibition inspired by Arthur was opened to much acclaim. This one was a collection of paintings, 28 in all, by a Berowra-based artist named David Lever. Each painting depicted a scene from Arthur's life. Lever had begun his research the year before and 'discovered a story that was far more complex and inspiring than I first expected.' In an email to Elizabeth Meyers some years later, he elaborated: 'I have always gained inspiration from people who I regard as high achievers. Stace was one of those people. I have also been attracted to people who are prepared to 'walk the beat of a different drum.''[44]

Lever's paintings were exhibited in October 2001 at Glenmore Gallery, a prestigious space in the inner-Sydney suburb of Paddington. As a promotion, *Eternity* was chalked around the local streets.[45] Most of the paintings sold on opening night, many for four-figure sums.

In November 2001, the Victorian Tapestry Workshop completed production of its monumental *Federation Tapestry*, comprising ten stand-alone pieces hung together in a row from left to right. The intention was to 'capture the history and spirit of Australia.' Relevantly, the tenth and final piece, *Celebrations 2001*, was designed by Martin Sharp around the *Eternity* theme. It features the word *Eternity* inside an ochre-coloured map of Australia as part of a line from Patrick White's novel *Riders in the Chariot*: 'Because a moment can become Eternity depending on what it contains.'[46] The *Federation Tapestry* is now displayed at the Melbourne Museum.

On 23 July 2003, in yet another twist, Arthur's story reached London – the ancestral home of his father, William Wood Stace, and generations of Staces before him.

The occasion was the premiere of a chamber opera, *The Eternity Man*, composed by Jonathan Mills (score) and Dorothy Porter (libretto). It is a powerful work, but more an ode to Sydney than to Arthur. In Porter's words, 'It's not presenting him as a sort of folk saint. He is a much more feral and complex character than that.'[47] A concert version was performed at the Sydney Festival in January 2005[48] and a screen version for ABC Television was filmed in Sydney in mid-2007. The latter was broadcast in Australia and overseas, winning the prestigious international Rose d'Or Award for Best Performing Arts program.[49]

And so it has gone on, right up to the present day.

In March 2005, as part of the KrossArts community festival, students from Ultimo TAFE decorated the streets of Kings Cross with chalk art images. The creator of the best artwork received an 'Arthur Award'.[50]

In late September 2006, the second annual 'Chalk the Walk' festival took place on Sydney's Pyrmont Bridge. Inevitably there was an entry depicting Arthur (by Jamieson Lawrance) and coverage in the local press.[51]

In June 2008, Debra Adelaide published her wonderful novel *The Household Guide to Dying*, in which the central character, author Delia Bennet, must come to terms with terminal cancer. Delia visits Arthur Stace's grave and reflects that 'Eternity contained everything he needed to say.' Later she plants clover in a neighbour's lawn to spell out *Eternity*, 'Arthur Stace's perfect word.'[52]

In October 2008, a world-renowned British graffiti artist, Mohammad Ali, visited Sydney on his way to the Melbourne International Arts Festival. Ali, a Muslim, was told about the work of Arthur Stace and was much impressed. On a visit to students at the Al-Ghazzali Centre in Lakemba, he produced a four-by-two-metre painting featuring the Sydney Harbour Bridge that blended Arthur's *Eternity* with the Arabic phrase *As-Samad*, which loosely corresponds to 'the eternal.' The painting was given to the Australian Catholic University as an 'interfaith gift.'[53]

In October 2009, journalist John Sandeman founded a Christian newspaper called *Eternity*. Later acquired by Bible Society Australia, but still edited by Sandeman, it is published monthly and distributed free of charge to churches around the country. It boasts a circulation of 100,000.

In March 2010, there was a retrospective of Martin Sharp's work at the Museum of Sydney. In the lead-up, Sharp was interviewed by Rachael Kohn on ABC Radio National and had much to say about Arthur Stace and *Eternity*. His overall verdict: 'I love the idea of Arthur, and he must be one of Australia's greatest writers. I think he wrote so simply, just one word but it said everything.'[54]

Later in 2010, in October, Delia Falconer published her exquisite little book *Sydney*. In a page-long passage about Arthur's *Eternity* mission, she described it as 'a kind of poetry, a meditation on the city's combination of the infinite and fragile.'[55]

In October 2012, veteran rock musician Russell Morris released a blues-style album, *Sharkmouth*. It was a collection of tracks about famous Australian 'characters' of the 1920s and 30s – the likes of 'Squizzy' Taylor and Les Darcy, as well as racehorse Phar Lap and the Sydney Harbour Bridge. The final track, 'Mr Eternity', was a tribute to Arthur. *Sharkmouth* was the highest-selling Australian album of 2013.[56]

In February 2013 came yet another art exhibition. This one, at the Damien Winton Gallery in Redfern (the suburb of Arthur's birth), was called, simply, 'Eternity'. It displayed the work of numerous artists, including Liane Rossler, a co-founder of the 'Dinosaur Designs' jewellery business. Rossler's husband had proposed to her on 1 January 2000 as *Eternity* lit up the Harbour Bridge.[57] Again, the media was fascinated. The headline of the article run by the *Sydney Morning Herald* said it all: 'And the word was eternal: Stace lives on.'

In July 2013, a talented 'guerrilla' street artist, Will Coles, affixed a number of casts of old drink cans to the stanchions of Sydney's defunct monorail, in Pitt Street. Each bore the word '*Eternity*' – 'an invitation,' according to one admirer of Coles' work, 'to think deeply about the shallowness of present-day [consumer] culture.'[58]

Martin Sharp died on 1 December 2013. His funeral service was held nine days later at Christ Church St Laurence on Broadway, where he had worshipped for many years. Back in 13 October 1885, Christ Church St Laurence had also been the venue for the wedding of Arthur Stace's parents, William Wood Stace and Laura Lewis.[59] The symmetry was charmingly apt. Sharp, in life, had thought of himself as 'continu[ing] Arthur's work', of 'keep[ing] it alive.'[60] After Sharp's funeral – attended by around 800 people – pieces of chalk were passed around. Within half an hour, *Eternity* had been written many times on surrounding pavements.[61]

In 2016, one of Australia's foremost photographers, Robyn Stacey, produced a superb image for Sydney City Council using the camera obscura method, *Martin Sharp's Eternity, Wirian, Bellevue Hill.*[62]

Most recently – on 30 July 2017, at a memorial service at Sydney's St Andrew's Cathedral to mark the 50th anniversary of Arthur's death – the much-loved artist/entertainer Colin Buchanan performed a new song, 'Eternity (Arthur Stace)', the chorus of which highlighted themes of challenge, promise and redemption.[63]

Epilogue: Reflections on eternity

We are all totally hooked in our moment to moment troubles. Mr Stace's word is like a bucket of cold water, a wake-up call that puts these things into perspective. This effect transcends all religious points of view or perspectives.

Mrs Jenny Story, spotter of a chalked *Eternity* as a child, writing in 2011[1]

What might Arthur make of events since his death – both the ongoing legacy of his mission, and the state of Christianity and society in Australia today?

We can be sure that he wanted his message to get out. That message was everything to him, and incredibly, as we have seen, it has now been relayed many times to most of the adult population of Australia. Twice, during the year 2000, it reached billions of people across the globe. In the words of a distinguished Baptist historian, the Rev. Dr Ken R. Manley, 'the single word sermon of a Baptist layman was shared with the whole world.'[2]

Since 30 July 1967, and especially since New Year's Day 2000, many Australian Christians have utilised Arthur's story for evangelistic purposes. Colin Buchanan is the latest in a very long line, one that includes John Barwick, Nigel Chapman, Peter Rahme, Ramon Williams, Colin Mackeller and Michael Jensen. There are also at least two marvellous examples from overseas.

In mid-2012, the founder of the Vertical Church movement in North America, James MacDonald, published a bestselling book in which Arthur was held up as an exemplar of the Christian life.[3] And in early 2016, as part of an outreach program in Moldova, Christian Mission International (an Australian body) opened its Sydney Café. Arthur's story is presented pictorially and in writing throughout; his copperplate *Eternity* is even printed on the coffee cups. According to leader Matthew Hillier, 'one of our workers, Sergey, used it several times in Gospel work and found that people could identify with it because Arthur Stace was an alcoholic and poor – both things that people know well in Eastern Europe.'[4]

On the other hand, one has to wonder how many people in Australia *not already Christian* have understood properly – let alone taken to heart – the message Arthur wanted to convey. He would surely be disappointed that his fundamentally religious message has so often been watered down and reinterpreted. Of course, that is anyone's (certainly any artist's) right. But even so ...

Take the 2003 Jonathan Mills–Dorothy Porter opera, *The Eternity Man*. Asked about the depiction in it of Arthur's Christianity, Mills hedged his bets: 'It's not anti-religious. But we don't have a message to carry in this.'[5] On another occasion, Mills admitted that Arthur saw himself as 'trying to save the soul of city.' Nevertheless, Mills expressed concern about 'nasty evangelism' in Sydney, even complaining that Arthur's memory was 'being used by the churches.'[6] Martin Sharp made a glorious response: 'Is he being used by the churches? Probably. Is he being used by God? Definitely.'[7]

Dorothy Porter drew attention to the word *Eternity* itself: 'It has incredible resonance. Heaven or hell, it doesn't promise anything, which is quite a terrifying thing.'[8]

This came closer to the heart of the matter. *Eternity* still has near-universal resonance precisely because, as a word, it is ambiguous, open to all sorts of interpretations and associations. Arthur's original choice remains an inspired one. But times change. In the 50-year period since Arthur's death, the proportion of the Australian population who self-identify as Christian has fallen from 88 per cent to 52 per cent.[9]

Nowadays, many fewer people than in Arthur's era are likely to connect *Eternity* with Christian conceptions of the afterlife – and fewer still with Isaiah 57:15 or the prospect of Jesus' judgement. In that respect, Dorothy Porter was atypical. In his heartfelt article for the *Sydney Morning Herald* on New Year's Eve 1999, Simon Townsend admitted that *Eternity* was, for him, 'still a mystery.' And Clive James' epic 1995 poem, though not unsympathetic to Arthur, contained a flat rejection of *Eternity*'s biblical meaning:

> Where will we spend it? Nowhere except here.
> Life everlasting ends where it begins,
> On Earth, but it is present at every moment.[10]

Some have been positively hostile. In January 2005, a person calling himself 'Strapemhard' complained in a letter to the *Sydney Morning Herald* that 'the quaint sentiment behind "Eternity" belongs to a different era. Arthur's scribblings might [have been] well intentioned, but are a sanctimonious admonition to Sydneysiders who are now full of fun and creativity.'[11]

Author Peter Carey has described the continuing appeal of *Eternity* to the 'utilitarian' people of Sydney as a 'puzzle':

> We generally do not like religion in this town, are hostile to *God-botherers* and *wowsers* and *bible-bashers*. We could not like Arthur because he was 'saved', hell no! We like him because he was a cockatoo outside the brothel, because he was a drunk, a ratbag, an outcast. He was his own man, a slave to no one on this earth.[12]

When the filmed version of *The Eternity Man* was first screened on ABC Television in January 2009, comments were sought from the actor/baritone who played Arthur, Grant Doyle. He ascribed motives to Arthur that bordered on the psychotic: 'It seemed a kind of primitive obsession with a Christian songline to it. His was the life of an addict. He may have given up the bottle but he never really overcame his addiction.'[13]

It is safe to say that, as regards such notions, Arthur would be shaking his head.

He and R.B.S. Hammond would certainly be dismayed by Sydneysiders' ongoing problems with the demon drink – including the extraordinary backlash against the New South Wales government's mild 'lockout laws' of 2014. These were designed to minimise alcohol-fuelled violence late at night and have achieved good results. The tragedy suffered by the Kelly family[14] would have made both Arthur and Hammond weep. Six o'clock closing (repealed in 1955) has become something close to open slather. The liquor and other commercial interests that Hammond battled still wield great power.

Hammond and Arthur would be much happier about the continuation of the archdeacon's magnificent work for the needy and vulnerable. In 2017, HammondCare is an independent Christian charity specialising in dementia and aged care, palliative care, rehabilitation and older persons' mental health.[15] It does superb work and is highly respected.

Arthur would have bittersweet feelings about the state of the two churches to which he belonged.

St Barnabas' on Broadway is still going strong. The old church building was destroyed by fire on 10 May 2006, but Barneys (as it is now known) continues to flourish. The congregation is housed in a sleek, high-tech new building opened in June 2012.[16] R.B.S. Hammond is still venerated. By contrast, the Burton Street Tabernacle in Darlinghurst ceased to operate as a place of worship in 1996.[17] The building was purchased in 2004 by Sydney City Council (for $3.5 million) and now has a very different use. Since September 2013 it has been the home of the Darlinghurst Theatre Company.[18]

In its capacity as a Baptist church, the Tabernacle was a victim of the gentrification of the inner-city suburbs of Sydney, a long-term process that began during Arthur's life. The places in which he grew up and later lived as an adult – Redfern, Newtown, Balmain, Surry Hills, Darlinghurst, Pyrmont and the rest – are now prime real estate. Their residents still vote Labor (or Green) but for very different reasons than a century ago. And an ever-dwindling proportion of their residents take Christianity seriously. According to the 2016 census, these parts of Sydney are among the most irreligious places in Australia.[19]

Nonetheless, the Tabernacle still stands. What is more, in the process of its being converted to a theatre, it was painstakingly and lovingly restored.

Sydney City Council is no longer an institution renowned for its ties to the Christian churches (if indeed it ever was). But those presently in charge at the Town Hall – pre-eminently the longtime Lord Mayor of Sydney, Clover Moore, who is a believing Catholic[20] – certainly have an appreciation of aesthetics and history. The Tabernacle's restorations cost $7.9 million and the result was superb.

In December 2011, the Council decided to rename the building the 'Eternity Playhouse' in tribute to Arthur Stace.[21] A large *Eternity* sign in Arthur's distinctive copperplate adorns the entrance. Inside, above the stage, is an original inscription: 'Reverence My Sanctuary.' And nestled under a stage-floor trap door is the baptismal bath in which Arthur was once immersed.[22]

The Eternity Playhouse in Darlinghurst, opened in 2013. Sydney City Council restored and converted the old Burton Street Baptist Tabernacle for the purpose.

Arthur and Pearl Stace, John Gotch Ridley, R.B.S. Hammond, Lisle and May Thompson – one would like to think that all of them, if they know about these things, are smiling. And yet, if they are, it must be somewhat ruefully.

Perhaps the most that contemporary Christians can hope for is that the 'average' fair-minded Australian reflects upon *Eternity* in the manner of Mrs Jenny Story, now 59, who first saw the word as a child of nine chalked on the wall of a Sydney underground railway station. (See Chapter 18.) Decades later, Mrs Story mused thoughtfully about *Eternity* in words quoted at the outset of this chapter. She continued:

> Mr Stace's dedication to bringing us his word is a testimony to his faith. It is partially this dedication and conviction which leads me to treat his views with respect. His life demonstrates the

> possibility of making a radical change in how you live, right now and in a lasting way.
>
> This brings us the hope that no matter how dark things are, tomorrow things may be better. The importance of a person's life, the brightness of their gift and the size of their legacy to others do not have to be destroyed by an unfortunate start. Mr Stace's work is a sure sign that miracles can and do happen.[23]

Let the last word go to King Solomon:

> I have seen the burden that God has laid on men. He has made everything beautiful in its time. He has also set eternity in the hearts of men; yet they cannot fathom what God has done from beginning to end (Ecclesiastes 3:11, NIV).

Notes

Please note that where it occurs, '†' indicates that a copy of the document is in the possession of the authors.

Introduction

1 N. Jamal, 'Fireworks to reign over the rain', *The Sydney Morning Herald (SMH)* 29 Dec. 1999, p. 5. The precise crowd estimate was 1.2 million.
2 See *SMH*, 9 Nov. 1887, p. 5.
3 See, e.g., A. Dennis, 'Enigma variation for fireworks', *SMH*, 21 Dec. 1999, p. 1.
4 M. Knox, 'One man's message of salvation, yours eternally', *SMH*, 29 Dec. 1999, p. 5.
5 John Job Crew Bradfield, address in 1926 to the General Assembly of the Presbyterian Church in NSW. Quoted in P. Lalor, *The Bridge: The Epic Story of an Australian Icon – The Sydney Harbour Bridge*, Allen & Unwin, Crows Nest NSW, 2006, p. 152.
6 D. Marr, *The High Price of Heaven*, Allen & Unwin, Crows Nest NSW, 1999.
7 *SMH*, 31 Dec. 1999, p. 1.
8 Dionysius Exiguus (c. 470–544) and the Venerable Bede of Northumbria (672–735) are the gentlemen traditionally credited. Both were monks.
9 Quoted in N. Chapman, 'Eternity in the heart of Sydney', 15 Jan. 2000, http://www.bereanpublishers.com/eternity-in-the-heart-of-sydney/.
10 See, e.g., letters to the editor of *SMH*, 4 Jan. 2000, p. 10; editorial in the *Daily Telegraph* (Sydney), 6 Jan. 2000, p. 10.
11 P. Carey, *30 Days in Sydney: A Wildly Distorted Account*, Bloomsbury, London, 2001, p. 74.
12 *Sunday Telegraph* (Sydney), 16 Jan. 2000, p. 11.
13 See http://empathynation.co/.
14 P. Koch, 'Arthur's resting place for Eternity', *Sunday Telegraph* (Sydney), 16 Jan. 2000, p. 7.
15 P. Conolly, 'From the battlefield to saving souls', *SMH*, 11 Nov. 2009, p. 10.
16 A. Young, *Street Art, Public City: Law, Crime and the Urban Imagination*, Routledge, London, 2014, p. 21.
17 Interview of Bernard G. Judd on camera in Lawrence Johnston's 1994 documentary film, *Eternity*. See also A. Gill, 'Eternity and the miracle of Burton Street', *SMH*, 4 Oct. 1994.
18 Though, as we shall see in Chapter 2, Arthur Stace's father was born into the English upper-middle class family with close links to the aristocracy.
19 See A.B. Facey, *A Fortunate Life*, Fremantle Arts Centre Press, Fremantle WA, 1981.
20 'Testimony to Arthur Stace by John Starr', 24 Feb. 2009.†

1. Born unto trouble

1 Birth certificate of Arthur Malcolm Stace, NSW reg. no. 1885/010246.
2 See description in *New South Wales Police Gazette (NSWPG)*, 2 Nov. 1892, p. 364.
3 Most of William's neighbours in Morehead Street, Redfern, were artisans or small shopkeepers – *Sands' Sydney and Suburban Directory* (*SSSD*) of 1885 lists carpenters, drapers, butchers, grocers, boot-makers, engine-fitters and the like.
4 William's occupation was given as 'labourer' on the birth certificates of both Minnie (NSW reg. no. 1880/23831) in 1880 and Arthur in 1885, and on the death certificate of Ellen (NSW reg. no. 1889/5724) in 1889.
5 Marriage certificate of William Wood Stace and Laura Lewis, NSW reg. no. 1589/1885.
6 *SSSD*, 1886 (p. 297), 1887 (p. 758), 1888 (p. 775) and 1889 (p. 828). See also the death certificate of Ellen Stace, NSW reg. no. 1889/5724, which lists Ellen's place of death as Kings Clear Road, Alexandria – presumably the Stace family home by 26 Mar. 1889.
7 C. Pearl, *Wild Men of Sydney*, Universal Books, Melbourne, 1970, p. 11.
8 Death certificate of Ellen Stace, NSW reg. no. 1889/5724. Ellen was eleven months old when she died, on 26 Mar. 1889, placing her birth in Apr. 1888. For reasons unknown, she was born in Maitland, some 100 miles (165 km) north of Sydney.
9 *SSSD*, 1889, p. 828 (entries for both Malcolm Stace and William Stace).
10 Death certificate of Ellen Stace, NSW reg. no. 1889/5724.
11 Ibid.
12 Biloela or Parramatta Training School – *Court Ordered Admissions, 1867–1924*, p. 205; *NSW Industrial School Registers, 1867–1925*, pp. 205–6 (entry for Clara Mabel Stace). Clara was incorrectly described as being 12 years old. She was 13.
13 Ibid.
14 See the discussion at http://www.parragirls.org.au/parramatta-girls-home.php.
15 Ibid.
16 By the time of the taking of the 1891 UK census, Malcolm and Ellen Stace were living at 15 Camberwell Station Road in Lambeth.
17 *NSWPG*, 10 Oct. 1888, p. 808.
18 *SSSD*, 1891, p. 124.
19 C.M.H. (Manning) Clark, *A History of Australia, Volume V: The People Make Laws 1888–1915*, Melbourne University Press, Melbourne, 1981, chapter 4, esp. pp. 92–94.
20 *NSWPG*, 2 Nov. 1892, p. 364.
21 Register of the Benevolent Society of New South Wales, entry for 'Stace, Laura' and children, 29 Oct. 1892.[†]
22 See the discussion in Stephen Garton, 'Health and welfare', *The Dictionary of Sydney*, 2008, at http://dictionaryofsydney.org/entry/health_and_welfare.
23 L.M. Thompson, *Crooked Made Straight*, Christian Broadcasting Association Ltd, Sydney, 1955.
24 Ibid.
25 *Evening News* (Sydney), 7 Aug. 1891, p. 3.

26 *Evening News* (Sydney), 1 Jan. 1892, p. 6.
27 *Sydney Mail and New South Wales Advertiser*, 6 Feb. 1892, p. 331 (death notice).
28 *NSWPG*, 2 Nov. 1892, p. 364. Interestingly, William's age was overstated by 7 years – he was 37, not 44.
29 Register of the Benevolent Society of NSW, entry for 'Stace, Laura' and children, 29 Oct. 1892.

2. Sins of the fathers

1 'Statement of the Services of Walter Samuel Stace of the Royal Engineers', c. 1868.†
2 General W.H. Askwith, *List of Officers of the Royal Regiment of Artillery from the Year 1716 to the Year 1899*, printed by William Clowes & Sons Ltd, London, for the Royal Artillery Institution, 1900, p. 194.
3 The Order of the Bath was a prized order of chivalry (see *London Gazette*, 4 Jan. 1815, p. 17).
4 Askwith, *List of Officers*, p. 194.
5 W.R. O'Byrne, 'Pasley, Thomas Sabine', in *A Naval Biographical Dictionary*, John Murray, London, 1849.
6 Marriage register of the parish church of St John Pater in the County of Pembroke, p. 45, entry no. 89, 16 June 1851.†
7 *The Royal Kalendar, and Court and City Register, for England, Scotland, Ireland, and the Colonies for the Year 1847*, p. 148.
8 The Crimean War was fought from Oct. 1853 to Mar. 1856. It pitted Tsarist Russia against an unlikely coalition of Britain, France and the Ottoman Empire.
9 For the dates and places of birth of Malcolm and Georgina Stace, see the 'Statement of the Services of Walter Samuel Stace' (note 1 above).
10 UK census, 1861.
11 *The London Gazette*, 4 Oct. 1867, p. 5341.
12 UK census, 1871. The Stace family lived at 4 Sion Hill Place.
13 *Colburn's United Service Magazine and Naval and Military Journal*, 1869, Part III.
14 Notice of the proving of the will of Walter Samuel Stace on 13 Oct. 1869.†
15 *The London Gazette*, 27 Oct. 1874, p. 5114.
16 *The Times* (London), 21 Mar. 1877, p. 8.
17 'Names and Descriptions of Cabin Passengers', SS *City of Santiago*, 20 Oct. 1887.†
18 *Sydney Mail and New South Wales Advertiser*, 20 Jul. 1878, p. 102.
19 *SSSD*, 1879, pp. 122, 577 (entry for W. Stace).
20 See Major-General Sir Eustace F. Ticknell, 'The Eustace Family of Castlemore and Newstown, County Carlow', *Journal of the County Kildare Archaeological Society*, vol. XIII, no. 6, 1955, pp. 375–382.
21 *British Medical Journal*, 22 Feb. 1879, p. 295.
22 *The London Gazette*, 11 Feb. 1881, p. 609.
23 *The London Gazette*, 4 Dec. 1883, p. 6265.
24 Birth certificate of Minnie Lewis, or Stace (NSW reg. no. 1880/23831).
25 *NSW Gaol Description and Entrance Books 1818–1930* (Windsor), 15 Sep. 1876, p. 74.

26 *SMH*, 26 Sep. 1876, p. 3.
27 Ibid.
28 *NSWPG*, 27 Sep. 1876, p. 300.
29 There is no reference to any subsequent trial in the *SMH* or the *NSWPG*, nor, until the mid-1880s, is there any further entry for a 'Margaret Lewis' in the *NSW Gaol Description and Entrance Books*.
30 *NSWPG*, 24 Dec. 1879, p. 480; 18 Feb. 1880, p. 64. See also *NSW Gaol Description and Entrance Books 1818–1930*, 10 Feb. 1880, p. 97 (Windsor); 18 Feb. 1880, p. 109 (Parramatta). Lewis was released from custody on 9 Jul. 1882.
31 Register of the Benevolent Society of NSW, entry for 'Stace, Laura' and children, 29 Oct. 1892, listing the ages of William John and Samuel Stace as at that date as 11 and 9 respectively. See also the death certificate of Samuel Seaward Stace (NSW reg. no. 1949/22625), according to which Samuel was 66 years old when he died, on 18 June 1949.
32 N. Gould, *Stray Notes on Australia*, George Routledge & Sons Ltd, London, 1896, ch. VI, available online at http://www.monalena.me/static/html/b0398.html.
33 Ibid, ch. II.
34 NSW Registers of Coroners Inquests 1821–1937, pp. 44–47.
35 See, for example, *Windsor and Richmond Gazette*, 28 Jan. 1893, p. 4; *Evening News* (Sydney) 27 Jan. 1897, p. 4.

3. The road to perdition

1 Edward Smith Hall (1786–1860) was a remarkable man. In 1817, he had been a founder of the NSW auxiliary of the British and Foreign Bible Society (now Bible Society Australia).
2 See M.J.B. Kenny, 'Hall, Edward Smith (1786–1860)', *Australian Dictionary of Biography (ADB)*, National Centre of Biography, Australian National University, http://adb.anu.edu.au/biography/hall-edward-smith-2143/text2729, viewed 13 Apr. 2017.
3 See generally T. Evans, *Fractured Families, Life on the Margins in Colonial New South Wales*, UNSW Press, Sydney, 2015, and the discussion at http://www.sydneybenevolentasylum.com/index.php?page=what-was-the-sydney-benevolent-asylum.
4 J. Ramsland, 'Children's institutions in nineteenth-century Sydney', *Dictionary of Sydney*, 2011, http://dictionaryofsydney.org/entry/childrens_institutions_in_nineteenth-century_sydney, viewed 5 Jul. 2017.
5 NSW State Children's Relief Boarding-Out Registers 1881–1923, p. 1895.
6 Ibid. See also https://www.findandconnect.gov.au/guide/nsw/NE00003.
7 Register of the Benevolent Society of NSW, entry for 'Stace, Laura' and children, 29 Oct. 1892.
8 Ibid.
9 See M. Murray, 'Working Boarders: The Boarding Out Scheme in New South Wales, 1880–1920', Working Paper 99–10, Department of Economics, University of Wollongong, 1999, p. 3.
10 Register of Dependent Male Children (NSW), p. 1985 (entry for Arthur Stace).[†]

11 Ibid., pp. 1983, 1984 (entries for William Stace and Samuel Stace respectively).†
12 This was a good opportunity for Sam. The Nobles, with whom he lived for five years, were decent people with three children of their own.
13 In Sep. 1898, when he was 17, William was relocated from Berry to Kangaroo Valley. His new foster parents were John Nelson, farmer and auctioneer, and his wife Susannah. He was discharged from their care on 11 June 1899.
14 L. Thompson, *Crooked Made Straight*, p. 3.
15 Despite persistent myths to the contrary, Arthur was *not* illiterate. As we shall see in later chapters, he could write basic letters and read the Bible with considerable insight. He must have learned to read and write somewhere, and by far the most likely possibility is that he did so at a government school at some stage between the ages of 8 and 14 while living in Goulburn with Mrs Campbell.
16 Murray, 'Working Boarders', *passim*.
17 Quoted in Murray, 'Working Boarders', p. 6.
18 In the official report of Clara's entry to Parramatta Training School in 1889 (see note 12 to Chapter 1), there appeared the notation 'Education: neither read nor write.' Minnie signed her name with an 'X' – for example, on her mother's death certificate in 1912. Dora Stace should have attended school during her time in foster care at Parramatta with Mrs Brown and may have acquired a basic level of literacy.
19 William and Samuel Stace should have attended school while they were wards of the state. Samuel most probably did so, at least until the age of twelve when he was sent to the Nobles in Jamberoo. William's level of literacy must be accounted less certain than that of his two younger brothers. He was already eleven when he entered the Asylum and may not have received much additional schooling.
20 See *SSSD*, 1897, p. 906 (listing William as resident in Moore's Lane, Balmain); it seems Laura was definitely living at Moore's Lane by Dec. 1898, since it was the scene of her robbery and assault of John Bain.
21 *Australian Star* (Sydney), 1 Apr. 1897, p. 6.
22 H. Montgomery-Massingberd (ed.), *Burke's Irish Family Records*, Burkes Peerage Ltd, London, 1976, p. 383.
23 C. Mosley (ed.), *Burke's Peerage, Baronetage & Knightage*, Burke's Peerage (Genealogical Books) Ltd, London, 2003, vol. 3, p. 3066.
24 See the entry for Malcolm Vincent Stace at http://www.ozgenealogy.info/genealogy/familygroup.php?familyID=F1175&tree=cressie1.
25 *Australian Star* (Sydney), 12 Nov. 1894, p. 5; *NSW Gaol Description and Entrance Books 1818–1930*, 12 Nov. 1894 (entry for Laura Stace).
26 *Australian Star* (Sydney), 7 Dec. 1898, p. 6.
27 *NSW Gaol Description and Entrance Books 1818–1930* (page headed 'GENERAL INDEX of PRISONERS received in BILOELA GAOL during 1898 and 1899', entry for Laura Stace).
28 Register of Dependent Female Children (NSW), p. 1625 (entry for Dolly Stace).†
29 NSW Industrial School Registers 1867–1925, Discharges 1869–99, 16 May 1893, pp. 199–200.
30 Ibid., 15 Nov. 1894, pp. 225–6; *NSWPG*, 21 Nov. 1894, p. 893.

31 NSW Industrial School Registers 1867–1925, Discharges 1869–99, 21 Oct. 1895, pp. 217–8.
32 Birth certificate of Henry Stace, NSW reg. no. 28038/1897. Henry took his mother's surname because Clara Lewis and John Go-Hing were not married at the time of their child's birth. They did marry in 1912 and then, in accordance with the custom of the day, re-registered Henry's birth so as to 'legitimise' it.
33 Birth certificate of Ethel Edith Stace, NSW reg. no. 17657/1899. Ethel also took her mother's surname and had her birth re-registered in 1912.
34 L. Thompson, *Crooked Made Straight*, p. 3.
35 *SSSD*, 1900, p. 216.
36 Register of Dependent Male Children (NSW), p. 1985 (entry for Arthur Stace).
37 *SMH*, 26 Jun. 1901, p. 10.
38 Ibid.
39 F. Moore, P. Gorman & R. Harrison, *At the Coalface: The Human Face of Coalminers and Their Communities; An Oral History of the Early Days*, CFMEU Mining and Energy Division, Sydney, 1998, p. 8.
40 L. Thompson, *Crooked Made Straight*, p. 3.
41 Ibid.
42 Moore et al., *At the Coalface*, p. 8.
43 Ibid.
44 Register of Dependent Male Children (NSW), p. 1985 (entry for Arthur Stace).
45 Ibid.
46 *Illawarra Mercury* (Wollongong, NSW), 28 Jun. 1912, p. 2.
47 Ibid; *South Coast Times and Wollongong Argus* (NSW), 5 Jul. 1912. Other newspapers of the period show that both the Dalgleishes served on various community bodies.
48 *South Coast Times and Wollongong Argus* (NSW), 19 Apr. 1902, pp. 8-10.
49 Jamie Radford, 'What happened tragic day of Mt Kembla Mine disaster', *Illawarra Mercury*, 25 Jul. 2014.
50 *The Kiama Reporter and Illawarra Journal*, 27 Jul. 1904, p. 2.
51 *Register of Dependent Children (NSW)*, p. 1985 (entry for Arthur Stace).
52 *Daily Telegraph* (Sydney), 25 Jun. 1956 (J. Macdougall's 'Contact' column). According to Macdougall, Arthur spent a night in a hollow log in the company of a tiger snake.
53 L. Thompson, *Crooked Made Straight*, p. 3.

4. And lead us not into temptation

1 The year of Arthur's move back to Sydney, 1905, is calculated as follows. According to *Crooked Made Straight* (pp. 3–4), Arthur spent eight years living in 'the underworld' before making 'attempts to stop on the downward path.' His first attempt came in 1916, when he enlisted in the AIF. Working backwards, that places the beginning of his eight years in 'the underworld' at 1908. Before that he had spent three years in Sydney in the employ of the city council, bringing us back to 1905.
2 As to William and Laura's address in 1905, see the arrest warrant for William issued on 10 Oct. 1906 in *NSWPG*, 10 Oct. 1906, p. 346.

3 L. Thompson, *Crooked Made Straight*, p. 3.
4 Quoted in C. Keating, *Surry Hills: The City's Backyard*, illustrated edn, Halstead Press, Sydney, 2008, p. 74.
5 Ibid., p. 78.
6 Ibid. Keating drew upon observations from a 1902 Sydney Municipal Council survey.
7 Marriage transcription from NSW Registry of Births, Deaths and Marriages, reg. no. 07526 – marriage of John Joseph Harmon and Minnie Stace on 3 Nov. 1903.[†]
8 The Unitarian Church was known for its liberal attitudes to theology and morality.
9 Marriage transcription from NSW Registry of Births, Deaths and Marriages, reg. no. 07526.
10 L. Thompson, *Crooked Made Straight*, pp. 2, 3.
11 Ibid, p. 4. As to the unemployment rate in 1905 – about 4% and falling – see the chart headed 'Australia's unemployment rate, 1901–2001' at https://archive.treasury.gov.au/documents/110/PDF/round3.pdf.
12 L. Thompson, *Crooked Made Straight*, pp. 3–4.
13 On Minnie's marriage certificate (1903), the occupation of her father was recorded as 'sculptor'. By the time William entered the care of the Parramatta Asylum in 1908, he was describing himself as a 'chainman'. But Sam remembered his father's occupation as 'tea agent' (see Sam's death certificate).
14 *NSWPG*, 10 Oct. 1906, p. 346.
15 Birth certificate of Eileen Stace, NSW reg. no. 43917/1911. Eileen was born at the Royal Women's Hospital, Paddington on 28 Sep. 1911.
16 L. Thompson, *Crooked Made Straight*, p. 2. The reference was to 'both sisters' running houses of ill-fame: presumably Arthur meant his full-blood sisters, Minnie and Dora. In any event, it seems clear that Clara, his half-sister, never resorted to prostitution. She was a full-time wife to John Go-Hing and a good mother to her two children.
17 *NSW Hospital Asylum Records 1840–1913*, entry for William Woods (sic.) Stace, Jun.–Sep. 1908.[†]
18 NSW Death Registration Transcription, ref. no. 1908/14972 – death of William Wood Stace on 24 Nov. 1908.[†]
19 *NSW Hospital Asylum Records 1840–1913*, entry for William Woods (sic.) Stace, Jun.–Sep. 1908.
20 See NSW Death Registration Transcription, ref. no. 1908/14972 – death of William Wood Stace on 24 Nov. 1908.
21 *Evening Star* (Sydney), 25 May 1909, p. 1.
22 L. Thompson, *Crooked Made Straight*, p. 4.
23 Ibid.
24 Typewritten document entitled 'Our Friend – Arthur Stace – Sydney's Mr. Eternity' prepared in 1969 by May Thompson at or around the time of his burial service.[†]
25 Marriage certificate of Samuel Seaward Stace and Edith Ann Geary, NSW reg. no. 3073/1909.
26 *South Coast Times and Wollongong Argus* (NSW), 12 Jun. 1909, p. 11

27 *SSSD*, 1910, p. 474. Minnie was listed as 'Mrs Minnie Harmon' of 61 Cambridge Street, Newtown. If she and Harmon had still been living together, the entry would have been under his name.
28 *SMH*, 26 Oct. 1910, p. 6.
29 M. Thompson, 'Our Friend'.
30 *SMH*, 25 Nov. 1909, p. 6.
31 Ibid.
32 Death certificate of John Lewis, NSW reg. no. 4332/1910.
33 England and Wales National Probate Calendar (Index of Wills and Administrations), 1858–1966, entry for William Wood Stace, 11 Feb. 1911.†
34 Death certificate of Laura Stace, NSW reg. no. 1912/4322.
35 Marriage certificate of John Go-Hing and Clara Lewis, NSW reg. no. 4464/1912.
36 *SMH*, 15 May 1912, p. 17.
37 *SMH*, 13 May 1913, p. 8.
38 In the electoral roll of 1913, an 'Arthur Stace' was listed as living at 87 Bathurst Street in the CBD. He had given his occupation as 'bricklayer'. It is not entirely clear that this was our Arthur Stace – there were one or two others alive in the same period.

5. He that doeth

1 See generally B.W. Butcher, *Darwinism and Australia 1836–1914*, PhD thesis, Department of History and Philosophy, University of Melbourne, 1992, https://minerva-access.unimelb.edu.au/bitstream/handle/11343/36461/273463_Butcher%20B%20W%20%281%29.pdf?sequence=1.
2 Reid was Premier of NSW, 1894–99.
3 McGowen was the Leader of the parliamentary Labor Party in NSW, 1894–1910; premier of NSW, 1910–13. In the period 1900–08, McGowen also served on the State Children's Relief Board.
4 See R. Williams, *In God They Trust? The Religious Beliefs of Australia's Prime Ministers, 1901–2013*, Bible Society Australia, Sydney, 2013.
5 S. Garton, 'Health and welfare', 2008, http://dictionaryofsydney.org/entry/health_and_welfare.
6 Basic biographical details on Hammond are drawn (unless otherwise indicated) from J. Mansfield, 'Hammond, Robert Brodribb (1870–1946)', *ADB*, http://adb.anu.edu.au/biography/hammond-robert-brodribb-6543/text11243, viewed 20 Apr. 2017.
7 *SMH*, 15 Mar. 1890, p. 11. For Drummond's influence on Hammond, see B.G. Judd, *He That Doeth: The Life Story of Archdeacon R.B.S. Hammond, O.B.E.*, Marshall, Morgan & Scott, Ltd, London, 1951, pp. 17–9.
8 See E.C. Millard (ed.), *The Same Lord: An Account of the Mission Tour of the Rev. George C. Grubb, M.A. in Australia, Tasmania, and New Zealand from April 3rd, 1891, to July 7th, 1892*, Marlborough, London, 1893.
9 S. Judd, 'Hammond, Robert Brodribb Stewart (1870–1946)', *Australian Dictionary of Evangelical Biography*, 2004, http://webjournals.ac.edu.au/ojs/index.php/ADEB/article/view/1112/1109.

10 Judd, *He That Doeth*, p. 22.
11 Ibid, p. 51.
12 See D.W.A. Baker, 'Archdall, Mervyn (1846–1917)', *ADB*, http://adb.anu.edu.au/biography/archdall-mervyn-5044/text8401, viewed 1 Aug. 2017.
13 B. Nairn, 'McGowen, James Sinclair (1855–1922)', *ADB*, http://adb.anu.edu.au/biography/mcgowen-james-sinclair-7360/text12785, viewed 20 Apr. 2017.
14 Keating, *Surry Hills*, pp. 80–1.
15 See R. Fitzgerald & T. Jordan, *Under the Influence: A History of Alcohol in Australia*, ABC Books, Sydney, 2009, pp. 160–65.
16 Judd, *He That Doeth*, p. 41.
17 O.A. Piggott, quoted in Judd, *He That Doeth*, p. 148.
18 Judd, *He That Doeth*, p. 41.
19 Ibid.
20 S. Judd, 'Hammond, Robert Brodribb Stewart'.
21 M. Lake, *Faith in Action: HammondCare*, UNSW Press, Sydney, 2013, p. 16.
22 See J.D. Bollen, 'The temperance movement and the Liberal Party in New South Wales politics, 1900–1904', *Journal of Religious History*, vol. 1, 1961, pp. 160–82.
23 For the results of the local option polls in 1907, 1910 and 1913, see *Official Yearbook of the Commonwealth of Australia*, 1922, p. 1028.
24 Ibid. See also Judd, *He That Doeth*, p. 149.
25 *Official Yearbook of the Commonwealth of Australia*, 1922, p. 1028. In 1910 only 14 of 90 electorates voted for prohibition/reduction, and in 1913 only 15 of 90 did so. In both years, there was a clear absolute majority across NSW for continuation of the status quo. The powerful liquor interests had won.
26 Judd, *He That Doeth*, p. 60.
27 Ibid, pp. 34–5.
28 Ibid, p. 63 ('he gloried in it').
29 Quoted in Judd, *He That Doeth*, p. 62.
30 Lake, *Faith in Action*, p. 20.
31 Judd, *He That Doeth*, p. 58.
32 St Simon's and St Jude's stood on the corner of East and Campbell Streets, Surry Hills; the building was resumed and demolished in 1923 as part of the Sydney Municipal Council's ongoing slum clearance program. St David's in Arthur Street still stands, but it is no longer used as a church.
33 Judd, *He That Doeth*, p. 48.

6. The lot is cast into the lap

1 R. White, 'Motives for joining up: self-sacrifice, self-interest and social class, 1914–18', *Journal of the Australian War Memorial*, Oct. 1986, pp. 4, 14.
2 Speech by Cook at Horsham, Victoria, on 1 Aug. 1914. Quoted in 'World War I: How Australia reacted to the outbreak of conflict', ABC News, 4 Aug. 2014, http://www.abc.net.au/news/2014-08-04/world-war-i-australian-reaction-to-outbreak-of-conflict/5603588.

3 Labor won the election on 5 Sep. 1914, and Fisher became prime minister for the third and final time.
4 Cf. M. McKernan, *Australian Churches at War: Attitudes and Activities of the Major Churches 1914–1918*, Catholic Theological Faculty and Australian War Memorial, Sydney, 1980, p. 29. According to McKernan, this was 'an almost universal belief.' He overstated the position.
5 Ibid, p. 26.
6 *SMH*, 10 Aug. 1914, p. 7.
7 J. Beaumont, *Broken Nation: Australians in the Great War*, Allen & Unwin, Crows Nest NSW, 2013, p. 21.
8 *SSSD*, 1914, p. 1625 (Arthur listed at 237 Commonwealth Street); *SSSD*, 1915, p. 38 (Dora listed at 237 Commonwealth Street).
9 In 1914, the minimum height requirement was 5 feet 6 inches. See https://www.awm.gov.au/encyclopedia/enlistment/.
10 See J. Kershaw & B. Thornton (eds.), *Born to be a Soldier: War Diary of Lieutenant John G. Ridley MC*, Baptist Historical Society of NSW, Sydney, 2010, p. 73.
11 H.E. Evans, *Soldier and Evangelist: The Story of Rev. John G. Ridley, M.C.*, Baptist Historical Society of NSW, Sydney, 1980, pp. 9–11.
12 Undated letter from Ruth Ridley to E. Meyers.†
13 Kershaw & Thornton, *Born to be a Soldier*, p. 73.
14 *SMH*, 15 Apr. 1887, p. 5.
15 J. Starr, 'A Brief History of the Building of the Baptist Tabernacle, Burton St. Darlinghurst', in the Order of Service for the 119th Church Anniversary Service, 23 Jun. 1991 †; Colin Scott, 'Continuing Baptist witness in Woolloomooloo: a history of the Burton Street Baptist Tabernacle', *Baptist Recorder*, no. 4 (Oct. 2003), p. 12.
16 J.G. Ridley, *Milestones of Mercy*, Christian Press, Sydney, 1957, pp. 20, 24–5.
17 J.G. Ridley, *William Lamb: Preacher and Prophet*, Australian Baptist Publishing House, Sydney, 1944, p. 39.
18 See M. Petras, 'The life and times of the Reverend William Lamb (1868–1944)', *Baptist Recorder*, no. 101, May 2008, http://www.baptisthistory.org.au/journals/tbr/tbr101_may2008.
19 See W.A. Elwell (ed.), *The Concise Evangelical Dictionary of Theology*, Baker Book House Co., Grand Rapids MI, 1991, p. 313. The key Scripture is Revelation 20:1–10.
20 Ridley, *William Lamb*, p. 17.
21 Quoted in Evans, *Soldier and Evangelist*, p. 12.
22 Evans, *Soldier and Evangelist*, p. 12.
23 Kershaw & Thornton, *Born to be a Soldier*, p. 73.
24 See Ridley, *Milestones of Mercy*, p. 32.
25 Kershaw & Thornton, *Born to be a Soldier*, pp. x, 1.
26 Ibid, pp. 1–16, esp. at p. 8. See also, re Ridley's first ever 'sermon', Evans, *Soldier and Evangelist*, p. 19.
27 Kershaw & Thornton, *Born to be a Soldier*, p. 14.
28 Ibid, p. vii. The 53rd Battalion became part of the 14th Brigade of the 5th Australian Division.

29 Evans, *Soldier and Evangelist*, p. 19.
30 *Daily Telegraph* (Sydney), 22 Dec. 1915.
31 White, 'Motives for Joining Up' (see note 1 above).
32 See https://www.awm.gov.au/encyclopedia/enlistment.
33 Beaumont, *Broken Nation*, p. 23.
34 For details of Storey's war record, see https://www.aif.adfa.edu.au/showPerson?pid=290113.
35 Details are taken from Arthur's AIF service records held in the National Archives of Australia: Barcode 8091454 (35 pages), Series B2455. Although Storey completed the paperwork relating to Arthur on 18 Mar. 1916, it is certain from the column in the *Evening Star* of 17 Mar. 1916 that Arthur had enlisted on the previous day.
36 *Evening Star* (Sydney), 17 Mar. 1916, p. 4.
37 L. Murray, 'Soldier's riot of 1916', *Dictionary of Sydney*, 10 Feb. 2016, at http://home.dictionaryofsydney.org/soldiers-riot-of-1916/.
38 L. Murray, 'The liquor referendum and the six o'clock swill', *Dictionary of Sydney*, 18 May 2016, at http://home.dictionaryofsydney.org/the-liquor-referendum-and-the-six-oclock-swill/.
39 Ibid. Out of 579,106 votes cast, 347,049 (60 per cent) were in support of 6 o'clock closing. Only 178,842 voted for 9pm. Small numbers of votes were cast for other options. On Hammond's role in the 1916 campaign, see Judd, *He That Doeth*, pp. 140–1.
40 Kershaw & Thornton, *Born to be a Soldier*, p. vii.

7. The furnace of affliction

1 Quoted in Kelshaw & Thornton, *Born to be a Soldier*, p. 48.
2 Beaumont, *Broken Nation*, p. 186ff.
3 Ibid, p. 190.
4 Ridley, *Milestones of Mercy*, p. 38.
5 Kelshaw & Thornton, *Born to be a Soldier*, p. 49.
6 Evans, *Soldier and Evangelist*, p. 17.
7 Kelshaw & Thornton, *Born to be a Soldier*, p. 59.
8 Ibid, pp. 60–70
9 Ibid, pp. 72–83.
10 See the discussion on the Australian War Memorial website at https://www.awm.gov.au/encyclopedia/fromelles/.
11 Ibid.
12 Kelshaw & Thornton, *Born to be a Soldier*, p. 70.
13 Ibid.
14 Ibid, p. 97.
15 Ibid, p. 77
16 AIF service records of Arthur Stace.
17 P. Martin, 'A word in time from Mr Eternity', *The Herald* (Melbourne), 13 Jul. 1963 (quoting Arthur: 'When the First World War broke out I enlisted as a side drummer in the 19th Battalion's band').

18 Tony Sillcock, quoted in G. Hoskin & T. Joy, 'Bandsmen and stretcher-bearers: Why were bandsmen also stretcher-bearers?', Military History and Heritage Victoria Inc., 2012, article available online at http://www.mhhv.org.au/?p=811.
19 See the discussion on the Australian War Memorial website at https://www.awm.gov.au/unit/U51459/.
20 Martin, 'A Word in Time from Mr Eternity' (quoting Arthur: 'But in France I became a stretcher-bearer').
21 Set out in the discussion on the Australian War Memorial website at https://www.awm.gov.au/exhibitions/1918/medical/.
22 J.G. Ridley, *The Passing of Mr Eternity*, n.p., Sydney, 1967, p. 3.
23 From an oral account by Arthur Stace of his war service during a street mission in 1951, quoted in an unpublished article titled 'Meet Mr Eternity' written for *Reader's Digest* in 1957 by Lisle Thompson.†
24 AIF service records of Arthur Stace.
25 Letter dated 17 May 1917 from the AIF to Mrs Minnie Harmon.†
26 Years later, Arthur told a close friend at Burton Street Baptist Tabernacle, John Starr, that he did not like writing letters. In an undated letter to E. Meyers, Starr wrote: 'he was not comfortable writing, seeming embarrassed by his variable letting and odd spelling mistakes and he avoided it where he could, though it was quite legible.'
27 Official citation for the award of Ridley's Military Cross, quoted in Kelshaw & Thornton, *Born to be a Soldier*, p. 117.
28 Ridley, *Milestones of Mercy*, p. 91.
29 J.J. Kennedy, quoted in Evans, *Soldier and Evangelist*, p. 16. The tribute is all the more impressive for the fact that Kennedy was a Roman Catholic during an era of bitterly fierce Protestant-Catholic sectarianism.
30 Kelshaw & Thornton, *Born to be a Soldier*, pp. 127–8, 132.
31 Ibid., p. 116.
32 Matthew 18:20: 'For where two or three are gathered together in my name, there am I in the midst of them'; Romans 8:35, 37: 'Who shall separate us from the love of Christ? shall tribulation, or distress, or persecution, or famine, or nakedness, or peril, or sword? ... Nay, in all these things we are more than conquerors through him that loved us'.
33 Kelshaw & Thornton, *Born to be a Soldier*, pp 118–27, esp. p. 125 (re Péronne). See also Evans, *Soldier and Evangelist*, pp. 22, 70–8.
34 Evans, *Soldier and Evangelist*, p. 24. See also Ridley, *Milestones of Mercy*, pp. 62–3.
35 'The World War I Diary of Percy Smythe', 2016, http://www.smythe.id.au/diary/ch8.htm (entry for 9 Jan. 1917).
36 See the discussion in 'Following the Twenty-second: the First World War through the eyes of an Australian Infantry Battalion', n.d., https://anzac-22nd-battalion.com/training-camps-england/.
37 Ibid.
38 AIF service records of Arthur Stace.
39 *SMH*, 17 Feb. 1919, p. 6.
40 AIF service records of Arthur Stace.

41 Ibid. See also L. Thompson, ‘Meet Mr Eternity’.

8. Lost in the wilderness

1 R. Ward, *Australia Since the Coming of Man*, Lansdowne Press, Sydney, 1982, p. 185.
2 G. Souter, *Lion and Kangaroo, Australia: 1901–1919, The Rise of a Nation*, Fontana Books, Sydney, 1978, p. 290.
3 Lake, *Faith in Action*, pp. 30–1.
4 L. Thompson, *Crooked Made Straight*, p. 4.
5 *Sunday Telegraph* (Sydney), 24 Jun. 1956, p. 3.
6 On 25 Aug. 1927, Arthur’s address was 379 Riley Street, Surry Hills – see his letter to the AIF quoted in the text and referenced in note 10 below.
7 Letter dated 23 May 2011 from Denis Padgett to E. Meyers, recounting Arthur’s testimony to Padgett about his early life.[†]
8 Memorandum dated 13 Sep. 2002 by E. Summergreene (a fellow parishioner of Arthur and Pearl Stace at Burton Street Tabernacle in the period 1942–53).[†]
9 L. Thompson, ‘Meet Mr Eternity’, p. 2.
10 AIF service records of Arthur Stace. This letter, and others written by Arthur that are quoted in this book, disprove the myth of his ‘illiteracy’.
11 *SMH*, 27 Oct. 1927, p. 5 (funeral notice of John Harmon).
12 The wedding took place at St David’s, Surry Hills – formerly the church of R.B.S. Hammond. Arthur was one of the two witnesses on Minnie and Campbell’s marriage certificate.
13 Marriage transcription from NSW Registry of Births, Deaths and Marriages, marriage of Alexander Stewart and Minnie Harmon, 30 May 1925, reg. no. 04961.
14 Clara Go-Hing together with her husband John Go-Hing and their daughter Ethel Edith Go-Hing departed Sydney for China in early Nov. 1915 on the SS *St Albans*, returning on 16 Jun. 1920 on the SS *Eastern*. See http://recordsearch.naa.gov.au/scripts/Imagine.asp?B=1569491&I=1&SE=1.
15 *South Coast Times and Wollongong* Argus, 7 Jan. 1921, p. 11; *Illawarra Mercury* (Wollongong), 3 Mar. 1922, p. 2; *South Coast Times and Wollongong* Argus, 29 Aug. 1924, p. 5; *Illawarra Mercury* (Wollongong), 29 Jul. 1928, p. 12. It is fair to point out that Sam and Edith lost their ten-year-old son Raymond in 1921 to a sudden illness.
16 Samuel Stace enlisted in the AIF in Sydney on 29 Jun. 1918.
17 L. Thompson, *Crooked Made Straight*, p. 3.
18 Ibid.
19 Letter dated 23 May 2011 from Denis Padgett to E. Meyers.
20 Evans, *Soldier and Evangelist*, p. 25; cf. Ridley, *Milestones of Mercy*, p. 100.
21 J.G. Ridley, *William Lamb: Preacher and Prophet*, Australian Baptist Publishing House, Sydney, 1944, p. 108.
22 W. Lamb, *The Advent Herald*, 15 Jan. 1920, quoted in Ridley, *William Lamb*, p. 102.
23 Ridley, *Milestones of Mercy*, pp. 102–3, 122–3. See also *SMH*, 22 Oct. 1932, p. 14 (report of the death of John Complin).
24 Evans, *Soldier and Evangelist*, p. 25.

25 Ibid. See also *SMH*, 29 May 1920, p. 20; 31 Jul. 1920, p. 11; 2 Apr. 1921, p. 10; 7 May 1921, p. 4 (advertisements for Ridley's preaching at Maroubra Baptist).
26 Evans, *Soldier and Evangelist*, p. 25.
27 *SMH*, 11 Mar. 1921, p. 8 (report of the death of Thomas Ridley).
28 Ridley, *Milestones of Mercy*, p. 107.
29 Ibid, p. 108. See also Evans, *Soldier and Evangelist*, p. 25.
30 Ridley, *Milestones of Mercy*, pp. 108–9; Evans, *Soldier and Evangelist*, p. 26.
31 Evans, *Soldier and Evangelist*, p. 28.
32 Italics added.
33 Ridley, *Milestones of Mercy*, pp. 125–6.
34 Evans, *Soldier and Evangelist*, pp. 28–9.
35 Undated letter from Ruth Ridley to E. Meyers.†
36 Ibid.
37 R. Teale, 'Chapman, Henry George (1879–1934)', *ADB*, http://adb.anu.edu.au/biography/chapman-henry-george-5557/text9475, viewed 2 May 2017. See also article entitled 'Professor Chapman – Gifts to Secretary – Long Friendship', *The Scone Advocate* (NSW), 20 Jul. 1934, p. 3.
38 Teale, 'Chapman, Henry George'. See also *SMH*, 24 Sep. 1919, p. 10.
39 Evans, *Soldier and Evangelist*, p. 29.
40 For example, during Ridley's 'Echoes of Eternity' sermon of 1 Feb. 1970. See Chapter 19.
41 Evans, *Soldier and Evangelist*, pp. 31–3. For example, in early Mar. 1928, Ridley was the principal speaker at a special mission service in Lithgow (*Lithgow Mercury*, 2 Mar. 1928, p. 4).
42 *Evening News* (Sydney), 25 May 1929, p. 3.
43 Judd, *He That Doeth*, pp. 69, 197).
44 See the 'Who We Are' section of the St Barnabas', Broadway ('Barneys') website at https://www.barneys.org.au/who-we-are/our-story/.
45 See Mansfield, 'Hammond, Robert Brodribb (1870–1946)'.
46 Judd, *He That Doeth*, pp. 68–9, 192–3.
47 Ibid, p. 69.
48 Ibid, p. 72.
49 See Lake, *Faith in Action*, p. 40.
50 Judd, *He That Doeth*, pp. 134–35.
51 *SMH*, 11 Jan. 1928, p. 19.
52 The question posed to the voters of NSW on 1 Sep. 1928 was: 'Are you in favour of Prohibition with Compensation? (Liquor (Amendment) Act 1919).' There were 357,684 votes for 'Yes' and 896,752 for 'No'.
53 Quoted in Judd, *He That Doeth*, p. 136.
54 Lake, *Faith in Action*, p. 39.
55 S. Judd, 'Hammond, Robert Brodribb Stewart (1870–1946)'.

9. From darkness to light

1 J.H. (Jim) Scullin (1876–1953) was arguably the most devout Christian ever to occupy the prime ministerial office in Australia. See Williams, *In God They Trust?*
2 See generally B. Nairn, *The 'Big Fella': Jack Lang and the Australian Labor Party 1891–1949*, Melbourne University Press, Melbourne, 1986; W. Denning, *Caucus Crisis: The Rise and Fall of the Scullin Government*, Hale & Ironmonger, Sydney, 1982.
3 *SMH*, 18 Jan. 1930, p. 3.
4 Electoral roll, 1930.
5 In Tom Farrell's account of Arthur's conversion story ('The Man That Sydney Wondered About', *Sunday Telegraph*, 24 Jun. 1956, p. 5), three key incidents – Arthur's appearance before the magistrate who spoke of 'power', Arthur's request at Regent Street police station to be locked up, and Arthur's attendance at Hammond's Wednesday night men's meeting at St Barnabas' – are related *consecutively*, as if they all occurred on the same day (6 Aug. 1930). It is quite possible that things happened that way. Elizabeth Meyers firmly believes that they did. But the historical record is unclear. In Judd's account at p. 82 of *He That Doeth*, the appearance before the magistrate is not mentioned, and the temporal link between Arthur's request to be locked up and his subsequent attendance at St Barnabas' is vague ('I went back to the park, and then I heard'). In Thompson's *Crooked Made Straight*, there is no mention of the request to be locked up, and the appearance before the magistrate is described as a stand-alone incident. In Ridley's *Passing of Mr Eternity*, there is no mention of the appearance before the magistrate, and the request to be locked up is related as a stand-alone incident. In the authors' view, all the incidents undoubtedly occurred. The most likely order of events, in Roy Williams' view, is as related in the text.
6 L. Thompson, *Crooked Made Straight*, p. 4.
7 See P. Reynolds, 'Broughton Hall Psychiatric Clinic', *Dictionary of Sydney*, 2008, http://dictionaryofsydney.org/organisation/broughton_hall_psychiatric_clinic.
8 See Chapter 4.
9 L. Thompson, *Crooked Made Straight*, p. 2.
10 Farrell, 'The Man That Sydney Wondered About', p. 5.
11 L. Thompson, *Crooked Made Straight*, p. 2.
12 Farrell, 'The Man That Sydney Wondered About'. For a slightly different version of this episode, see Judd, *He That Doeth*, p. 82. Arthur told Judd in or before 1951: 'My system was ... poisoned with methylated spirits [and] I was so miserable I just wanted to forget about existing. But the sergeant told me to "clear out".'
13 Ridley, *Passing of Mr Eternity*, p. 4.
14 Lalor, *The Bridge*, pp. 12–27.
15 See note 5 above.
16 Quoted in Farrell, 'The Man That Sydney Wondered About', p. 5.
17 Judd, *He That Doeth*, p. 92.
18 The text of one of Hammond's typical addresses at a Wednesday night men's meeting is set out in *He That Doeth*, pp. 107–11. In this one, delivered in 1933, Hammond

took it as a given that many in his audience were 'doing it tough.' He urged them not to complain, or to wish for worldly things, but to 'learn to trust in Him.'

19 Memorandum dated 13 Sep. 2002 by E. Summergreene.†
20 Judd, *He That Doeth*, p. 82.
21 L. Thompson, *Crooked Made Straight*, p. 5. See also Judd, *He That Doeth*, pp. 82–83.
22 Given that Arthur was previously unschooled in the gospel, it seems most unlikely that he would have known to use this phrase otherwise.
23 Letter dated 23 May 2002 from Denis Padgett to E. Meyers.†
24 L. Thompson, *Crooked Made Straight*, p. 6.
25 Ibid.
26 Ibid.
27 Ibid. See also Judd, *He That Doeth*, p. 83.
28 L. Thompson, *Crooked Made Straight*, pp. 6–7.
29 Judd, *He That Doeth*, p. 63.
30 Letter dated 23 May 2002 from Denis Padgett to E. Meyers.†
31 Ibid.
32 Farrell, 'The Man That Sydney Wondered About'. As to the Maroubra sand hills work, see C. Ford, *Sydney Beaches: A History*, NewSouth, Sydney, 2014, p. 125ff.
33 Lake, *Faith in Action*, pp. 59–60 (Game), 61–2, 64, 115 (Walder).
34 *SMH*, 26 Nov. 1930, p. 14
35 *SMH*, 16 May 1931, p. 14. For three years the Hammond Hotel No. 2 in Buckland Street operated in tandem with another men's shelter in Buckland Street run by the Salvation Army.
36 *SMH*, 4 Jun. 1931, p. 10
37 *Maryborough Chronicle, Wide Bay and Burnett Advertiser*, 2 Jun. 1932, p. 8; Judd, *He That Doeth*, p. 161.
38 See generally Lake, *Faith in Action*.
39 *The Sun* (Sydney), 15 Apr. 1932, p. 12.
40 According to the 1933 electoral roll, William John Stace was living at 23 Abercrombie Street, Philip (now Chippendale).
41 *The Sun* (Sydney), 15 Apr. 1932, p. 12.

10. Echoes of Eternity

1 Evans, *Soldier and Evangelist*, pp. 47–48.
2 Scott, 'Burton Street Baptist Tabernacle', p. 8.
3 *Australian Baptist*, 1 and 8 Nov. 1932.
4 *SMH*, 5 Nov. 1932, p. 19
5 *SMH*, 12 Nov. 1932, p. 7.
6 The opening Test of that immortal 'Bodyline' series of 1932–33 was played at the Sydney Cricket Ground – just a short walk from the Burton Street Tabernacle.
7 Ridley, *Passing of Mr Eternity*, p. 8. See also Farrell, 'The Man That Sydney Wondered About'.
8 Ibid.

9 The authors have in their possession a copy of an eight-page typewritten document headed 'Echoes of Eternity.' The text of the typewritten document differs significantly from the text of the 'Echoes of Eternity' sermon as re-delivered by Ridley in Feb. 1970 at Burton Street Baptist Tabernacle (and tape recorded). Among other things, the typewritten document contains references to imperial currency. In the authors' view, the typewritten document is clearly a record of the original 1932 sermon, presumably utilising Ridley's original handwritten notes. Peter Rahme, a Sydney Baptist pastor, acquired a copy of it in the late 1990s from Ridley's daughter, Ruth.
10 In accordance with the custom of the day, Ridley was using the King James Version of the Bible. In some modern translations of Isaiah 57:15, the word 'eternity' does not appear: in the NIV, the relevant phrase is translated as 'he who lives forever.'
11 Ridley, *Passing of Mr Eternity*, p. 8.
12 Ibid., pp. 14–15.
13 Quoted in Ridley, *Passing of Mr Eternity*, p. 8. See also 'An End to Eternity', *Sunday Telegraph* (Sydney), 12 Jun. 1965, p 14.
14 The myth of Arthur's near-illiteracy is traceable to a statement attributed to him in Jun. 1965 by a reporter from Sydney's *Sunday Telegraph* (and re-quoted by Ridley in his 1967 *Passing of Mr Eternity*). Arthur was quoted: 'The funny thing is that before I wrote it ['Eternity' on 14 Nov. 1932] I could hardly write my own name. I had no schooling and I couldn't have spelled 'eternity' for a hundred quid.' Assuming he was accurately quoted, we must forgive Arthur some poetic license. As we saw earlier, he received some schooling as a boy and could write basic letters, albeit in a stilted style. He was a very old man in Jun. 1965, and had recently been admitted to the Hammondville nursing home.
15 Undated letter from J. Starr to E. Meyers.† According to Starr, 'all his other writing never came close' to the consistent beauty of *Eternity*.
16 Farrell, 'The Man That Sydney Wondered About'.
17 Until the mid-1950s, Arthur often had other daytime work commitments. Presumably during these periods he was required to arrive at work by 9am or thereabouts, which would have limited his *Eternity* hours.
18 Farrell, 'The Man That Sydney Wondered About'.
19 'An End to Eternity', *Daily Telegraph* (Sydney), 12 Jun. 1965, p. 14 ('I've been writing it at least fifty times a day ever since [14 Nov. 1932]').
20 Typewritten document entitled 'Mr Eternity' prepared in early 1968 by May Thompson.†
21 *Australian Baptist*, 29 Nov. 1932, p. 10.

11. Rivers in the desert

1 Electoral roll, 1933.
2 Judd, *He That Doeth*, pp. 24–25.
3 *SMH*, 21 Oct. 1933, p. 21.
4 The first edition of *Crooked Made Straight* (1955), contained this statement: 'Realising that he must go out into the open air to reach men, Arthur Stace led an open-air

meeting on the corner of George and Bathurst Streets, Sydney, for 24 years.' Based on available information, it seems unlikely that Arthur began to *lead* weekly open-air meetings in the CBD as early as 1931 (i.e. 24 years before 1955). However, it is perfectly possible that he began dabbling in open-air missioning in 1931, with the help and encouragement of men such as R.B.S. Hammond and Cairo Bradley.

5 C.J. Pittendrigh, 'Bradley, William 'Cairo' (1870–1945)', *Australian Dictionary of Evangelical Biography*, http://webjournals.ac.edu.au/ojs/index.php/ADEB/article/view/1364/1361.

6 *SMH*, 3 Jun. 1939, p. 17 (the Hammond Hotel at the former Danks & Son premises in Buckland Street had then been operating for 'four and a half years'). See also *Maitland Daily Mercury* (NSW), 21 Jun. 1934, p. 6 (the Salvation Army was still then running the Buckland Street hostel).

7 See Judd, *He That Doeth*, pp. 155–9. Judd's main source was an eight-page pamphlet compiled by G.M. Dash, *The Hotel Hammond (For Single Unemployed Men), Buckland Street, City: Sydney's Largest Hotel*, c. 1939.

8 R.B.S. Hammond, 'Amazing helpfulness', in Dash, *Hotel Hammond*, p. 4 ('Nearly two years ago my friends made it possible to start an "Emergency Depot". Arthur Stace is in charge'). See also L. Thompson, *Crooked Made Straight*, p. 7; Judd, *He That Doeth*, p. 161; Lake, *Faith in Action*, p. 4.

9 Judd, *He That Doeth*, p. 161.

10 Lake, *Faith in Action*, p. 4. See also Judd, *He That Doeth*, p. 161.

11 Lake, *Faith in Action*, pp. 2–3.

12 'The Hotel Hammond: very unlike the common idea of charity', in Dash, *Hotel Hammond*, pp. 3, 7. Quoted in Judd, *He That Doeth*, p. 159.

13 Ibid, p. 7.

14 *Sun* (Sydney) 29 Dec. 1935, p. 12; *Westralian Worker* (Perth), 10 Jan. 1936, p. 3.

15 In Arthur's letter to the AIF of Oct. 1935, he gave his address as 419 Liverpool Street (see note 19 below), further proof that his work in the Emergency Depot at Buckland Street started later, in 1937.

16 'The Hotel Hammond: very unlike the common idea of charity', in Dash, *Hotel Hammond*, p. 3. Quoted in Judd, *He That Doeth*, p. 157. See also a note about Arthur dictated by C.K. Hemmingway in or about 1978.† Hemmingway recalled Arthur telling him that he had studied the properties of coal at a municipal library.

17 Document dated Jan. 2000 written by Bruce Leghorn entitled 'My Recollections of a Remarkable Man – Mr Arthur Stace – "Mr Eternity"'.†

18 Undated letter from Arthur to the AIF, received at the AIF on 11 Oct. 1935 (Arthur's AIF service records).

19 Statutory declaration of Arthur Stace sworn 14 Oct. 1935 (Arthur's AIF service records).

20 L. Thompson, *Crooked Made Straight*, p. 7. Note about Arthur dictated by C.K. Hemmingway in or about 1978.†

21 *Courier Mail* (Brisbane), 26 Nov. 1935, p. 17. See generally re the Francis Street hostel: https://www.findandconnect.gov.au/ref/nsw/biogs/NE00283b.htm.

22 L. Thompson, *Crooked Made Straight*, p. 7; Ridley, *Passing of Mr Eternity*, p. 7.

23 M. Hoctor, 'Heritage: the early history of leprosy', *Illawarra Mercury*, 8 Sep. 2013, http://www.illawarramercury.com.au/story/1758917/heritage-the-early-history-of-leprosy/.
24 B. Burgess, 'A look at life at Little Bay in the 30s and 50s', Prince Henry Community, 2017, http://www.princehenrycommunity.com.au/the-neighbourhood/special-interest-groups/ward-24-the-non-club-for-non-members-who-like-to-swim/a-look-at-life-in-little-bay-in-the-30s-and-50s/.
25 L. Thompson, *Crooked Made Straight*, p. 7.
26 Ibid, p. 2.
27 Samuel Seaward Stace remained living on the NSW south coast until his death in 1949. Sam's daughter Edna, Arthur's niece, had moved to Sydney by 1936 but the extent of her contact with Arthur is unknown. Edna married Alfred McKay in 1952 and died in the year 2000 – making her the closest blood descendent of Arthur to see *Eternity* lit up on the Sydney Harbour Bridge.
28 In 1936 Minnie was living at 36 Botany Road, Alexandria (death certificate). In 1933 William was living at 23 Abercrombie Street, Chippendale (electoral roll) and by 1937 at 29 Bulwara Road, Pyrmont. In 1933 Dora was living at 67 Macarthur St, Ultimo (electoral roll).
29 Death transcription from NSW Registry of Births, Deaths and Marriages, Minnie Campbell, reg. no. 09522.
30 *SMH*, 20 May 1946, p. 5.
31 Information supplied by J. Starr.
32 *SMH*, 3 Jun. 1939, p. 7; 7 Jun. 1939, p. 17.
33 Ridley, *William Lamb*, pp. 36–7.
34 Scott, 'Burton Street Baptist Tabernacle', p. 9.
35 After undergoing a believer's baptism, the believer would receive an invitation to be placed on the Tabernacle's roll of members. Since Arthur's name first appeared on the roll in 1939, we know he must have undergone baptism in that year.
36 The baptistery was rediscovered during renovation of the Tabernacle in the early twenty-first century. See Steve Dow, 'Curtain up at last – seems like an eternity', *SMH*, 20 Sep. 2013, p. 9.
37 The main proponents of this view – that Arthur did not begin chalking *Eternity* on Sydney footpaths until the 1940s – are descendants of R.M. Leghorn, pastor at Burton Street in the period from May 1942 to Feb. 1953, and a former member of the congregation there, Rex Beaver. They rely on Arthur's comment about 'twenty years' during the Jim Waugh radio interview of 1964 (see following note and the corresponding text in Chapter 17).
38 Interview of A. Stace by Jim Waugh broadcast on Sydney radio station 2GB in 1964. An audio recording is accessible online via a link at http://simplyaustralia.net/article-jkl-eternity.html. For the origin of the recording, see note 23 to Chapter 17.
39 See Chapter 15, and the discussion of Tom Farrell's *Sunday Telegraph* article of 24 Jun. 1956. Italics added.
40 Ridley, *Passing of Mr Eternity*, pp. 8–9.

41 L. Thompson, 'Meet Mr Eternity'. On the day in 1951 that Thompson first discovered Arthur writing *Eternity*, Thompson asked Arthur straight out why – and when – he had started doing it. Arthur explained about the Ridley sermon and said: 'That was just two years after I became a Christian. I have written it ever since.'
42 See also 'An End to Eternity', *Daily Telegraph* (Sydney), 12 Jun. 1965, p. 14 ('I've been writing it at least fifty times a day ever since [i.e. since Ridley's sermon of 14 Nov. 1932], and that's thirty years ago').
43 See *The Australian Women's Weekly*, 25 Mar. 1944, p. 20.
44 Letter dated 25 Aug. 2009 from Ron Barker to E. Meyers, attaching an article written by Mr Barker about Arthur Stace and signed and dated by him.†

12. More precious than rubies

1 Ridley, *Passing of Mr Eternity*, pp. 3, 12.
2 It appears that for many years Ridley was unaware of the effect that his 'Echoes of Eternity' sermon had had on Arthur.
3 Evans, *Soldier and Evangelist*, p. 33.
4 See Ridley, *Milestones of Mercy*, pp. 144, 188, 193. Ridley suffered two other serious nervous breakdowns, in 1934 and 1950. Each one laid him low for about two years.
5 Teale, 'Chapman, Henry George', *ADB*. For accounts of the scandal in contemporary newspapers, see, e.g., *Wagga Wagga Express* (NSW), 23 Jun. 1934, p. 13; *The Scone Advocate* (NSW), 20 Jul. 1934, p. 3.
6 Kelshaw & Thornton, *Born to be a Soldier*, p. 29.
7 Undated letter from Ruth Ridley to E. Meyers.†
8 Undated letter from Stella Hesse (niece of Pearl Stace) to Bronson Symes, received in Aug. 2002.†
9 Arthur and Pearl's meeting occurred in the late 1930s or early 1940s. If it was before Jun. 1939, which seems more probable than not, then the venue was almost certainly the Hammond Hotel in Buckland Street. Many meals were cooked there on site, so Stella Hesse's use of the term 'soup kitchen' would apply well enough.
10 In the 1930 *SSSD* there was a 'Miss E. Dawson, dressmaker' listed as living at 166 Victoria Avenue, Chatswood (pp. 978, 1278) – it is very likely that this was Pearl, before she took the housekeeping job with the doctor and his family. She was a talented seamstress. Notification to the publishers of the 1930 *SSSD* would have been made by Oct. 1929. Thereafter Pearl lived variously at 25 Gordon Road, Roseville (1930 electoral roll), 7 Highfield Road, Lindfield (1931 electoral roll), 60 Treatts Road, Lindfield (1936 electoral roll) and, by Jan. 1942, Wollstonecraft (marriage certificate).
11 Letter from S. Hesse to Bronson Symes.
12 Ibid. Stella Hesse recalled eleven children, but other records indicate that Sophy gave birth to 15 children in all. Thus four died in infancy.
13 Letter dated 25 Jul. 2002 from Dorothy Osborne (niece of Pearl Stace) to Bronson Symes.†

14 A photo survives of Pearl Dawson at the age of about 20. She looks slender and demure. In Johnston's *Eternity*, the former assistant minister at St Barnabas' from 1942, George Rees, recalled a 'a very lovely looking lady ... quite a joy to the eye.'
15 Letter from S. Hesse to Bronson Symes; letter dated 25 Jul. 2002 from Dorothy Osborne to Bronson Symes.
16 Letter from S. Hesse to Bronson Symes read in conjunction with the electoral roll information.
17 See note 10 above.
18 Bruce Leghorn, 'My Recollections of a Remarkable Man'.
19 *Leader* (Orange, NSW), 27 Jul. 1915, p. 3; 7 May 1917, p. 6; 6 Mar. 1918, p. 5.
20 Recollection of Bob McDonald, co-worker of Arthur's at open-air meetings at Paddy's Markets, relayed to John Barwick in a telephone conversation on 13 Mar. 2000. (Attachment to letter dated 1 Aug. 2017 from Barwick to editor of *Eternity* newspaper.)
21 Memorandum dated 13 Sep. 2002 by E. Summergreene. The prayer meetings took place at 4A Bligh Street, Sydney.
22 Cf. L. Thompson, *Crooked Made Straight*, p. 7. If the relevant passage in *Crooked Made Straight* is read literally, Arthur began open-air missioning at the corner of George and Bathurst Streets in 1931. After consideration of all the evidence, a starting date of 1941 – shortly before the arrival of R.M. Leghorn at the Burton Street Tabernacle – seems much more likely. The 1943 electoral roll was the first in which Arthur described his occupation as 'missioner'.
23 Letter dated 28 Aug. 2011 from Denis Padgett (a fellow parishioner of Arthur and Pearl Stace at Burton Street Tabernacle) to E. Meyers.† According to Padgett, the two ladies who most often accompanied Arthur on Saturday evenings were Florence Biggers and Pearl Rash.
24 Leghorn, 'My Recollections of a Remarkable Man'.
25 Ibid.
26 Ibid. See also letter dated 28 Aug. 2011 from Denis Padgett to E. Meyers.
27 Letter dated 25 Jul. 2002 from Dorothy Osborne to Bronson Symes. Cliff Hemingway confirmed that this was the case (see M. Thompson, 'Memorial? for Mr. Arthur Stace – Sydney's Mr. Eternity', prepared in 1969).
28 Letter dated 25 Jul. 2002 from Dorothy Osborne to Bronson Symes.
29 M. Thompson, 'Memorial?'
30 Hammond was appointed Archdeacon of Redfern in 1939.
31 M. Thompson, 'Memorial?' The date of Arthur and Pearl's wedding, 11 Jan. 1942, is recorded in NSW Certificate of Marriage no. 410 of 1942.†
32 M. Thompson, 'Memorial?'
33 Electoral roll, 1943. It is possible that Arthur and Pearl moved straight into the house at 12 Bulwara Road, Pyrmont, immediately after their marriage in late Jan. 1942.
34 Memorandum dated 13 Sep. 2002 by E. Summergreene.
35 Letter dated 25 Jul. 2002 from Dorothy Osborne to Bronson Symes.

13. Growing in faith

1 Bruce Leghorn, 'My Recollections of a Remarkable Man'. See also letter dated 23 May 2011 from Denis Padgett to E. Meyers, p. 3.†
2 Memorandum dated 13 Sep. 2002 by E. Summergreene.
3 *SMH*, 9 May 1942, p. 1.
4 Leghorn, 'My Recollections of a Remarkable Man'.
5 Scott, 'Burton Street Baptist Tabernacle', p. 8. See also Ridley, *William Lamb*, p. 64, describing Leghorn as a 'devoted and dynamic man of God.'
6 Ibid, p. 9. See also Leghorn, 'My Recollections of a Remarkable Man'.
7 Memorandum dated 13 Sep. 2002 by E. Summergreene.
8 Ibid.
9 John Ridley volunteered again, joining the 9th Field Ambulance Unit as a military chaplain. After service in the Middle East, curtailed by ill health, he returned to Australia and ministered to troops in training camps in both NSW and QLD.
10 Scott, 'Burton Street Baptist Tabernacle', p. 8.
11 R. Wilson, *Jenner of George Street: The Story of Frank Jenner, Australia's Soul-winning Sailor*, self-published, Hurstville NSW, 2000, *passim*.
12 Ibid, pp. 37, 73.
13 Ibid, p. 66.
14 Ibid, pp. 37–9.
15 R. Armstrong, *The Wheel Tracks of the Pioneer Preachers: Bob's First Album of Aussie Gospel Waggons*, R.M. & E.L. Armstrong, Mumbil NSW, 1999, pp. 51–3.
16 Leghorn, 'My Recollections of a Remarkable Man'.
17 For example, on Sunday 29 Jul. 1945 at 7pm, Arthur appeared as a speaker at the Paddington branch of the Sydney City Mission (*SMH*, 28 Jul. 1945, p. 16).
18 Judd, *He That Doeth*, p. 207.
19 Ibid, p. 217. Unfortunately, no record survives of what Arthur said at this service.
20 Ibid. See also 'Sydney's Mr Eternity remembered 50 years on', 26 Jul. 2017, http://www.hammond.com.au/news/sydney-s-mr-eternity-remembered-50-years-on (a copy of the register is reproduced).
21 Letter dated 1 Aug. 1967 from Bernard G. Judd to Stewart Mitchell.†
22 Shortly before his death Arthur gave his copy of *The New Testament* to May Thompson. It is now in the possession of E. Meyers.
23 Leghorn, 'My Recollections of a Remarkable Man'.
24 Ibid. See also note by C.K. Hemmingway (note 17, Chapter 11).
25 Memorandum dated 13 Sep. 2002 by E. Summergreene.
26 Letter dated 23 May 2011 from Denis Padgett to E. Meyers.†
27 See Scott, 'Burton Street Baptist Tabernacle', p. 10.
28 Letter dated 23 May 2011 from Denis Padgett to E. Meyers.
29 *Wellington Times* (NSW), 24 Jun. 1948, p. 8.
30 Ibid., 8 Jul. 1948, p. 8.
31 *Goulburn Evening Post* (NSW), 30 Jun. 1950, p. 3.
32 Letter dated 1 Jun. 2009 from Les Nixon to E. Meyers.†

33 Ibid.
34 Email dated 22 Jun. 2010 from Suzanne Grunstein, Australian Red Cross [NSW], to E. Meyers.†
35 Shirley Wood and Helen Livingstone, who had worked with Arthur Stace at the Red Cross' offices in Sydney in the early 1950s and were interviewed on camera in Johnston's *Eternity*, recalled Arthur as 'the essence of politeness ... a very gentle man.'
36 In mid-1950, the Australian Red Cross (NSW Division) purchased Petty's Hotel at 1 York Street, Sydney, for use as its blood transfusion service headquarters and laboratories. This was the building in which Arthur Stace worked for five years.
37 Leghorn, 'My Recollections of a Remarkable Man'.
38 Ashfield: telephone conversation c. 2009 between John M. Smith and E. Meyers. Mosman: conversation on 16 Jul. 2017 between Barry Breeze and R. Williams.
39 Discussion between Joan Reilly and R. Williams on 30 Jul. 2017 at Sydney's St Andrew's Cathedral, on the occasion of a special service to mark the 50th anniversary of Arthur Stace's death.
40 Undated letter from S. Hesse to Bronson Symes received in Aug. 2002.†
41 *Sunday Telegraph* (Sydney), 12 Jun. 1965, p. 14. During this interview Arthur estimated that his use of the capital 'E' had started 'about eight years ago' – i.e. c. 1957, but it must have been considerably earlier.
42 'Testimony to Arthur Stace by John Starr'.
43 Farrell, 'The Man That Sydney Wondered About'; 'An End to Eternity', *Daily Telegraph* (Sydney), 12 Jun. 1965, p. 14.
44 Farrell, 'The Man That Sydney Wondered About'. Arthur told Tom Farrell in Jun. 1956 that he had begun writing 'Obey God' about eight or nine years after he started writing *Eternity* (i.e. in 1940 or 1941) and that he added 'God or Sin' five years after that (i.e. in 1945 or 1946).
45 Re the *Herald of Hope*, see http://heraldofhope.org.au/index.php/our-purpose/.
46 *Sun* (Sydney), 20 Sep. 1947, p. 1.
47 *Tribune* (Sydney), 21 Jan. 1948, p. 4.
48 Letter dated 23 May 2011 from Denis Padgett to E. Meyers.
49 Memorandum dated 13 Sep. 2002 by E. Summergreene.
50 Memorandum dated 19 Feb. 2009 by Mrs Betty Pickering (née Smith).†
51 Arthur was asked directly about his encounters with the police during the 1964 radio interview with Jim Waugh. He told Waugh that he had been 'held up' 21 times.
52 Ibid. See also *Sun Herald* (Sydney), 22 Sep. 1963, p. 41; Ridley, *Passing of Mr Eternity*, p. 7.
53 Graffiti Control Act (NSW), s. 4 (5), inserted in 2014 by way of amendment to the original 2008 act. During debate in the NSW parliament on 24 Nov. 2009 as regards the Graffiti Control Amendment Bill, Greens MLC Ian Cohen expressed concern about the draconian nature of some provisions. He invoked Arthur Stace: 'He would not hold a fond place in the colourful history of Sydney if he were merely treated as a petty criminal and defacer of the pavement.'
54 Dorothy Hewett (1923–2002) was interviewed on camera in Johnston's *Eternity*. She explained that at the time she wrote *Bobbin Up* (which was in the winter of 1958),

it had been 'nine years' since she saw the man writing *Eternity* outside the Oxford Street ice works – i.e. in 1949.

55 *SMH*, 20 Jun. 1949, p. 1. See also *South Coast Times and Wollongong Argus* (NSW), 23 Jun. 1949, p. 1.

56 *South Coast Times and Wollongong Argus* (NSW), 23 Jun. 1949, p. 12.

57 Ibid., 30 Jun. 1949, p. 14. Samuel's only son, William Stace, a West Wollongong store-keeper, was not a party to this notice. It appears he was something of a black sheep himself: later in 1949 he was convicted (not for the first time) of illegal SP bookmaking. It is not known what contact, if any, Arthur Stace still had with his nephew.

58 Ibid., 23 Jun. 1949, p. 12.

59 Electoral roll, 1949. Re the Waterfall Sanatorium, see https://www.findandconnect.gov.au/guide/nsw/NE01214.

14. As iron sharpens iron

1 'The Municipal Gallery Revisited' (1937) from *The Collected Poems of W.B. Yeats*, Shribner, New York, 1996.

2 Unless otherwise indicated, all information in this book in relation to Lisle and May Thompson was supplied by their daughter, Elizabeth Meyers (née Thompson), from her own personal knowledge and recollection.

3 R.B. Henson, *And One was a Doctor – A Life of Rev Dr A J Waldock*, Baptist Historical Society of NSW, Eastwood NSW, 2003.

4 See K.R. Manley, 'Jarvis, Wilfred Lemuel (1895–1977)', *Australian Dictionary of Evangelical Biography*, http://webjournals.ac.edu.au/ojs/index.php/ADEB/article/view/1083/1080.

5 L. Thompson, 'What Our Grads are Doing – a State Evangelist Speaks', *Suma Supremo*, Sep. 1949.†

6 See E.R. Rogers, 'Morling, George Henry (1891–1974)', *Australian Dictionary of Evangelical Biography*, http://webjournals.ac.edu.au/ojs/index.php/ADEB/article/view/1020/1017.

7 *Lithgow Mercury* (NSW), 21 Mar. 1947, p. 5.

8 Ibid.

9 *Argus* (Melbourne), 22 Jun. 1939, p. 2.

10 See Judd, *He That Doeth*, pp. 20–21; Mansfield, 'Hammond, Robert Brodribb'.

11 *Cessnock Eagle and South Maitland Recorder* (NSW), 6 Aug. 1948, p. 5.

12 See, e.g., *Lithgow Mercury* (NSW) 21 Mar. 1947, p. 5; *Mudgee Guardian and North-Western Representative* (NSW), 26 Apr. 1948, p. 2; *The Macleay Chronicle* (Kempsey, NSW), 2 Feb. 1949, p. 2; *Goulburn Evening Post* (NSW), 2 Feb. 1951, p. 5.

13 *Molong Express and Western District Advertiser* (NSW), 8 Sep. 1950, p. 3.

14 See, e.g., annual report, 1947, Department of Evangelism (NSW Baptist Union), discussing successful missions by Rev. Thompson to Stanmore, Dundas, Undercliffe, Dubbo, Granville, Lithgow, East Chatswood, Parramatta, Park Hill, Concord West.†

15 L. Thompson, 'Meet Mr Eternity'.

16 Scott, 'Burton Street Baptist Tabernacle', p. 13.

17 Armstrong, *Wheel Tracks*, pp. 53–54.
18 Ibid.
19 L. Thompson, 'Meet Mr Eternity'.
20 Ibid.
21 Ibid.
22 M. Thompson, 'Our Friend – Arthur Stace'.
23 *SMH*, 5 Dec. 1951, p. 2 (advertisement); 19 Jan. 1952, p. 9 (review).
24 *Wellington Times* (NSW), 31 Jul. 1952; *Wellington Star* (NSW), 7 Aug. 1952.
25 L. Thompson, *Crooked Made Straight*, p. 8. The authors' estimate of 1952 as the year in which Thompson wrote *Crooked Made Straight* was arrived at after discussion with J. Starr.
26 Arthur chose the title of the tract and the two principal colours, red and white, in which it was published. Jesus's (red) blood had washed Arthur's sins white as snow.
27 May Thompson, on-camera interview in Johnston's *Eternity*.
28 L. Thompson, *Crooked Made Straight*, p. 7.
29 For example, Arthur's confessions to the crowd at the 1951 open-air meeting on the George and Bathurst Street corner witnessed by Lisle Thompson (set out verbatim in Thompson's unpublished article for *Reader's Digest*) had covered a lot of the ground traversed in *Crooked Made Straight*.
30 *SMH*, 27 Dec. 1951, p. 10. Clara's death notice made mention of Arthur: she was described as his 'dear sister.'
31 Scott, 'Burton Street Baptist Tabernacle', p. 8.
32 A breakaway group of about 70 people went off to worship separately at a room in the city premises of the NSW Teachers' Federation (166 Phillip Street). In Jul. 1953, under Leghorn, they formed the Phillip Street Baptist Church. In Dec. 1957, they made their permanent home at the Belvoir Street Particular Baptist church at Surry Hills.

15. Knock and it shall be opened

1 J. Starr, telephone conversation with R. Williams on 27 Mar. 2017. However, cf. Scott, 'Burton Street Baptist Tabernacle', p. 11: Scott put the numbers much lower.
2 M. Thompson, 'Memorial?'
3 M. Thompson, 'Our Friend – Arthur Stace'.
4 Undated letter from J. Starr to E. Meyers.† At least three of the hymn books used by Arthur at the Tabernacle and at open-air meetings (and annotated by him) are still in existence. They are in the possession of Rex Beaver, Les Nixon and J. Starr.
5 The Thompsons drove from their home in Haberfield; the Staces walked, or caught public transport, from theirs in Pyrmont.
6 Letter dated 24 Oct. 2010 from J. Starr to E. Meyers.†
7 Recollections of E. Meyers.
8 'Testimony to Arthur Stace by John Starr'.
9 J. Starr, telephone conversations with R. Williams on 20 and 26 Jul. 2017. The refuge in question was based at 141–155 Commonwealth Street, Surry Hills.
10 S. Townsend, 'Still wondering About Eternity', *SMH*, 31 Dec. 1999, p. 11.

11 S. Townsend interview with Peter Thompson, 'Talking Heads', ABC Television, 8 Aug. 2005, transcript online. See also Townsend's article, 'Still wondering about Eternity'.
12 Martin Sharp interview with Rachael Kohn, *The Spirit of Things*, ABC Radio National, 7 Mar. 2010, transcript available online.
13 Memorandum dated 13 Sep. 2002 by E. Summergreene. This exchange must have occurred by 1953 at the latest, because Edith moved to Tamworth in that year.
14 *Catholic Weekly*, 31 Aug. 1994, p. 10.
15 *Sun* (Sydney), 18 Jun. 1953, p. 2.
16 *Sun* (Sydney), 22 Sep. 1953, p. 1.
17 *Sun* (Sydney), 26 Sep. 1953, p. 1.
18 *Sun-Herald* (Sydney), 22 Nov. 1953, p. 57.
19 *Sun-Herald* (Sydney), 1 Nov. 1953, p. 3. See also *SMH*, 2 Sep. 1954, p. 1 – Column 8 noted that 'the Harbour Bridge footpaths are littered with chalked messages about sinful Sydney, Armageddon, eternity.' This sounds more like the work of the couple seen by Mrs Scott than that of Arthur.
20 *Sun-Herald* (Sydney), 27 Jun. 1954, p. 54.
21 *Farmer and Settler* (Sydney), 15 Apr. 1954, p. 21.
22 *Farmer and Settler* (Sydney), 11 Mar. 1955, p. 2.
23 Typewritten document headed 'Mr. Eternity' prepared by M. Thompson c. 1978.†
24 M. Thompson, interviewed on camera in Johnston's *Eternity*.
25 Matthew 6:28.
26 Email dated 22 Jun. 2010 from Suzanne Grunstein to E. Meyers.
27 Rebecca Senescall, 'From here to Eternity?' *Camden Advertiser* (NSW), date unknown.
28 Interview of Arthur Stace by Jim Waugh on Sydney radio station 2GB in 1964 (audio recording in the possession of the authors). Arthur claimed in this interview to have been 'right around Melbourne', but by that he almost certainly meant the CBD only.
29 Farrell, 'The Man That Sydney Wondered About'.
30 M. Thompson, 'Our Friend – Arthur Stace'. Although the words quoted had been crossed out by Mrs Thompson in pen, it is the authors' firm view that she did so because she had second thoughts about mentioning Arthur's 'secret' at or very soon after his burial, not because she was in any doubt as to the truth of what she had written.
31 L. Thompson, *Crooked Made Straight*, p. 3. It should be noted that *Crooked Made Straight* also incorrectly stated Arthur's year of birth (it was 1885, not 1884) and place of birth (it was Redfern, not Balmain). These, no doubt, were honest errors of detail on Arthur's part, repeated by Thompson. Evidently Arthur did not have a copy of his birth certificate. The first suburb of Sydney in which he lived at an age advanced enough for him to take note of its name was, probably, Balmain, in 1899.
32 Ibid., p. 8.
33 This tall ginger-headed man was referred to by Arthur in his 1964 radio interview (see Chapter 17) and by M. Thompson in her 1978 typewritten document, 'Mr Eternity'.
34 Undated article by L.M. Thompson, 'I Survived Three Coronary Occlusions'.†
35 Ibid.
36 M. Thompson, 'Mr. Eternity'.

37 *Daily Telegraph* (Sydney), 15 Jun. 1956, p. 2 ('Town Talk' column).
38 M. Thompson, 'Mr. Eternity'.
39 Ibid.
40 Tom Farrell's article referred to an interview conducted 'yesterday'. Tom Farrell (1917–2012) was a Sydney icon in his own right. In 1959 he went over to the *SMH* and spent the rest of his career at Fairfax in increasingly senior editorial and management roles. He retired in 1982.
41 Farrell, 'The Man That Sydney Wondered About'.
42 Letter dated 25 Jul. 2002 from Dorothy Osborne to Bronson Symes.
43 Helen Livingstone, Red Cross employee in the 1950s, interviewed on camera in Johnston's *Eternity*.
44 In his 'Echoes of Eternity' sermon of 1 Feb. 1970 (29 mins in), Ridley said 'for years I didn't know anything about it.' In Jul. 2017, the recollection of Ridley's daughter, Ruth, was that her father was 'probably' not aware until 1956 of Arthur's identity as Mr Eternity or of his own role in inspiring Arthur on the evening of 14 Nov. 1932. Miss Ridley recalls seeing *Eternity* chalkings as a child (i.e. before 1956), but she never met Arthur (telephone interview of R. Ridley by R. Williams on 4 Jul. 2017).
45 J. Starr, telephone conversation with R. Williams on 27 Mar. 2017.
46 L. Thompson, 'I Survived Three Coronary Occlusions'.
47 See Farrell's obituary in *SMH*, 1 Dec. 2012, p. 21.
48 Interview of Tom Farrell on camera in Johnston's *Eternity*.
49 L. Thompson, 'I Survived Three Coronary Occlusions.'
50 Ibid.
51 M. Thompson, 'Memorial?' It is clear that the hospital visit by Arthur that is described by Mrs Thompson in this document (prepared in 1969) must have taken place in Sep. or Oct. 1956, not Jun. 1956. She wrote herself in the same document that Arthur's hospital visit occurred after Lisle's '*third* and massive coronary', i.e. the one of 28 Aug. 1956. It follows that Mrs Thompson was eliding two separate memories – the hospital visit in Sep./Oct. 1956 (at which the officious nursing sister initially challenged Arthur's entry) and Arthur's visit to the Thompson home in Jun. 1956 (at which Lisle persuaded him to reveal himself to the press as Mr Eternity).
52 Ibid.
53 Ibid.
54 Ibid.
55 M. Thompson, 'Our Friend – Arthur Stace'.

16. Fruits of the Spirit

1 R. Cotton, 'Hamilton Baptist Church', 3 Sep. 2015, http://hiddenhamilton.blogspot.com.au/search/label/Hamilton%20Baptist%20Church.
2 Memorandum dated 13 Sep. 2002 by E. Summergreene.
3 Recollection of E. Meyers.
4 Document written by J. Starr entitled 'Pastor Lisle Matthew Thompson, Minister of the Burton St. Baptist Tabernacle 1951–64'.†

5 Letter dated 10 Jun. 2014 from J. Starr to E. Meyers.†
6 Letter dated 14 Jul. 2014 from J. Starr to E. Meyers.†
7 'Testimony to Arthur Stace by J. Starr'.
8 Ibid.
9 Letter dated 10 Jun. 2014 from J. Starr to E. Meyers.
10 Ibid.
11 Ibid.
12 *SMH*, 5 Jun. 1937, p. 10.
13 Letter dated 10 Jun. 2014 from J. Starr to E. Meyers.
14 J. Low, 'Mr Eternity: Arthur Stace', at http://simplyaustralia.net/article-jkl-eternity.html.
15 See further Chapter 20.
16 G. Fay, online comment posted on 31 Jul. 2017 at https://www.eternitynews.com.au/australia/eyewitness-to-arthur-staces-secret-life-comes-forward/.
17 J. Weaver, *Much Love, Jac x*, Allen & Unwin, 2005, Crows Nest NSW, p. 18.
18 Apart from newspapers of record, the anecdotal evidence is overwhelming. For example, in 2002–03, Sydney artist David Lever spoke at numerous Sydney nursing homes about his 28-piece exhibition of Arthur Stace paintings (see Chapter 20). His talk was always accompanied by a slide show. Lever recalled that this 'always prompted numerous questions and statements about first-hand experiences with Arthur Stace.'
19 *SMH*, 24 May 1958, p. 11. Gavin Souter (b. 1929) was already a prominent journalist when he interviewed Arthur in 1958. But, like Tom Farrell, he went on to even bigger things, including stints as the *SMH*'s correspondent in Washington and London, and as assistant editor. Arthur excited the interest of some of the finest journalists in Australia.
20 Bea Miles' (1902–73) life trajectory was almost the opposite of Arthur's. She was educated at exclusive Abbotsleigh School for Girls on the North Shore. After a falling out with her father in 1923, she was committed to a mental asylum. Released two years later, she became famous in Sydney for outrageous conduct in public places and highly unorthodox views about 'free love.' She was also an atheist. It is not known whether she and Arthur ever met, but Arthur would have been delighted to know that as she lay dying and contemplating eternity, Bea Miles converted to Christianity.
21 *SMH*, 28 May 1959, p. 2.
22 Ibid.
23 Ibid.
24 Ibid. For a rare example of a less than glowing reference to Arthur, see *Nepean Times* (NSW), 2 Apr. 1959, p. 3. In the context of a council debate about graffiti, one speaker questioned whether Arthur's efforts had converted even one person. 'So what's the use?' this cynical gentleman asked.
25 Starr, 'Pastor Lisle Matthew Thompson'.
26 Hemmingway lived from 1920–97. The whole Thompson family attended his funeral at Mayfield Baptist Church in Newcastle, each member travelling a long distance to get there.
27 Starr, 'Pastor Lisle Matthew Thompson'; recollections of E. Meyers.

28 See S. Piggin, 'Billy Graham in Australia, 1959 – Was it Revival?', *Lucas: An Evangelical History Review*, no. 6, Oct. 1989.
29 Starr, 'Pastor Lisle Matthew Thompson'.
30 J. Starr, telephone conversation with R. Williams on 20 Jul. 2017.
31 Conversation on 4 Aug. 2017 between Peter Holland and R. Williams. Mr Holland was a student at Moore College in 1959–60, placing this event in that period.
32 *Sun* (Sydney), 10 Oct. 1961, p. 27.
33 Lisle Thompson filled out a card in relation to each person who presented themselves at the Clinic. By the time of his death there were about 1000 cards in existence.
34 *Sun* (Sydney), 10 Oct. 1961, p. 27.
35 Note dictated by C.K. Hemmingway in or about 1978.†
36 *Sun* (Sydney), 10 Oct. 1961, p. 27.
37 For biographical details on W.T. Stace, see the *Encyclopaedia Britannica* entry online at https://www.britannica.com/biography/W-T-Stace.
38 Arthur and Walter Stace had a common great-grandfather – William Stace (1755–1839), whom we met at the beginning of Chapter 2. (He was the Stace ancestor who served during the Battle of Waterloo.) Arthur's father, William Wood Stace, and Walter's father, Major Edward Vincent Stace (1841–1903), were first cousins.
39 These four books, all published while W.T. Stace was employed by the Ceylon Civil Service, were *A Critical History of Greek Philosophy* (1920), *The Philosophy of Hegel: A Systematic Exposition* (1924), *The Meaning of Beauty* (1929) and *The Theory of Knowledge and Existence* (1932).
40 Of all W.T. Stace's books, the one generally regarded as the most important is *Mysticism and Philosophy*, Macmillan & Co Ltd, London, 1961.
41 Stace, *Mysticism and Philosophy*, p. 82.
42 See Chapter 2.
43 Arthur Stace died on 30 Jul. 1967. W.T. Stace died in California on 2 Aug. 1967.

17. The valley of the shadow of death

1 Undated letter from J. Starr to E. Meyers.†
2 'Testimony to Arthur Stace by John Starr'.
3 Undated letter from Stella Hesse to E. Meyers, received in Aug. 2002.†
4 Letter dated 25 Jul. 2002 from Dorothy Osborne to Bronson Symes.†
5 *SMH*, 14 Jul. 1961, p. 26 (death and funeral notices of Pearl Stace).
6 Bernard Judd, interviewed on camera in Johnston's *Eternity*.
7 Conversation on 4 Aug. 2017 between R. Williams and Peter Holland.
8 Recollections of E. Meyers.
9 Ibid. For good measure, Arthur also got an extra pair of trousers.
10 Note dictated by C.K. Hemmingway c. 1978.†
11 Letter dated 1 Aug. 1967 from B. Judd to Stewart Mitchell. † See also the interview of Judd on camera in Johnston's *Eternity*.
12 M. Thompson, 'Our Friend – Arthur Stace'.

13 M. Trembath, 'He took a photo of Eternity', *St George & Sutherland Shire Leader* (Sydney), 2 Sep. 2008, pp. 1, 10.
14 P. Martin, 'A word in time from Mr Eternity', *Herald* (Melbourne), 13 Jul. 1961.
15 '"Mr Eternity" still undaunted', *Sun Herald* (Sydney), 22 Sep. 1963, p. 41.
16 *Canberra Times*, 4 Nov. 1964, p. 3.
17 Sydney Davies, retired quantity surveyor, interviewed on camera in Johnston's *Eternity*.
18 In 1970, Thelma Dodds gave her piece of black cardboard with *Eternity* chalked on it by Arthur to Stan Levit, a guest preacher at Burton Street Tabernacle that year. Levit took the object to Woy Woy when he retired and it was affixed to his back door until 2000. See the National Museum of Australia website entry, http://collectionsearch.nma.gov.au/object/60237.
19 Undated letter from J. Starr to E. Meyers.†
20 Letter dated 19 Jan. 1964 from J. Ridley to M. Thompson.†
21 Quoted by J. Starr, 'Man of God', tribute to L. Thompson, Order of Service on the occasion of the of the opening of Rev. Lisle M. Thompson Memorial Therapy Room, 11 Sep. 1965.†
22 *Canberra Times*, 13 May 1964, p. 2.
23 The original recording was made on a reel-to-reel tape recorder by John Barwick, who listened to the interview in 1964 through his local radio station in Gunnedah, 2MO. Barwick had been converted at the 1959 Billy Crusade and had developed an interest in Arthur after being told about him by his Uncle Ken in the late 1950s or early 1960s who had heard Arthur speak at a Methodist Men's Brotherhood meeting in Regentville (near Penrith). In Feb. 2000, Barwick sent the recording to ABC Radio's Ian McNamara, who played it on his Sunday morning program *Australia All Over* (letter dated 1 Aug. 2017 from J. Barwick to the editor of *Eternity* newspaper).
24 See, for example, http://simplyaustralia.net/article-jkl-eternity.html.
25 See M. Sheather, 'From here to Eternity', *WHO Weekly*, 7 Nov. 1994, p. 57.
26 From the on-camera interview of George Gittoes in Johnston's *Eternity*.
27 Letter dated 1 Aug. 1967 from B. Judd to Stewart Mitchell.
28 'An end to Eternity', *Daily Telegraph* (Sydney), 12 Jun. 1965, p. 14.

18. At home with the Lord

1 'An End To Eternity', *Daily Telegraph* (Sydney), 12 Jun. 1965, p. 14.
2 Ibid.
3 Ibid.
4 G. Souter, *Sydney*, Angus & Robertson, Sydney, 1965.
5 J. Morgan, *Martin Sharp*, Allen & Unwin, Sydney, 2017, p. 45. For the 1965 SUDS revue *Look, No Pinky*, Sharp did some of the design and his girlfriend was an usher.
6 Colin R. Anderson (1937–2014) was interviewed on camera in Johnston's *Eternity*.
7 Scott, 'Burton Street Baptist Tabernacle', p. 11.
8 Letter dated 10 Jun. 2014 from J. Starr to E. Meyers.

9 Document headed 'Message preached at the funeral of Arthur J. [sic] Stace, Botany Cemetery, Tuesday, Oct. 7, 1969, 2p.m. by Stewart Mitchell', p. 2.†
10 Undated letter from A. Stace to M. Thompson received by Mrs Thompson in Dec. 1965.†
11 Undated letter from A. Stace to a Baptist pastor named Malcolm, written in or about Apr. 1966.†
12 Letter dated 25 Jul. 2002 from Dorothy Osborne to Bronson Symes.†
13 Letter dated 1 Dec. 1966 from A. Stace to John Osborne.† Mr Osborne was married to Pearl's sister Amy.
14 Letter dated 1 Aug. 1967 from B. Judd to Stewart Mitchell.†
15 Ibid.
16 Email dated 18 Jul. 2011 from Jenny Story to E. Meyers.†
17 *SMH*, 2 Aug. 1967, p. 1 ('three months ago').
18 Document headed 'Message preached at the funeral of Arthur J. [sic] Stace, Botany Cemetery', p. 3.
19 Paddy Newnham, interviewed on camera in Johnston's *Eternity*.
20 Memorandum dated 13 Sep. 2002 by E. Summergreene. According to Edith, her visit to Arthur took place on 'the night before he went home to Jesus.'
21 Ibid.
22 *SMH*, 2 Aug. 1967, p. 1. See also *Daily Telegraph* (Sydney), 1 Aug. 1967, p. 6 (Ray Castle column).
23 Quoted in Ridley, *Passing of Mr Eternity*, p. 10.
24 Letter dated 1 Aug. 1967 from J. Ridley to Stewart Mitchell.†
25 Letter dated 1 Aug. 1967 from B. Judd to Stewart Mitchell.
26 Undated letter from J. Starr to E. Meyers.†
27 Ridley, *Passing of Mr Eternity*, pp. 12–3.
28 Order of Service, 13 Aug. 1967.†

19. If what has been built survives

1 1 Corinthians 3:13–15, NIV.
2 2 Corinthians 5:10, NIV.
3 Ridley, *Passing of Mr Eternity*.
4 *SMH*, 12 May 1968 ('Candid Comment' column by 'Onlooker'); David Griffin, letter to the editor, *SMH*, 20 Nov. 1976, p. 8. Sir David Griffin (1915–2004) was a former Lord Mayor of Sydney (1972–73) and the councillor who had first proposed the idea of a memorial to Arthur Stace in Aug. 1967. In his 1976 letter, Sir David wrongly attributed the final 'killing' of the plaque idea to the Labor Party: in fact, the villains in Apr. 1968 were the (Liberal Party-appointed) 'Treatt troika'(Sir Vernon Haddon Treatt [1897–1984] was a former leader of the NSW parliamentary Liberal Party. From late 1967 to Sep. 1969 he served as Chief Commissioner of the City of Sydney. His two fellow commissioners were J.A.L. Shaw and W.W. Pettingell). As ever, lack of vision cut across party-political lines. However, Sir David made this accurate prediction: 'eternity has a way of having the last say.'

5 *SMH*, 12 May 1968 ('Candid Comment' column by 'Onlooker').
6 Letter of Jun. 1968 from Messrs Church and Grace, solicitors, to C.K. Hemmingway.†
7 Unidentified Christian journal, 13 Aug. 1967.†
8 See https://www.eternitynews.com.au/australia/eyewitness-to-arthur-staces-secret-life-comes-forward/.
9 M. Thompson, 'Our Friend – Arthur Stace'.
10 *SMH*, 23 Aug. 1969, p. 18. Stewart's poem was reprinted in the *Herald* in full on 30 Dec. 1999, in the lead-up to the millennium celebrations. It is included in *Douglas Stewart: Selected Poems*, Angus & Robertson, Pymble NSW, 1992, first published c. 1973. The words are used here with permission.
11 I. Indyk, 'Stewart, Douglas Alexander (1913–1985)', *ADB*, http://adb.anu.edu.au/biography/stewart-douglas-alexander-15726/text26914, viewed online 12 Jun. 2017.
12 Letter dated 1 Sep. 1969 from Prof. Michael J. Blunt, UNSW, to C.K. Hemmingway.†
13 *Sunday Telegraph* (Sydney), 5 Oct. 1969, p. 11.
14 Cf. Luke 7:47.
15 John 8:8.
16 M. Thompson, 'Our Friend – Arthur Stace'.
17 Ibid. The authors also rely on May Thompson's letter to J. Ridley of 22 Jan. 1970 ('I do feel that hearing the message as you have so kindly consented to give will help me very greatly in my little task Lisle promised Arthur to do for him').†
18 Letter dated 13 Jan. 1970 from J. Ridley to M. Thompson.†
19 See, e.g., *SMH*, 17 Jan. 1970, p. 67.
20 See note 9 to Chapter 10.
21 Letter dated 23 Feb. 1970 from J. Ridley to M. Thompson.†
22 Letter dated 20 Feb. 1970 from M. Thompson to J. Ridley.†
23 To listen to the sound recording, go to http://eternitynews.com.au/mreternity.
24 J.G. Ridley, *Eternity! Where?* (s.n., c. early 1970s), p. 5. The publication date was not printed on the tract, but J. Starr recalls that a period of a few years had passed between Arthur's death and the conversation at the Tabernacle between Ridley and Mitchell that is related in the text. Hence Ridley's agitation: he felt he had let Arthur down. (Telephone conversation on 3 Aug. 2017 between J. Starr and R. Williams.)
25 K. Dunstan, *Ratbags*, Golden Press, Sydney, 1979, pp. 177–9.
26 Ibid.
27 See, for example, Psalms 1:1, 14:1, Proverbs 3:34, 13:20, 19:29, 29:8, John 15:18-19, Acts 13:41, 2 Peter 3:3.
28 Email dated 11 Aug. 2017 from Alana McDiarmid to E. Meyers.
29 Ibid.
30 Letter dated 22 Feb. 1974 from M. Thompson to Mrs Ruby Bond, oldest sister of Pearl Stace.†
31 Letter dated 23 Feb. 1970 from J. Ridley to M. Thompson.
32 *SMH*, 28 Sep. 1976, p. 1 (Column 8).
33 Evans, *Soldier and Evangelist*, pp. 66–7.
34 Ibid, p. 66.
35 See Smith's obituary in the *SMH*, 21 Mar. 2014, p. 31.

36 Quoted in A. Gill, 'An unusual memorial for Mr Eternity', *SMH*, 12 Jul. 1978, p. 12. Italics added.
37 *SMH*, 13 Jul. 1977, p. 1.
38 Martin Sharp interview on camera in Johnston's *Eternity*. See also Morgan, *Martin Sharp*, p. 45.
39 J. Gemes, 'Reflection on Martin Sharp', *Old Cranbrookians' Association Newsletter*, 13 Dec. 2013, http://oca.org.au/news/reflection-martin-sharp.
40 See http://nga.gov.au/federation/Detail.cfm?WorkID=77190&ZoomID=2. Sharp produced another *Eternity Haymarket!* screenprint in 1981, the original of which was sold at auction in 2015: see http://www.lawsons.com.au/asp/searchresults.asp?pg=1&ps=100&st=D&sale_no=8103A++.
41 G. O'Brien, 'Eternal hope a Stace original exists', *SMH*, 8 Mar. 2001, p. 5.

20. What do these stones mean?

1 Quoted in C. Chisholm, *The Daily Telegraph Mirror* (Sydney), 28 Oct. 1994, p. 81. Patrick White once wrote: 'I suppose what I am increasingly trying to do in my books is to give professed unbelievers glimpses of their own unprofessed faith.'
2 See the Introduction.
3 *Canberra Times*, 4 Nov. 1990, p. 26.
4 C. Cunneen, 'Stace, Arthur Malcolm (1885–1967)', *ADB*, http://adb.anu.edu.au/biography/stace-arthur-malcolm-8615/text15049, published first in hardcopy 1990, viewed 16 Jun. 2017.
5 See, e.g., O. Spate, 'All sorts and conditions', *The Canberra Times*, 3 Nov. 1990, p. B5; A. Connolly, 'Looking back from here to eternity', *The Australian*, 6 Nov. 1990, p. 9.
6 See the 'Our Story' section of the REMO website at https://remogeneralstore.com/.
7 Email exchange between Remo Giuffre and R. Williams, 27–28 Jul. 2017.
8 'The Spiritual Vision of Martin Sharp', *The Spirit of Things*, ABC Radio National, 7 Mar. 2010, http://www.abc.net.au/radionational/programs/spiritofthings/the-spiritual-vision-of-martin-sharp/3118558.
9 See R. Kohn, 'Fire and faith: the spiritual vision of Martin Sharp', 3 Dec. 2013, http://www.abc.net.au/radionational/programs/spiritofthings/5131110.
10 See http://www.printsandprintmaking.gov.au/impressions/28639/.
11 See http://remogiuffre.com/post/100398058282/general-thinker-44-crown-street-windows-the.
12 R. Giuffre, 'Eternity', 27 Jun. 2016, posted at https://remogeneralstore.com/blogs/news/eternity.
13 Ibid.
14 One person whose initial interest in Arthur Stace was sparked by the REMO catalogue of 1990 was filmmaker Lawrence Johnston. See M. Sheather, 'From Here to Eternity', *WHO Weekly*, 7 Nov. 1994, p. 57 ('I saw a photograph of him ... and just became enamoured by it').
15 For a summary of the 1992 radio program see http://www.abc.net.au/rn/legacy/programs/lifeandtimes/stories/2009/2690199.htm.

16 *Canberra Times*, 12 Dec. 1992, p. 25.
17 From the on-camera interview of George Gittoes in Johnston's *Eternity*.
18 For the lyrics of the Jim Low song, see http://jimlow.net/lyrics-eternity.htm.
19 *Filmnews* (Sydney, NSW), 1 Jun. 1994, p. 7.
20 Quotes from a newspaper advertisement for the film in late 1994.
21 *SMH*, 12 Sep. 1995, p. 1 ('Column 8').
22 *Catholic Weekly*, 31 Aug. 1994, p. 10.
23 S. Hunt, 'Tales of immortality', *Sydney Star Observer*, 17 Nov. 1994, p. 44.
24 *New Life*, 30 Jun. 1994 and 25 Aug. 1994 ('Australia's Weekly Christian Newspaper' – a Protestant publication).
25 *Daily Telegraph* (Sydney), 28 Oct. 1994, p. 81 (story by Caroline Chisholm), 3 May 1995, p. 10 (column by Mike Gibson).
26 *WHO Weekly*, 7 Nov. 1994, p. 57.
27 A. Gill, 'Eternity and the miracle of Burton St.', *SMH*, 4 Oct. 1994, p. 18.
28 D. Anderson, 'Eternal signature of a gentle mortal', *SMH*, 25 Oct. 1994, p. 20.
29 Quoted in Chisholm, 'An eternal word for a lost world'.
30 Quoted in Hunt, 'Tales of immortality'.
31 R. Begbie, 'On eccentrics, choice and eternity in chalk', *The Canberra Times*, 26 Mar. 1995, p. 8.
32 *London Review of Books*, Vol. 17 No. 14, 20 Jul. 1995, p. 16.
33 P. Kirkpatrick, 'That Shy Mysterious Poet Arthur Stace', *Journal of Australian Studies*, Vol. 21, Iss. 54–55, 1997, http://www.tandfonline.com/action/showCitFormats?doi=10.1080%2F14443059709387338.
34 M. Skelsey, 'Once he wrote on streets, now he's saved for Eternity', *Daily Telegraph* (Sydney), 21 Oct. 1997, p. 3. Arthur was in interesting company. Among the other 'Legends of King's Cross' were Henry Lawson, Bea Miles and Brett Whiteley.
35 D. Dale, 'The Moving Finger', Spectrum section, *SMH*, 18 Jul. 1998, p. 7s.
36 See the discussion at http://www.imdb.com/title/tt0120595/trivia.
37 For an image of Sharp's 1999 *Eternity* tapestry and a discussion of it, see https://www.unisa.edu.au/Global/Samstag/Exhibitions/2008/Documents/SMAFromHere-toEternitymediarelease.pdf. See also *SMH*, 19 Nov. 1999, p. 67.
38 L. Morris, 'Eternity must have its limits, Sartor decrees', *SMH*, 12 Jan. 2001, p. 1.
39 Council minutes online at http://meetings.cityofsydney.nsw.gov.au/documents/meetings/2001/cosc_cm_minutes_2001_cl260201.pdf. Trademark no. is 817532: see http://brizdazz.blogspot.com.au/2013/06/eternity.html.
40 Quoted in Morris, 'Eternity must have its limits'.
41 A transcript of Howard's speech is online at http://pandora.nla.gov.au/pan/10052/20030821-0000/www.pm.gov.au/news/speeches/2001/speech810.htm.
42 In fact, the exhibition ran for 16 years, closing permanently on 1 Jun. 2017.
43 S. Jensen, 'The end of Eternity', 29 May 2017, at http://www.nma.gov.au/about_us/news/articles/the-end-of-eternity.
44 Email dated 12 Nov. 2009 from David Lever to Lionel Meyers.†
45 *Daily Telegraph* (Sydney), 25 and 26 Oct. 2001 ('Confidentially Speaking' column).

46 For images of the 2001 *Federation Tapestry* and a discussion of it, see https://museumvictoria.com.au/discoverycentre/infosheets/federation-tapestry/viewing-the-federation-tapestry/.
47 Quoted in P. Fray, 'Here to Eternity on a faraway stage', *SMH*, 12 Jul. 2003, p. 2.
48 S. Verghis, 'One-word sermon we can't forget', *SMH*, 19 Jan. 2005, p. 16.
49 S. Molitorisz, 'A write of passage', The Guide, *SMH*, Jan. 12–18, 2009, p. 4. The screen version of *Eternity Man* premiered at the Sydney Film Festival in Jun. 2008, was shown in the Piazza Grande at the Locarno Film Festival in Italy in Aug. 2008, and was broadcast on ABC Television on 18 Jan. 2009. The Rose d'Or Award was given in May 2009.
50 *SMH*, 12 Mar. 2005, p. 5.
51 *SMH*, 25 Sep. 2006, p. 2.
52 D. Adelaide, *The Household Guide to Dying: A Novel*, Picador Australia, Sydney, 2008, pp. 145, 157–8, 365.
53 D. Snow, 'Sydney's eternal message crosses the religious divide', *SMH*, 20 Oct. 2008, p. 17.
54 'The Spiritual Vision of Martin Sharp'.
55 D. Falconer, *Sydney*, NewSouth, Sydney, 2010, p. 53.
56 See http://russellmorris.com.au/.
57 A. Taylor, 'And the word was eternal', *SMH*, 11 Feb. 2013, p. 10.
58 S. Taylor, 'Images of Eternity', 21 Jul. 2013, https://www.meganix.net/pavement/page/4/.
59 See Chapter 1.
60 Carey, *30 Days in Sydney*, p. 78. Carey and Sharp were friends. During Carey's visit to Sydney in Apr. 2000, they discussed *Eternity* at some length.
61 D. Dumas, 'Sharp farewelled to eternity on a larger canvas', *SMH*, 11 Dec. 2013, p. 2; E. Fortescue, 'Sydney farewells Martin Sharp with Vincent's sunflowers and Arthur Stace's "Eternity"', *Daily Telegraph* (Sydney), 9 Dec. 2013, http://www.dailytelegraph.com.au/news/nsw/sydney-farewells-martin-sharp-with-vincents-sunflowers-and-arthur-staces-eternity/news-story/fd756e9b40ff95ccb276a731fabfa71f.
62 See the article 'Three artworks you didn't know about from our unique collection', 13 Mar. 2017, on the City of Sydney's website 'Creative City Sydney' at http://www.creativecitysydney.com.au/blog/3-artworks-didnt-know-unique-collection/.
63 Order of Service, 50th Anniversary, Arthur Stace Commemorative Service, St Andrew's Cathedral, 30 Jul. 2017.

Epilogue: Reflections on eternity

1 Email dated 18 Jul. 2011 from Jenny Story to E. Meyers.†
2 K.R. Manley, *From Woolloomooloo to 'Eternity': A History of Australian Baptists*, Volume 1: Growing an Australian Church (1831–1914), Paternoster, Milton Keynes, 2006, pp. 5–6.
3 J. MacDonald, *Vertical Church: What Every Heart Longs For. What Every Heart Can Be* David C. Cook Publishing Company, Colorado Springs, 2012, Chapter 1.

4 'CMI-AID expands work in Moldova', *newlife*, vol. 78, no. 11, 1 Dec. 2015, p. 1.
5 Quoted in Fray, 'Here to Eternity on a faraway stage'.
6 Quoted in Verghis, 'One-word sermon we can't forget'.
7 Ibid.
8 Quoted in Verghis, 'One-word sermon we can't forget'.
9 1966 Australian census; 2016 Australian census.
10 *London Review of Books*, vol. 17, no. 14, 20 Jul. 1995, p. 16.
11 *SMH*, 20 Jan. 2005 (letters page).
12 Carey, *30 Days in Sydney*, p, 79.
13 See Molitorisz, 'A write of passage'.
14 18-year-old Thomas Kelly was killed by a drunkard's unprovoked 'coward's punch' on Thomas' first night at King's Cross in 2012. His family campaigned successfully for the 'lockout laws', which mandate non-admission of new patrons at bars, pubs and clubs in the Sydney CBD after 1.30am, and 'last drinks' at 3am.
15 See HammondCare website, http://www.hammond.com.au/about; Lake, *Faith in Action*.
16 See Barneys' website at https://www.barneys.org.au/.
17 Scott, 'Burton Street Baptist Tabernacle', p. 13.
18 S. Dow, 'Curtain up at last – seems like an eternity', *SMH*, 20 Sep. 2013, p. 9.
19 2016 Australian census.
20 'John Paul II – Australian Legacy', *Compass*, ABC Television, 10 Apr. 2005, available online at http://www.abc.net.au/compass/s1342889.htm.
21 Website of Darlinghurst Theatre Company, sub-section headed 'Eternity Playhouse – History', at http://www.darlinghursttheatre.com/eternity-playhouse/history.
22 Dow, 'Curtain up at last'.
23 Email dated 18 Jul. 2011 from Jenny Story to E. Meyers.

Sources

The authors wish to thank the following individuals and organisations for permission to reproduce their material in this book:

ROBERT ARMSTRONG: Figs 13.1, 14.3 (both from R.M. & E.L. Armstrong, *The Wheel Tracks of the Pioneer Preachers: Bob's First Album of Aussie Gospel Waggon*, Mumbil NSW, 1999, pp. 51–3).

REMO GUIFFRE: Figs 20.1, 20.2; Plate 4.

ROBYN HACK: Fig. 13.3 (photo: E. Summergreene).

STEPHEN JUDD: Figs 9.2, 9.3, 18.1 (all from B.G. Judd, *He That Doeth: The Life Story of Archdeacon R.B.S. Hammond, O.B.E.*, Marshall, Morgan & Scott, Ltd, London, 1951).

DAVID LEVER: Figs 1.2 (*Sanctuary*), 1.3 (*Daily Bread*), 4.3 (*Cockatoo*), 7.2 (*Stretcher-bearer*), 10.4 (*The Enlightenment*); Plates 2, 5 (*Tea and Rock Cakes at Barneys, August 1930; The Bell*). Oil on board, 2000/2001.

JIM LOW: 'Mr Eternity' lyrics (http://jimlow.net/lyrics-eternity.htm).

ELIZABETH MEYERS: Figs 14.1, 14.2, 15.1 (L.M. Thompson, *The Crooked Made Straight*, Christian Broadcasting Association Ltd, Sydney, 1955), 16.2, 17.1 (photo: Ramon Williams), 17.5, 18.3, 19.1 (photo: Alana McDiarmid), 19.2 (photo: Ramon Williams), 19.3 (photo: Ramon Williams); Plates 3, 6.

DOROTHY OSBOURNE: Figs 12.1, 12.2, 12.3.

RUTH RIDLEY: Figs 6.1 (J. Kershaw & B. Thornton, *Born to be a Soldier: War Diary of Lieutenant John G. Ridley MC*, Baptist Historical Society of NSW, Sydney, 2010), 8.3 and 10.3 (both from H.E. Evans, *Soldier and Evangelist: The Story of Rev. John G. Ridley, M.C.*, Baptist Historical Society of NSW, Sydney, 1980).

JOHN STARR: Fig. 16.1.

HAMMONDCARE ARCHIVES: Figs 5.1, 5.2, 11.2, 11.3 (all from *Faith in Action: HammondCare* by M. Lake) and 18.2 (courtesy of HammondCare Archives).

ST ANNE'S ANGLICAN CHURCH, HAMMONDVILLE: Fig. 13.2.

Sources and details for figures not listed above or supplied in main text are as follows:

CHAPTER 1. Fig. 1.1: 'Rear of 93 Cumberland Street, The Rocks (NSW)', 01/10/1901, digital ID: 4481_a026_000109. Courtesy State Archives NSW.

CHAPTER 2. Fig. 2.1: Title page, *Sermons on Christian Duties* (Montagu John Wynyard, J.G. & F. Rivington, London, 1832, https://archive.org/details/sermonsonchrist00wynygoog); Fig. 2.2: 'Government House' & 'View on Port

Louis – Citadel', Port Louis, Mauritius, 1880–1899. The National Archives UK, CO 1069-745-5; Fig. 2.3: Photo: Jen Harding, 2017, used with permission; Fig. 2.4: Google Street View image, © 2017 Google.

CHAPTER 3. Fig. 3.1: NSW, Australia, Police Gazettes, 1854–1930 (database online). Provo UT, USA: Ancestry.com Operations, Inc., 2010. Original data: NSW Government. Police Gazettes. Series 10958, Reels 3129–3143, 3594–3606. State Records Authority of NSW; Fig. 3.2: 'Benevolent Asylum corner of Pitt and Devonshire Streets, Railway Square Sydney, c. 1901', NSW State Archives; Fig. 3.3: Register of the Benevolent Society of NSW, entry for 'Stace, Laura' and children, 29 October 1892. Mitchell Library; Fig. 3.4: 'Railway Station – Goulburn, c.1879', Photographic Collection from Australia, CC by 2.0, https://commons.wikimedia.org/w/index.php?curid=17620866; Fig. 3.5: 'Assault and Robbery at Balmain', 7 December 1898, *The Australian Star* (Sydney, NSW: 1887–1909), p. 6. National Library of Australia, CDC-10619529; Fig. 3.6: 'Mount Kembla Colliery, 1901.' Image from opposite page 100 of the Annual Report, Department of Mines, NSW, for the year 1901. Sydney, 1902. University of Wollongong Archives, collection D158/8/1.

CHAPTER 4. Fig. 4.1: 'Riley Street, Surry Hills, c. 1905–10.' State Library of NSW, Mitchell Library, Government Printing Office 1-37992; Fig. 4.2: NSW, Australia, Police Gazettes, 1854–1930 (database online). Provo UT, USA: Ancestry.com Operations, Inc., 2010. Original data: NSW Government. Police Gazettes. Series 10958, Reels 3129-3143, 3594-3606. State Records Authority of NSW; Fig. 4.4: 'Family Notices', 13 May 1913, SMH (NSW: 1842–1954), p. 8. Retrieved 16 August 2017 from http://nla.gov.au/nla.news-article15420014.

CHAPTER 5. Fig. 5.3: Photo by John Sandeman, 2017, © *Eternity*.

CHAPTER 6. Figs 6.2, 6.3: Arthur Stace's AIF records, held by the National Archives of Australia. Used with permission; Fig. 6.4: 'Looking SW from the corner of Riley Street and William Street towards Yurong Lane. View showing horse drawn carts, advertising hoardings, and sign for the Liquor Referendum held on 10 June 1916.' Courtesy City of Sydney Archives: 002054. Used with permission.

CHAPTER 7. Fig. 7.1: https://commons.wikimedia.org/wiki/File:Australian_53rd_Bn_Fromelles_19_July_1916.jpg. Photo: Lance Corporal C.H. Lorking of the 53rd Battalion; Fig. 7.3: '*Takada*.' Photo: Allan C. Green 1878–1954. Courtesy State Library Victoria; Fig. 7.4: 'SS *Kildonan Castle* (1899) and ferry *Greycliffe* (1911–1927).' From Graeme Andrews 'Working Harbour' Collection: 78331 GKAC. Photo: Dufty. Courtesy City of Sydney Archives: 078331. Used with permission.

CHAPTER 8. Fig. 8.1: Darlinghurst Police Station, 2017. Photo: John Sandeman, 2017, © *Eternity*; Fig. 8.2: Arthur Stace's AIF records, held by the National Archives of Australia.

CHAPTER 9. Fig. 9.1: St Barnabas' Broadway, c. 1872. Photo: Charles Pickering. Courtesy State Library NSW; Fig. 9.4: Photo: John Sandeman, 2017, © *Eternity*.

CHAPTER 10. Fig. 10.1: 'Crowd of unemployed men queuing for the dole during the Great Depression, New South Wales, ca. 1932' (nla.pic-vn6255755). © Fairfax Media, Fairfax Syndication. Used with permission; Fig. 10.2: Burton Street Baptist Tabernacle, c. 1932. Photo: Esme Strauss.

CHAPTER 11. Fig. 11.1: *SMH*, 21 October 1933, p. 21. Courtesy National Library of Australia.

CHAPTER 13. Fig. 13.4: 'Jamison St, 1938.' Courtesy City of Sydney Archives: 033203. Used with permission.

CHAPTER 15. Fig. 15.2: Tom Farrell, 'The Man That Sydney Wondered About', *Sunday Telegraph* (Sydney), 24 June 1956, p. 5.

CHAPTER 16. Fig. 16.3: Front cover of *Time and Eternity: An Essay on the Philosophy of Religion* by Walter Terence Stace, Princeton University Press, 1952. Image used with permission.

CHAPTER 17. Figs 17.2, 17.3: Photos: Trevor Dallen, THE SYDNEY MORNING HERALD. © Fairfax Media, Fairfax Syndication. Used with permission; Fig. 17.4: Photo: George Serras, National Museum of Australia. Used with permission.

EPILOGUE. Photo: John Sandeman, 2017, © *Eternity*.

About the authors

Roy Williams won the Sydney University Medal in law in 1986 and spent 20 years in the legal profession before turning his hand to writing. His first and best-known book, *God, Actually* (2008), was a defence of Christianity for the educated layperson. A bestseller in Australia on release, it has since been published in Britain and North America. Roy's next two books – *In God They Trust?* (2013) and *Post-God Nation?* (2015) – focused on Australian history and society, and have been widely praised by believers and agnostics alike. *Mr Eternity* is his first full-length biography.

Elizabeth Meyers' father, Lisle Thompson, was the minister of Burton Street Baptist Tabernacle in Darlinghurst from 1951 to 1964 and also a dear friend and mentor of Arthur Stace. Elizabeth worked as a teacher for 26 years after attending Sydney Unversity and qualifying in early childhood/special education. She and her husband Lionel have two daughters and four grandchildren. Elizabeth has written this biography of Arthur Stace with Roy Williams to fulfil a promise to her mother, May, as Lisle Thompson received permission from Arthur to write his life story 'only after his death.'